A History
of the Swedish People

From Renaissance to Revolution

TOLD BY
Vilhelm Moberg

Translated from the Swedish by
PAUL BRITTEN AUSTIN

DORSET PRESS
New York

This edition published by Dorset Press,
a division of Marboro Books Corporation,
by arrangement with Random House, Inc.
1989 Dorset Press

ISBN 0-88029-313-6
(formerly 0-394-48973-X)

Printed in the United States of America

M 9 8 7 6 5 4

Contents

'Every true history must, by its human and vital presentation of events, force us to remember that the past was once real as the present and uncertain as the future ... it enables us, by the light of what men once have been, to see the thing we are, and dimly to descry the form of what we should be.'

G. M. Trevelyan, in *Clio, A Muse*, 1955

Foreword

IN THE FOREWORD to the first part of my *History of the Swedish People* I motivated its motto 'The history of Sweden is the history of her commons' by emphasizing that the word *allmoge*, in the original Swedish, was being used in its pristine sense of 'the whole people'. This has not prevented many people from understanding it in its modern, restricted sense of 'peasantry' and quite unjustifiably saddling me with the view that the history of Sweden is exclusively the history of her peasants, and that it is their history I have set out to write. Concerned to dispel this misunderstanding, I find I must reiterate what I wrote in my foreword to Volume I: *My history's main theme is the Swedish common man.* This comprehends for me all groups and classes of people who, down the centuries, have lived in our country, from the kings at the summit of the social pyramid, to the peasants, the outcroppers, the rank and file in our armies, the servants, the bondsmen and the unpropertied, at its base. Since this base consists of more than nine-tenths of the population of Sweden, it must necessarily dominate my narrative.

And it is for the commons of Sweden, in the sense of the whole Swedish people, I have written my *History*.

Since the first part was published I have – much to my surprise – received a wide variety of historical source materials from readers offering them to me for use in future parts of this work. Most of my correspondents are amateur historians, laymen and persons interested in local history. But some, too, are academics and professional historians. I have carefully filed away all these items of information and will go through and examine them in detail. Some will certainly prove useful as I proceed. Here I can only gratefully acknowledge their receipt.

My first book was published in 1921; that is to say I have been an author for fifty years. But to find my readers offering me their help for the work's continuation has been an entirely new experience. It is both remarkable and symptomatic. My compatriots' interest in their own history is apparently a great deal stronger than I had ever imagined. And this is above all true, to judge from these readers' letters, of the youngest generation.

To my good friend and Swedish publisher Ragnar Svanström, finally, I must proffer my warmest thanks. He has been the author's best imaginable adviser and support in the work's creation. In checking my facts and historical sources I have had the greatest possible use of his expertise. And his never-failing interest in my *History of the Swedish People* has been an invaluable stimulus to me.

V.M.

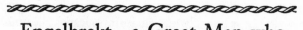

Engelbrekt—a Great Man who was Small of Stature

The man

ONE CHILLY EVENING IN APRIL 1436 a murder was committed with an axe on an island in Lake Hjälmaren. Today, more than five hundred years after the event, Swedes still refer to the victim in daily speech (but more especially on solemn or festive occasions) as the very symbol of our Swedish liberties. Only the other day I was reading in a newspaper that his name had been invoked at the annual meeting of the Centre Party, the speaker saying he could not pronounce it without feeling 'the wing-beat of history' above his head.

Everyone agrees that the man who met his death on the island in Lake Hjälmaren was a great liberator. Since freedom is a word which figures in the political programmes of all our parties it is a name which is in high degree serviceable as a rallying point. When Swedes speak of Engelbrekt it is without affectation, almost as if they were speaking of a contemporary. No other mediaeval personage enjoys so honourable a status. Together with Gustav Vasa, Engelbrekt would seem to be the figure from our Swedish past who appeals most vividly to our imagination.

Yet there is a paradox. As an individual, no historical personage from the Swedish Middle Ages is less known to us than Engelbrekt Engelbrektsson.

I have tried to absorb all available research into his life and achievements and as far as I know I have hardly overlooked any work of importance that deals with him. But when all the propaganda of the chronicles and annals has been sifted, and after cutting a path

through the thickets of myth and legend, the sum total of sub-
stantiated and incontestable source materials that remains is meagre.
Certainly they do not add up to a living portrait. Of his own writings
only two summary letters are extant. The sources leave us in the
lurch. Engelbrekt, as he really was, eludes investigation; he vanishes
into the jungle of mythology.

The man who was to become the very symbol of Sweden's liberties
and of our national freedom emerges from the darkness of the 15th
century and dominates events for a brief – and fleetingly brief –
while. All he achieved, he achieved between midsummer 1434 and
the end of April or early May 1436, a period of only one year and
ten months. In the ocean of time it seems but an instant. But the
events of that instant have filled more pages in Swedish history
books than any equivalent period in our past.

As to his person, historians are agreed on two points: Engelbrekt
was a great man, of small stature. In his *Song of Freedom* (*Frihetsvisa*)
Bishop Thomas calls him '*then litsla man*' – 'that little man';
and Ericus Olai, who wrote a Latin history of Sweden in the 15th
century, describes him as *statura pusillus*, 'of boyish stature'. An
epitaph, possibly the work of Bishop Thomas, presents the dead man
as *parvus corpore*, 'small or insignificant of stature'. Olaus Petri, too,
our famous 16th-century church reformer and historian writes that
Engelbrekt '*war en liten man till wext*' – 'was in stature a little man'.
A latter-day biographer, Henrik Schück, wonders whether the
expression '*then litsla man*' has not been wrongly interpreted: may
it not mean Engelbrekt was of low estate? But in point of fact
Engelbrekt can hardly be said to have been of low estate: he came
from the lesser aristocracy (*lågfrälse*), had a coat of arms, and sprang
from a family of prosperous miners in Kopparberget, as the hill
region in Central Sweden now known as Bergslagen was then called.

In his own part of the country, then, we may assume that Engelbrekt was a prominent personage. When the men of Bergslagen
wished to complain to the King of the Union in Copenhagen of
their distresses, the man they sent as their spokesman was naturally
the one in whom they felt they could repose most confidence –
they sent Engelbrekt.

Schück calls Engelbrekt 'the first Swede'. This is a rhetorical expression, more in place in a novel than in a biography. Undoubtedly men existed before Engelbrekt who could have been called Swedes, but we have every reason to doubt whether his peasants were nationalists. This 'first Swede', at all events, was of German extraction. Admittedly, a modern expert, Bertil Waldén (*Engelbrektsfejden*, 1934) is of the view that the documents 'provide no conclusive proof whatever' that he was of German origins. But in *Svenskt Biografiskt Lexikon* Professor Gottfrid Carlsson has gone into the question deeply and shows conclusively that a German by name Engelbrekt was a citizen of Västerås – the heart of Bergslagen – as early as 1367. Probably he was the great-grandfather of our national hero. That Engelbrekt was of German extraction is something this writer concludes from his name and its orthography.

Usually I find research into the ancestry of great men tedious to the point of boredom. Mostly they are no more than speculations on hereditary characteristics. But in Engelbrekt's case his German origins *are* of importance. It has been suggested that they were connected with Bergslagen's commercial transactions with the Hanseatic League, which could mean that there was a link between these transactions and the outbreak of the great rebellion. But proofs are lacking.

And already we are on shaky ground. We do not know, for instance, *when* Engelbrekt was born. But since at the time of his revolt he was obviously a middle-aged man, at least forty and probably older, he must have been born somewhere in the 1390's. In 1434, at all events, the year when he steps forward as the leader of the propular insurrection, he is already a man in the prime of life.

Nor do we know *where* he was born. Olaus Petri speaks of him as 'living in Kopparberget', but this could mean anywhere in the whole of Bergslagen, the country's oldest industrial region, where mining had already been in full swing in the 13th century. Dalarna and Västmanland each comprise a part of Bergslagen, and have competed for the honour of his birthplace. For a long while he was known as '*Engelbrekt dalkarl*' – 'Engelbrekt from Dalarna'. In our own century, however, the people of Västmanland have begun to lay claim to him. They assert that his birthplace lay in the Norberg mining district, a claim based on a court record from Norberg, dated January 23, 1432, concerning legal proceedings attended by a miner named Aengelbraeth, of that place.

Whether Engelbrekt came from Dalarna or Västmanland is thus a topic of local dispute, which we may ignore. Homer was born in seven different cities of Greece, and in the Middle West of the pioneer period in the United States fourteen log cabins can be seen, in all of which Abraham Lincoln first saw the light of day. So doubtless it is also quite in order that Sweden's great rebel should have more than one birthplace.

Engelbrekt, then, has neither a childhood nor a youth. When he first comes to meet us it is as a mature man. All his days up to the outbreak of the insurrection pass in obscurity. Every authority agrees that he was married, and tradition says his wife's name was Karin, and that she was his second. But he appears to have left no children, 'at all events none who reached maturity' (G. Carlsson), a childlessness which has not prevented quite a few Swedes from claiming descent from him. In his play *Engelbrekt*, Strindberg provides him with a Danish wife – poetic licence, the dramatist says, taken in order to find in the breach of sympathies between Swedes and Danes a source of the marital wrangling indispensable to his dramas. Strindberg also endows Engelbrekt's murderers with a hitherto unheard-of motive. He has Måns Bengtsson Natt och Dag declare: 'Engelbrekt took from me the bride of my youth'. On the Hjälmaren island he wreaks his revenge – just one more instance of how unhistorical Strindberg's historical dramas can be.

So much for what we know of Engelbrekt's private life. As to his social standing it has been established that as a member of the so-called '*bergsfrälse*' – i.e. those landed gentry of the mining regions who were exempt from taxation – he was entitled to a nobleman's coat of arms, with three demi-fleurs-de-lys set in a triangle. But the gap between this lower gentry and the Swedish nobility was a wide one, and the magnates certainly did not regard this Norberg mine-master as one of themselves. He was not a 'lord'. Perhaps we could even use a modern expression and call him middle-class, a man who would today simply be called the proprietor of an iron-works. For someone to have risen from this class to the highest position in the realm is unique in Sweden's mediaeval history.

Nor can the epoch show any counterpart to a situation where a propertied man comes forward as a leader of the oppressed common people. A contemporary German chronicler, Hermann Korner, bears witness that Engelbrekt did not initiate his revolt 'out of any overweening pride or lust for power, but out of compassion for those who were suffering'. Engelbrekt's actions, too, strongly suggest that if he sought power it was not for his own sake but to obtain justice for his people. Himself in no straits, he became the leader of a people who were. I am sceptical in principle of great men, place no faith in history's haloes and laurels; yet I cannot help conceding Engelbrekt his probity and altruism. Nothing in the sources blotches his escutcheon. The only men ever to denigrate him were King Erik of Pomerania and Måns Bengtsson, who murdered him.

Otherwise the sources are one long hymn of praise for the stumpy little mine-master. Noble, high-minded, heroic, resolute, a plain-dealer, eloquent, such are the epithets they use of him. And even if the real Engelbrekt did not perhaps exactly exemplify all these qualities, the man who, at the head of an exasperated and tormented population, went to the attack against the royal bailey of Borganäs around Midsummer 1434, was unquesionably a genuine man of the people.

The Insurgent

Engelbrekt's insurrection can only be fully understood against its European background. The late Middle Ages were an era of great popular risings. Peasants' revolts broke out in France, England, Germany and Denmark, all over Western Europe. The causes of these insurrections, which swept across the countries like a tidal wave, were mainly social. But they were also religious. The papacy and the universal Roman church were in a state of acute crisis.

As early as 1356 a revolt of the French peasantry against feudal oppression, the 'Jacquerie', had been crushed with appalling ferocity by the upper classes' well-equipped and war-seasoned legionnaires. In 1381, as a result of an agricultural crisis which was a consequence of the Black Death, severe disturbances broke out among the English peasantry. The English workers found an able leader in Wat Tyler; his fall meant their defeat. By his doctrinal ardour Wycliffe, an Oxford don, incited people's minds against the Church of Rome and precipitated an English revolt against its pretensions. As a reformer, Wycliffe anteceded Luther by a century and a half. On his own authority he quite simply excommunicated the Pope, whom he declared to be Anti-Christ.

At this time God had acquired two earthly representatives, one in Rome and another at Avignon, who were mutually excommunicating each other. The existence of two popes naturally meant a loss of prestige for the holy see in the eyes of the faithful. Which pope was the rightful one? But matters were to deteriorate still further. A General Council of the Church, held at Pisa in 1409, deposed not only God's representative in Rome but also his colleague at Avignon, and elected a pope of its own. Both the deposed pontiffs refused to recognize the validity of the Council's decision, and clung to their office. So now there were three popes, a trinity which immediately set about excommunicating one another. Confusion in Christendom was complete. Finally, another church council was held at Constance in 1414 and succeeded in prevailing upon all three popes to abdicate. In 1417, Martin V was elected sole pope, whereafter ecclesiastical law and order was considered to have been re-established.

But the Great Schism had loosened the Church's hold on the souls of all sensible and independently-minded people. It was the first tremor of the Reformation. The popes only had their own behaviour to thank if excommunication, that monstrous threat hovering over the head of every Christian, had now lost some of its terrors. Perhaps, after all, it was not so dangerous to be excommunicated as people had believed? The Church's grip on the rank and file of her followers had been loosened. And the proof came with the popular revolts. Men now had the audacity to rebel not only against worldly but also against spiritual oppression.

The greatest of these popular insurrections, and the one which lasted longest, was the so-called Hussite Rising in Bohemia. Breaking out in 1419, it lasted until 1436. Huss himself, whose doctrines had been inspired by Wycliffe, had been burnt as a heretic at Constance in 1415. According to Halvdan Koht, the Norwegian historian, the Bohemian conflagration sent sparks flying even into the remote North. Among peasants at Setesdal, in Norway, he has come upon German catchwords which clearly once incited them to rebel. And Swedish bishops went in fear that there might be some connection between the revolt of the commons in Sweden and the Hussite rising, still in full blaze at the time of Engelbrekt's insurrection.

The causes of the Engelbrekt rising have so often been described by Swedish historians that I have only dealt with them briefly. What Erik of Pomerania's régime was like we already know. As Erik XIII, he could not have had a more appropriate number to his name. The Kalmar Union, Queen Margareta's brilliant idea, had been thrown away by her niece's son. Only rarely did Erik ever visit his Swedish domains, which he left in the hands of his bailiffs. Yet at the same time he introduced into Sweden a novel system of taxation, requiring his subjects to pay cash. In converting the peasants' stores of grain, butter, meat, hay and other commodities into currency, the royal bailiffs had a free hand and naturally did not hesitate to under-value these products and put the profits into their own pockets. Here was a new chance for them to 'pill and poll' a peasantry already staggering under a grievous burden of taxation. One of Erik's new impositions obliged the peasants, in the teeth of all law and custom, to carry out days of compulsory labour on his royal estates.

At this juncture a general revolt would appear to have been inevitable. If ever a popular rising was spontaneous, it was this Swedish rising of 1434. The amazing thing is that it had not broken out earlier, for instance during Albrekt's German régime in the 1370's and 1380's. During the quarter-century when they had been subject to Albrekt, the Swedes had been probably more sorely tried than at any other time during the Middle Ages. These burdens had been relieved by Margareta's reduction of the noble estates. Schück is of the view that she saved the liberties of the Swedish peasant – that time. Perhaps he exaggerates slightly. Anyway, under Albrekt the tyranny had been even harsher and the peasants' existence even more intolerable than it was now under Erik's Danish rule. And indeed several insurrections had been attempted. Stifled at birth, these peasant revolts have been only summarily noticed by historians. Unfortunately they have been the object of very little research and, for the time being at least, we must be content with the indisputable fact that they did break out. My own view is that, if they failed, it was chiefly for lack of the right leader. This man had as yet not been found.

Not until 1434 did the peasants find him. The right man, in the right place, at the right moment. Engelbrekt Engelbrektsson.

On Midsummer Day, the contemporary *Rhymed Chronicle* tells us, the bailiff's castle at Borganäs was stormed and burnt to the ground. Borganäs lies in Southern Dalarna, near the present-day town of Borlänge, where there is a memorial tablet to the event. But the firewood for this great midsummer bonfire, as we have seen, had been gathering for a long time; and just how dry it was can be judged from the swiftness with which the conflagration spread throughout the kingdom.

A revolutionary state of affairs, as one can only call it, had long existed. Such a situation cannot be artificially brought about by writings or speechifyings. Nor can it be provoked from without. It can only spring from fertile soil; grow, like the grain in the fields, according to natural laws. 'Revolutions begin in men's stomachs', is a much later saying, but one which I believe to be applicable to the situation in Sweden in 1434. Only when their daily existence had become utterly insufferable did Engelbrekt's hosts take up their primitive weapons, their poleaxes, spiked clubs and bows and arrows. Most insufferable of all their torments was famine.

What the peasants wanted, the sources tell us, was the restoration of Sweden's ancient laws and customs, 'as in St Erik's day'. Like a popular refrain the memory of that monarch's reign was recalled by the people as a lost paradise, no little enhanced (no doubt) in a retrospect of three hundred years.

That the revolt should have broken out just in Bergslagen was not a mere matter of chance; it was a consequence of King Erik's unlucky war against the Hanseatic League and Holstein. Rich seams of Osmund ore and copper had been discovered in this part of Sweden, where mining was an ancient industry, and many vagrants, footloose men of no fixed abode, were finding their way up to Bergslagen and worked in its mines. During the war the Hanseatic cities had effectively blockaded Sweden's commerce; ore exports had been brought to a standstill, and unemployment was rife. Not that any real class structure is to be discerned in Bergslagen at this time: mine-owners and miners are more or less indistinguishable. What is certain is that they had common reasons for revolting. According to unverified statements, the revolt had been preceded by disturbances among the workers. If this was really so – it is a subject for future research – this would be the first strike of miners in Swedish history. We know that as early as the autumn of 1432 a rebellious crowd had made their way down to the bailiff's residence at Västerås. In the spring of 1433, too, there had been a march of dissatisfied and disgruntled folk to the same castle. Waldén, in his above-mentioned work, calls it 'the first demonstration known in our history'.

But, as transpires from Magnus Eriksson's charter for Kopparberget, granted on February 17, 1347, the workers of the famous copper mine at Falun were allowed no weapon but their knives: 'We further graciously forbid, under pain of our royal vengeance, any of the commons to bear whatsoever weapon may do harm to others, namely dagger, bow, club, spear, sword or broad axe, on pain of a fine of three marks a man; except at the utmost the knife where-with he eateth. Masters are permitted to own a sword, shield, iron hat and gauntlet. If, however, it be so, that the commons cause any disturbance that do harm to the mine, then may those of the masters as may be appointed by our bailiff be fully armed, until such time as they shall bring the commons back to order and each man goeth about his work without causing damage to other.'

The 1347 document further contains regulations stipulating severe punishments for 'troublemakers'. From which it seems likely that insurrections had been attempted in Kopparberget long before the outbreak of Engelbrekt's rebellion.

Västerås Castle was the seat of the Danish bailiff Jösse Eriksson, lord of Bergslagen. For me, ever since I first read about him in my school history book, Jösse Eriksson has embodied the concept of a bailiff. His cruelties to the 'poor peasants of Dalarna' threw me into a state of violent indignation. He 'hanged them up to smoke' and harnessed their pregnant wives to ploughs and haywains, so that their babes were stillborn. From childhood up, bailiffs of all sorts and sizes were hateful to me. They led my thoughts infallibly to Jösse Eriksson.

As a boy, of course, I swallowed my school books whole; took every word for gospel. Not until many years later did I realise that they were merely echoing the 15th-century *Engelbrekt Chronicle*, whose author wished to stir up hatred for the Danes and the Kalmar Union.

In this chronicle – which is a section of the *Karl Chronicle* – the misdeeds of Jösse Eriksson are detailed for posterity. Peasants hung up to smoke, pregnant women dragging heavy hay carts – here was propaganda with a vengeance! In the Bergslagen country-side, however, such sights cannot have been an everyday affair. Perhaps a few sporadic atrocities sufficed to inspire the chronicler's verses. But that peasants who rebelled or talked back at their masters were made an example of and subjected to gross mal-treatment is historical fact, cannot be disputed. The question is, how frequent were such occurrences? In the name of historical truth it must be stated that the Danes had no monopoly of cruel behaviour. Swedes indulged in it too.

Mediaeval legends about the inhumanity of bailiffs abound, but just how much truth they contain no one can say. Some were com-mitted to paper several centuries after the Engelbrekt rebellion, after being passed down through many generations of narrators. Probably these tales underwent successive changes; the bailiffs became steadily more cruel and inhuman. At the point where the Gullspång River flows out into Lake Vänern some large stones known as Plågan ('Torment') are to be seen. Here a bailiff by name Olov Stut is said to have obliged insubordinate peasants to sit on the stones in the icy lake water, naked as the day they were born, until they died of exposure.

For rebels and heretics, however, the penalty was usually the stake. Leaders of mediaeval rebellions commonly ended their days in flames. Neither hanging nor beheading were frightful enough to root out such evil – only fire sufficed. For this we have the word of

Archduke Leopold of Habsburg, in the true feudal spirit. Forcing his way into Switzerland in 1386 to suppress the freedom-loving people of the Alps who had taken up arms against him, he declared: 'I'll boil and fry this pack of rebellious peasants.'

The Union king's bailiffs undoubtedly followed continental practice. What the *Engelbrekt Chronicle* omits to mention, however, is that the leader of the Swedish nationalist party did exactly the same. In six known instances, Karl Knutsson, Earl Marshal and later King of Sweden, sent insurgent leaders to the stake. In 1437, four men of the commons of Västmanland, described as 'reputable', mounted the faggots outside Västerås Castle. And later, on the suppression of a revolt in Värmland in February 1438, two of its leaders, Torsten Ingelsson and Jösse Hansson, were burnt alive. Two Swedish historians, Gottfrid Carlsson and Kjell Kumlien, mention them by name.

But since the *Engelbrekt Chronicle* says not a word about these events, neither did any of my school history books; with the result that when I was at school I was never informed that this Swede, who thrice became King of Sweden, treated his own Swedish peasant just as ferociously as the Danish bailiff, Jösse Eriksson had done before him.

An eloquent instance, drawn from Swedish history, of E. H. Carr's thesis that facts do not speak for themselves until historians lend them a voice!

To posterity Jösse Eriksson's rampage has been made to appear the spark that lit the blaze. But his authority after all was limited to a single district – Dalarna and Västmanland – and therefore it cannot have only been this tormentor of peasants who was responsible for the revolutionary situation so soon to arise throughout the land. Several factors must have coincided.

All major Swedish histories describe the insurrection in detail. The best account, in my opinion, is that of Bertil Waldén. Here I shall only summarize.

Throughout the summer and early autumn of 1434 the skies of Sweden were darkened with smoke. Armies of peasants were marching through the land, leaving a trail of 'fire-blackened' ruins –

the bailiffs' castles. According to my reckoning, twenty-five famous castles, most of them in the south, were burnt to the ground. Probably the total number was greater. Most were no more than timber forts surrounded by palisades and earthen ramparts, and therefore easy enough to set fire to. Some were even smaller and more primitive. Thinly garrisoned, it seems they fell an easy prey to Engelbrekt's men, many times more numerous. After a brief resistance many of these fortresses simply surrendered on terms.

In his *History of the Nordic Peoples* written a century later, Olaus Magnus instructs us in the art of burning down castles. His lesson is probably based on a popular tradition dating from the Engelbrekt rebellion. The simplest way of setting fire to a castle, he says, is to fling red-hot iron balls over its walls. But there were also other admirable methods. Like foxes from a lair, the defenders could be smoked out. Great quantities of burning firewood piled up outside walls and ramparts could be used to fill the castle with smoke – whereupon the occupants would prefer capitulation to suffocation.

In his *Art of War* (*Stridskonst*) Bishop Peder Månsson, who died in 1534, tells us how the firebrands and fireballs used for setting wooden castles and fortresses ablaze were manufactured. There were four ingredients: willow wood, saltpetre, petroleum and brandy. There is no mention of brandy in Swedish annals until the 15th century, and then not as a drink but as a component in the manufacture of fireballs and gunpowder.

So Engelbrekt's rebellious army of peasants – a new phenomenon in Sweden's military history – were not only armed with axes, spiked maces and crossbows, but also with fire. Their leader, however, seems to have preferred to settle matters peacefully with the enemy, only resorting to force when all other arguments failed. In a number of instances Engelbrekt simply bought castles outright, paying large cash sums to their commanders, for whom capitulation became a smart stroke of business. We have descriptions of such proceedings, at Örebro Castle and elsewhere.

In the province of Halland, in the south, Engelbrekt purchased Laholm Castle, known in those days as Lagaholm. Reaching the Lagan River, his army had arrived at the frontier of Skåne, then part of Denmark. On the other side he found himself faced by an army in battle array. Immediately an armistice was concluded between the two peasant armies. This peace, concluded between two provinces, is historically remarkable; a forerunner, one might say, of many such peasant treaties afterwards concluded along the Swedish-Danish frontier. The last was reached as late as 1676.

Nothing succeeds like success. Engelbrekt was everywhere victorious. Soon other social classes and the lords spiritual and temporal supported him. They too had reasons for revolting against King Erik. Feeling themselves discriminated against as compared with the Danes who were really ruling Sweden, the Swedish nobles saw in Engelbrekt and his peasants a means of recovering their lost power. The Church, too, had long been in conflict with the Union king, notably concerning its right to appoint bishops – the most recent bone of contention had been the Uppsala archbishopric – and the lords spiritual were able to lend Engelbrekt military support. Some bishops were themselves military officers, commanding whole companies of men-at-arms, hundreds of soldiers. Gradually, well-equipped knights, squires and men-at-arms were absorbed into the ranks of the untrained and crudely armed peasants and supplied the need for officers. Little by little, from having been a genuine peasant insurrection, Engelbrekt's rising loses its original character. Nobles and commons participated in the revolution for quite different reasons, and were inspired by quite different aims. This became abundantly plain at its tragic dissolution. At Vadstena on August 16, 1434, the struggle took a dramatic and decisive turn. Here, in St Bridget's town, the lords of the council had met to confer. Among them were the highest potentates of the realm, including its leading bishops. Like a stupendous natural force the revolt's general dissemination throughout the realm had put them in an exceedingly sensitive position. Now they had to take sides. Which side?

At this juncture the little mine-master comes riding into Vadstena at the head of a great swarm of peasants – 'to the lords would he ride'. And a famous, dramatic scene is played out. The *Rhymed Chronicle* describes it vividly. As the lords are in the midst of their deliberations, there, unexpected and unannounced, he stands among them; the leader of the great revolt. Peremptorily, he demands that the highest personages in the realm shall join his struggle against King Erik's régime. Right now, on the spot, they must write a letter revoking their oath of fealty and obedience.

The lords refuse. Whereupon Engelbrekt, seizing Bishop Knut of Linköping and Bishop Sigge of Skara 'fast by the throat', threatens to throw them out to the furious peasants swarming and shouting outside in the market place. In the same way he threatens Bishop Thomas of Strängnäs. These are ungainsayable arguments, they prove decisive. Fearing for their lives, lords and bishops compose the required letter – but contrive to formulate it in such a fashion that King Erik will realise that they are acting under duress. Had they not bowed to Engelbrekt's will, writes Olaus Petri in his *Chronicle*, he and his men would have slain them and pillaged their estates.

Engelbrekt has been called 'the first democrat in Swedish history'. This honourable title, however, is a complete anachronism.

Throughout his brief career Engelbrekt showed himself to be a resolute man of action of the first order. Of this his behaviour at Vadstena is an instance. But the decision he then exacted from the council was certainly no majority decision, reached by a regular vote. Failing to move the lords by eloquence, he resorts to threats. It was his only recourse. In a revolution democratic law and order are suspended, and this was no action of a democrat but of a revolutionary. In the circumstances it was only natural that Engelbrekt should resort to violence.

This important historic confrontation between Engelbrekt and the lords of the council occurred on August 16, 1434 at Vadstena. But in which of its ancient buildings did it take place? In the days when I was working at Vadstena as a journalist I looked into this question and came to the conclusion that it must have been in the town hall where the city court still sits, and where I have often reported its proceedings. Vadstena's town hall, said to have been built in the early 15th century, is supposed to be the oldest still in use. At the time of the Engelbrekt rising it must have been new-built. Today its dark furnishings and low ceiling all seem heavily mediaeval. Outside is the little market place where, on that August day, 1434, the furious peasants are said to have stood shouting and clamouring. Sitting in the room, I have imagined the scene. There is another building on the market place, known as the Engelbrekt House; but since it dates from the 16th century it cannot come in question. In all likelihood it was in the old Council House that Engelbrekt threatened to fling the senior bishops of the realm to his peasants.

After three or four months' campaigning, Engelbrekt's work of liberation was in all essentials complete. Erik Puke, his faithful follower and second-in-command, brought out the commons of Northern Sweden, and it was not long before Finland, too, had declared for him. Yet the strongest fortresses still lay in King Erik's hands. Most such places, Stockholm, Stegeborg, Stäkeholm and Kalmar, lay along the east coast. The lord of Fågelvik in Tjust, on the south-east Baltic coast, young Karl Knutsson Bonde had joined forces with the peasant leader but failed to take Stäkeholm, which lay in his home district. Timber forts could be burned to the ground; but the castles at Stockholm and Kalmar had stone walls. They could only be taken by storm. Peasant armies were not storm troopers. In a later age Gustav Vasa and his Dalesmen, too, were to stand equally powerless before the walls of Stockholm Castle.

Marching through the countryside, Engelbrekt's host proceeded circumspectly. No outrages were committed against non-combatants; and there was no plunder. 'None suffered insult, none was deprived of his property, none lost so much as the value of a hen.' This touching and most unusual account of a mediaeval campaign, however, does not quite tally with the truth. There is evidence of another kind: Bishop Thomas of Strängnäs, namely, accuses Engelbrekt of stealing church property. In a letter to Karl Knutsson he calls the leader of the revolt, *ad hominem*, a thief: 'Engelbrekt, a ship's pound of pork in Romtuna church, that stole Johan Andersson on his behalf.' A ship's pound ('*skeppund*') was equal to about 400 ordinary pounds ('*skålpund*'), or upwards of two hundred kilos. This theft of pork conjures up a vivid picture of camp life during the Engelbrekt rising. By their camp fires a flock of famishing peasants sit roasting a few pounds of pork taken from a bishop. In view of the urgent business they had in hand one would hardly have thought that the Bishop of Strängnäs, the author of the famous *Song of Freedom*, would have begrudged them their supper.

Other contemporary documents imply that persons of rank were in fact plundered. Indeed it seems unlikely that the peasant host did not now and again eke out its meagre diet with food taken from others who were better supplied with it.

Yet this was no ordinary passage of men-at-arms feeding themselves by the forcible exaction of 'hospitality'. The peasant armies came to the countryfolk as their liberators, and were willingly given board and lodging. These were no mounted mercenaries in the service of great men and bishops, demanding to be fed and billeted with their horses. They were brothers and comrades in arms, welcome in the homestead. And probably Engelbrekt maintained what is called good military discipline among his folk; for as he was well aware, he exerted over them a magical influence, knew how to speak to them in their own language.

'He carried sword and club through the land.' This miner from Bergslagen, unknown outside his own part of the country until his middle years, suddenly appears as a successful commander-in-chief, a natural military genius. He also showed himself a political leader of substance. To enjoy the confidence of one's own parish by carrying out tasks equivalent to those of a county councillor or chairman of the local council is one thing; to lead an entire people in war, both militarily and politically, is quite another. Engelbrekt did both.

How can he have acquired these qualities? Here we have historical enigmas.

No one becomes a great commander overnight. Before appearing as leader of this rising the little man from Bergslagen must presumably have acquainted himself with the art of war. In his *Chronica regni Gothorum*, Ericus Olai, who had himself lived through the insurrection in his boyhood, writes that in his youth Engelbrekt had stayed in the houses and courts of great men and there been trained in the use of arms, in the manner usual among young noblemen. He is also mentioned as a squire. 'He had been abroad and stayed in many Courts,' writes our 18th-century author Olof von Dalin, without, however, producing any further evidence on this point.

Several historians assume that Engelbrekt had done military service under King Erik in his German war. Research has therefore sought Engelbrekt's name among Swedish gentlemen who had served under the King of the Union; but has not found it. Thus we know nothing with any certainty of Engelbrekt's military career prior to 1434. But that he lacked all previous experience of warfare is most unlikely.

Another and even more interesting question is: how did Engelbrekt finance this, his first great campaign? As yet he had no access to public funds, and his private fortune cannot possibly have sufficed. As far as I know, no expert has looked into this question, either.

Yet this peasant leader had to provide for an immense host, hitherto the largest ever to appear on Swedish soil. When he was about to blockade Stockholm his army is stated to have amounted to 100,000 men. Since this figure would mean that one in five of the entire population (then about half a million) had gone into the field, this can only be a gross exaggeration. Even an army of 40,000 or 50,000 (according to another statement) must also be excessive. Furthermore, the 1434 campaign was undertaken in haymaking and harvest time, when fields and meadows were crying out for peasants to reap them. But even if these figures must be greatly reduced, the number of troops who had to be equipped, fed and supplied, was still huge. That the leader of the revolt must have had a substantial war-chest at his disposal is also evident from his cash payments to a number of bailiffs, in exchange for their castles. But where did the money come from? How could Engelbrekt keep his great army supplied for four whole months as it marched through the kingdom?

Gustav Vasa, when his turn came, borrowed the necessary money from the Lübeckers; his war against the Danes was waged on credit. In Engelbrekt's rising, too, the name of Lübeck crops up. The insurgents were fighting the same foe as the Hanseatic League, namely King Erik of Pomerania. So the obvious question arises: did Engelbrekt receive economic support from the League?

Professor Erik Lönnroth (*En annan uppfattning*, 1949) finds a remarkable coincidence between the time of the insurrection's outbreak and an exceedingly sensitive juncture in the Union king's peace negotiations with the Hanseatic cities. For him the Swedish rising came at a most inconvenient moment. In fact it turned the tables against him. Was this pure coincidence? Or had it been agreed in advance?

There is evidence to show that Lübeckers owned mines at Norberg, in Bergslagen. Letters from German residents there have been found in the Hanseatic archives. As far as we can see from extant documents, however, no meetings were held between the men of Bergslagen and the Hanseatic League, other than those necessary in the normal way of business. There is no evidence whatever of any political links between Lübeck and the insurgents.

That a popular Swedish rising should have been financed by the great German capitalists of those days is an intriguing theory; but it can be nothing more. Research into this question has probably got as far as it ever will. So the historical enigma remains. Where did Engelbrekt obtain the money for his rising?

The Captain-General

After his war with the Hanseatic League had been brought successfully to a close, King Erik sought to open negotiations with his rebellious Swedish subjects. An armistice between the two parties followed, and thereafter compromise succeeded compromise. Soon the two parties were joined by a third: the Swedish aristocracy. By devious manoeuvres the nobles did all they could to get rid of Engelbrekt. As we have already surmised, the nobility and the commons had had entirely different motives for supporting the revolution. And now the popular leader finds himself seated beside the young Earl Marshal, Karl Knutsson Bonde, in the country's councils. From now on until Engelbrekt's death the sequence of events becomes so involved and complex that I shall not even attempt to survey it.

The meeting of the Estates of the Realm at Arboga, in 1435, had elected Engelbrekt Engelbrektsson 'Captain-General in Sweden' (*rikshövitsman*). This merely meant that he became in form what for more than six months he had already been in reality: commander-in-chief of all military forces in Sweden. As to Engelbrekt's other powers, experts disagree. There are two schools of thought. Lönnroth is of the view that his political importance dwindled swiftly after the Vadstena meeting, and that the country was thereafter ruled by the Council of State. Nils Ahnlund, however, is of another opinion, one which is shared by Gottfrid Carlsson. In the view of these two historians Engelbrekt remained 'the country's standard-bearer'. For a mere amateur to try to settle matters under dispute among professors of history would be presumptuous. Nevertheless I cannot see it in any other light than that, up to that fateful evening in April 1436, the popular leader continued to be the greatest single factor in the struggle for power. Having the commons behind him and pre-eminently enjoying their confidence, he could presumably at any time have led them to revolt against the Council of State and the aristocracy.

That Engelbrekt did not desire the end of the Kalmar Union is evident from the fact that he was party to the signature of a settlement with the Union king. But agreements with Erik XIII were not worth the paper they were written on. He kept no promises and abided by no agreements – behaviour quite normal in mediaeval potentates who, though they had not yet read Machiavelli, had no need to. They knew all his arts already. And when Erik, on his way home from Stockholm to Denmark, burned and ravaged the east coast of Sweden, his own kingdom, the revolt broke out a second time.

Early in 1436, therefore, Engelbrekt had to begin a second war of liberation. His second campaign passed through Southern Sweden. Being, unlike the first, a winter campaign, it was more troublesome. Yet it turned out fully as successful as its forerunner, and as brief. Once again the mine-master from Bergslagen showed himself a consummate field commander. Probably it was these months of winter warfare and this campaigning life during the cold season of the year, most of which Engelbrekt spent on horseback, which cost him his health. In the *Engelbrekt Chronicle* we read that he contracted 'a great sickness'. During his siege of Axvall Fortress in south-west Sweden, he had fallen sick and was 'rather ill'. What the nature of this illness may have been no one can now say, but we know that afterwards he could only get about on crutches. Probably it was some acute rheumatic disorder, contracted from the snows and freezing temperatures of his winter war.

At the end of April he left Axvall to recuperate at Örebro Castle, the province of Närke having been given him in fief. But there was to be no rest for the invalid. The question of a new agreement with King Erik was to be discussed, and the Council of State summoned him to a meeting in Stockholm. That the Captain-General could not absent himself from so important a meeting was obvious.

So Engelbrekt had to go up to Stockholm. What happened then we are informed not only by the *Rhymed Chronicle*, but also in other writings. All these accounts of the matter seem more or less to agree. By this time Engelbrekt's physical powers were so reduced that he could no longer even sit his horse and therefore it was decided to travel by water. Evidently in a crippled condition and accompanied by his wife and some servants, he was carried down to the boat. After the first day's voyage across Lake Hjälmaren the party decided to pass the night on one of its islets. The early spring evening was chilly. A fire is lit to warm them. Just then a boat with a number of men on board draws into sight. Among its occupants is Måns Bengtsson of the noble Natt och Dag family, son of Bengt Stensson, the lawman of Närke and lord of the nearby castle of Göksholm. Bengt Stensson and Engelbrekt had been enemies but had recently resolved their differences. Engelbrekt takes it for granted that the son of his former enemy is approaching on some peaceful errand, perhaps to invite him and his party to pass the night in his father's castle, and sends one of his servants down to the shore to show Måns Bengtsson the best spot to land.

The boat 'struck hard against the land', and Måns Bengtsson jumped ashore. Running up to Engelbrekt, who, on crutches, stands there awaiting his guest, he shouts: 'May I have peace from you in Sweden!' Engelbrekt refers to his reconciliation with Bengt Stensson. But Måns Bengtsson 'struck straightway at him with an axe'. With one of his crutches Engelbrekt tries to ward off the blow. The axe strikes his hand and cuts off three fingers. Turning, with his assassin at his heels, he tries to flee. With 'wrathful hands' Måns Bengtsson cuts a deep wound in Engelbrekt's neck, and then, with another blow of the axe, cleaves his skull. As Engelbrekt, his skull crushed, lies on the ground Måns Bengtsson is joined by his men, who shoot the corpse through 'with many arrows'. Wife and servants are taken prisoners to Göksholm. Later they are released.

The assassination of Engelbrekt who, completely defenceless, unsuspectingly had gone out to meet his murderers on crutches, was a crime of the first order. No other mediaeval event caused so loud an outcry. In popular fantasy and tradition it has survived for more than five centuries. As for its propaganda value, in the form it was disseminated in by the *Engelbrekt Chronicle*, it is beyond exaggeration.

The local peasantry 'in tears' took the people's leader's corpse to a nearby church, whence 'for greater honour sake' it was moved to the city church in Örebro. After his martyrdom Engelbrekt became a popular saint. At his tomb in Örebro church God caused many miracles to occur, and the lame and the halt were cured. In an entry in the Stockholm city records for 1487 mention is made of a pilgrimage to Engelbrekt's tomb. As Bishop Thomas's *Song of Freedom* bears witness:

> Many a pilgrim seeketh it out
> and there of his ill is quit,
> and harmless goeth home.

The subsequent fate of the popular leader's relics is a problem no one has ever been able to solve. At all events they have totally disappeared. Even his tomb is no longer to be seen in Örebro church, nor even any trace of it. But there is a chapel to his memory in one of the side-aisles. The fate of his original grave is an unexplored subject. Probably his relics were removed from the church as early as the 16th century at the time when the Lutheran faith was trying to extirpate the peasantry's worship of saints. A parallel may be drawn with the bones of St. Bridget which, as we have seen, were moved several times over. When the ground was being dug up for the construction of a new chapel in 1898, says Nils Finnhammar, director of Örebro Museum, numerous craniums and parts of skeletons were brought to light, and the rumour went round that some of them had belonged to Engelbrekt. But none of the craniums showed traces of an axe-blow.

What was the date of his murder? Research has had two Fridays to choose between: April 27, and May 4, 1436. It has settled for the former. But the site of Engelbrekt's murder has proved impossible to determine with any certainty. A promontory in Lake Hjälmaren, some six miles or so from Örebro, has long been known as 'Engelbrekt's Holm', the general rising of the land-level having joined it to the mainland. Here, in 1818, three hundred and eighty-two years after the murder, a monument was erected. It bears the legend: 'Here fell Engelbrekt Engelbrektsson, the Bulwark of Swedish Liberty, Gustav Vasa's forerunner, and Victim of a Vile Murder, April 27, 1436.' This memorial was put up by the then owner of Göksholm, G. M. von Rehausen. According to popular belief, no grass would ever again grow in this place; all the islet's vegetation was doomed to wither away. The ground was accursed for ever for having drunk Engelbrekt's innocent blood.

But today this promontory on the shore of Lake Hjälmaren is a lovely leafy grove with lush grasses and fresh and exuberant greenery. One day in June 1970 I saw how the most delightful lilies-of-the-valley were blooming there, like a white chaplet about the monument to the champion of our national liberties.

Popular belief thought a curse would rest for all futurity on the Natt och Dag family, one of whose members had done the deed. Yet Måns Bengtsson's real motives for his act are obscure. Probably it was some deep personal resentment against Engelbrekt. Between the murderer's father and Engelbrekt there had been a long-standing enmity. Olaus Petri tentatively suggests that father and son were in league, had jointly planned the murder. There are those who opine, he writes, 'that it was Herr Bengt who counselled him (Engelbrekt) to take boat.'

The Swedish 19th-century historian Anders Fryxell tells how the murderer was afterwards smitten by the bitterest remorse: 'But all his remorse did not suffice to wipe out his deed. The people always regarded Måns Bengtsson with deepest loathing.' For the commons, whom this act had deprived of their beloved leader, this reaction was most natural. But it was not shared by all classes of the country. Olaus Petri writes, briefly, that 'some counted it but small harm that Engelbrekt had been rid out of the way' – a mild way, to say the least of it, of describing the real state of affairs. The Danish historian Erik Arup, on the other hand, does not mince his words. In *Danmarks Historia* he writes that Engelbrekt

Engelbrektsson was murdered 'to the great relief of the Swedish nobility' – words which I believe to be the historical truth.

Presumably the man who drew the deepest sigh of relief was the young Earl Marshal, Karl Knutsson Bonde. After Engelbrekt's death, Karl Knutsson, his most dangerous rival out of the way, became the chief man of the realm. And therewith events took a new course. Wishing to be all-puissant in Sweden, the lords of the council and the rest of the nobility wanted to be quit equally of King Erik and of Engelbrekt. Thereafter the character of the Engelbrekt rising changed. It became a civil war. Engelbrekt's peasants had served their turn and were no longer needed.

Symptomatic is Karl Knutsson's immediate protection of the murderer. According to the usually reliable Ericus Olai, Knutsson issued a proclamation protecting Måns Bengtsson. It decreed that none might 'persecute, denigrate or libel him for his deed,' an injunction issued 'for the sake of peace and quiet in the realm.' Undisturbed by any considerations of justice, the murderer was to be allowed to continue his career. A member of the Council of State, one of the most important and respected men in Sweden, at the coronation of King Kristoffer in 1441 he was dubbed a knight. Finally, in 1451, Måns Bengtsson succeeded to his father's position as lawman of Närke. Thus the murderer of the Captain-General became the supreme representative of justice in the very assize where, seventeen years earlier, he had committed his own heinous crime. Had our present twenty-five year proscription period for murder then been in force, and Måns Bengtsson been prosecuted, he would have had to pass sentence on himself!

These latters patent, protecting Måns Bengtsson, implicated Karl Knutsson in the suspicion of being involved in Engelbrekt's murder. Undeniably, he had a strong motive for it. His family relationship to the murderer has also been pointed out: Måns Bengtsson's paternal uncle, Nils Stensson, a councillor of state, was Karl Knutsson's brother-in-law. But the connection was a distant one and most great 15th-century Swedish families were more or less related by marriage. So this is no valid evidence of his complicity; and for lack of evidence he must be acquitted. What is obvious is that he protected a murderer, who went scot-free. Current Swedish law metes out two years' imprisonment 'for protecting a criminal'. The parallel merely illustrates the difference between Swedish justice now and five hundred years ago.

No portrait of Engelbrekt exists; but his assassin can be viewed in a mediaeval wooden sculpture showing the descent of Christ from the cross. The work is part of an altar cupboard, now in Örebro Museum. Only about a fifth the size of the sculptor's other figures, Måns Bengtsson is a little figure down in one corner. His hands clasped, he kneels at the Redeemer's feet, imploring the crucified one to forgive him his sins.

Whether repentant or not, one thing is certain: the 'vile murder', as it is called on the monument, went unpunished. On the contrary, it seems to have been rewarded; a fact of historical interest.

The Living Engelbrekt : his achievement

The life of Engelbrekt Engelbrektsson was in high degree of the stuff of myths and legends. Therefore I must distinguish between Engelbrekt as he was when alive, and as a mystical figure. First, his living achievement.

As I have said, modern research, chiefly represented by Erik Lönnroth, has sought to reduce Engelbrekt's influence on political developments considerably. Further, the traditional view of his work, based mainly on the 19th-century historian Geijer, has been re-evaluated on two important points:

1. Engelbrekt's rising was not aimed at the Kalmar Union as such; its goal was therefore not the foundation of a national Swedish state.

2. The Arboga meeting of January 1435 'can in no circumstances be called Sweden's first parliament'; and consequently Engelbrekt is not the originator of the Swedish Diet.

Socially conditioned, the Engelbrekt rising had been a violent outbreak of fury and despair, fomented by starvation, oppression and general misery. If the peasantry had taken to their spiked clubs and followed their leader against the Danish bailiffs it was because their families' daily bread had been at stake. That is to say, the commons had not been incited by any hatred of the Danes, as such. Their hatred had been for particular individuals, as we see from the case of Jösse Eriksson who in due course was seized by resentful peasants in Östergötland, and beheaded at the town of Motala. Not that there were not other foreign bailiffs who had distinguished themselves by their decency and justice. Prominent among these was the German-born Hans Kröpelin of Stockholm Castle, of whom it has been said: 'The local population appreciated his just and humane administration and regarded him as virtually one of themselves.'

Nowhere in the sources does Engelbrekt appear to have been an opponent of the Kalmar Union. On the contrary, it must have in the highest degree lain in the peasants' interest to preserve a Union which, for more than forty years, had brought the Nordic peoples the blessings of continuous peace. Proof exists that in the provinces of Southern Sweden, which profited greatly from the free trade across the border, the commons were strongly pro-Union.

The second point which has been clarified is the question of the origin of the Swedish parliament. In 1935 the Quincentenary of the Arboga Assembly was celebrated with much official pomp and circumstance as the birthday of the Diet. Historians and poets were mobilized, publications came out in time for the jubilee praising Engelbrekt to the skies as the father of Sweden's five-centuries-old parliament, so deeply revered. Swedes felt they had every reason to be proud of themselves.

The jubilee, however, turned out to have been premature. The 1935 event lacked any historical basis. It had all been due to a misunderstanding, an erroneous reading of the *Karl Chronicle*. Something had been read into its pages which is not there: namely that the commons of Sweden had been represented at Arboga in January 1435. For this there is no evidence. Some nine-tenths of the Swedish people were in all probability *not* represented at it, hardly a cause for rejoicing.

Actually the Swedish parliament has no definite birthday on which historians can agree. Some of them are of the view that the Riksdag was founded at the election of King Magnus Eriksson on Mora Mead in 1319; while another scholar thinks it may have occurred at the 1464 meeting of the whole realm in Stockholm. As far as a layman can determine, the institution slowly grew into being as the result of a long process, from the meetings of the High Middle Ages to the definite establishment of the Estates of the Realm by Gustavus Adolphus' Parliament Act of 1617.

Engelbrekt's liberation movement also spread to Norway. The Norwegian peasants followed their Swedish brothers' example and flew to arms. But the Norwegian insurrection did not turn out so happily as the Swedish. Within a very short space of time it had ended in crushing defeat. Simultaneous disturbances among the Danish peasantry came to the same unhappy end.

In Sweden, Engelbrekt had had all classes of the population behind him and had been completely victorious in two campaigns. Yet even this did not suffice for his peasants' demands to be met. There were some changes in their conditions of life, of but little significance. Instead, the fruits of victory fell largely to the upper classes, a fact admirably expressed by a Norwegian historian: 'And, sure enough, the victorious insurrection was exploited by the indigenous aristocracy to its own advantage.'

And that, in a few words, was the final outcome of Sweden's first great popular rising.

The profound tragedy of Engelbrekt's insurrection has many parallels in world history. A revolution breaks out spontaneously, and for a while enjoys great success. But gradually it passes into new phases. The revolutionaries, it turns out, have been fighting for different goals; are therefore unable to unite; and their internecine strife is exploited by reactionary forces which finally gain the upper hand, whereupon the insurrection only leads to renewed oppression, sometimes harsher than the old.

When Engelbrekt's life was terminated, his achievement was still incomplete. Just how much he had meant to the commons in their struggle for freedom, however, was soon to become plain. The Council of State and the privileged classes rejected the peasants' social demands. What had been a general rising of the whole people was forthwith turned into a class war within the splintered structure of the Swedish community. From now on, Engelbrekt's folk had to turn their weapons against their own native lords. The country had been liberated from Danish rule. But from now on, as far as I can see, we are obliged to describe the rising as an *out and out class war within Sweden;* a sanguinary contest among Swedes.

The man who had been the peasant leader's right-hand man and his most capable commander and who now took up the dead man's mantle and attempted to bring his achievements to fruition, was Erik Nilsson Puke. Before long, open hostilities broke out between Puke and Karl Knutsson. Puke summoned the Dalesmen and the men of Västermanland to arms and for a while his fresh insurrection met with success. Over and above his class allies Karl Knutsson had on his side the city burghers, notably the citizens of Stockholm. With intent to deter the rank and file of the peasantry in other provinces from revolting, he behaved toward them with the utmost ferocity, causing as I have already said, four peasants to be burnt at the stake outside Västerås Castle.

After a preliminary settlement, Puke too fell into the hands of his enemy, by treachery. Breaking a promise of safe conduct, Karl Knutsson had him beheaded in Stockholm, in February, 1437. Bishop Thomas, the man who had guaranteed the safe conduct, bore witness to the Earl Marshal's treachery, and it aroused in him the profoundest indignation.

What the sources tell us about Erik Puke is little enough, and I should like to know more. He appears as an upright man of action, a lover of liberty and, after his death on the scaffold, a deeply tragic figure. In the *Karl Chronicle*, inspired by Karl Knutsson, he is for obvious reasons depicted as a scoundrelly rebel and an inciter of rebels. Gottfrid Carlsson writes of him: 'His epitaph was written by the hand of an enemy; having been deprived of his life, he was thereafter denied the honourable obituary he undoubtedly deserved.'

Now Engelbrekt's successor, too, had been disposed of. Once again the peasants lacked a leader. For the time being the insurrection had been crushed. The well-off and the privileged had triumphed. Måns Bengtsson's axe had cleared the Swedish aristocracy's road to power, personified now by Karl Knutsson Bonde. Up to 1441 he remains the most powerful man in Sweden.

On Palm Sunday 1437, about a year after the murder of Engelbrekt, a meeting of the lords, which can only be called a reactionary epilogue to the great popular rising, was held at Strängnäs.

At this meeting the Council of State issued an edict, known as the Strängnäs Decree. It gives us a reliable picture of the state of affairs in Sweden after the rising. Certain improvements are proclaimed in the commons' lot. Days of compulsory labour are to be reduced by one-third. They are also granted certain minor relief from other burdens. But this was their total gain. The so-called lawful tax (*laga skatten*) was still to be exacted as before. Another paragraph of this decree, though it may seem to imply an improvement, is, as an image of the times, horrific: children brought up by peasants and countryfolk may no longer be taken from their fathers and mothers against the latters' wishes. 'None shall have power so to do', we read. Which can only mean that, earlier, someone had: peasants' children had been taken from their parents and forced into service. Just how common this malpractice had been in reality is impossible to assess. The explanation is the usual one: 'detailed studies are lacking'.

Peasants who had fled to the cities during the Engelbrekt rising and were there wandering about as 'litherers'* were to be forced back to the countryside and there be degraded to the lowest class of servant ('*legohjon*'). But the most serious threat to the peasants' personal freedom was contained in a paragraph which reads: 'No peasant or countryman or their servants shall bear cross-bow, armour or the like weapons to church or council, market town or banquet; let those swords which are thus borne be forfeited.' Engelbrekt's peasants had inspired respect. The nobility, the upper classes, now wished to disarm them.

Karl Knutsson and his fellow nobles had made up their minds; there were to be no more peasant risings. Henceforward peace and quiet should reign in the land. But hardly six months after the lords' meeting at Strängnäs, in the summer of 1437, matters again came to a head. Once again, disturbances broke out. First, among the Dalesmen; then among the men of Värmland. The insurgents killed the bailiffs whom Karl Knutsson had sent to govern them.

Against these quarrelsome and rebellious peasants the Earl Marshal prepares to take new deterrent measures. The time has

* '*lättjades*' = 'lazed about'—the old English word about fits the bill.—
Transl.

come for someone to be made an example of. At a meeting of the Council at Arboga, at Christmas 1437, Karl Knutsson defines the nature of these measures. It is his intention to march up to Dalarna and there chop a hand and a foot off every Dalesman. Whereafter he will go on to Värmland and inflict on the peasants of that province 'the same pain'. The *Rhymed Chronicle* devotes eleven whole lines to Karl Knutsson's recipe against peasant risings, culminating in a declaration of principle, based on experience:

> For if the commons be not whipped full sore,
> None will obey us more.

Let no one suppose that Karl Knutsson Bonde was crueller than other men in his position in that century of peasant insurrections; perhaps he was even less so. I believe Bertil Waldén's assessment, in his work on the Engelbrekt rising, is correct: 'To deprive ... rebellious subordinates of a hand and a foot would have been regarded as a fairly humane disciplinary measure for the age.'

In the upshot the Dalesmen were not exposed to a general crippling. Perhaps the mere threat sufficed. Anyway, the Dalesmen made peace with the Earl Marshal, and had to pay heavy fines for slaughtering his bailiffs. But the men of Värmland did not throw in their hand. In the person of Torsten Ingelsson, earlier one of Karl Knutsson's lieutenants, they had found a leader of military skill, and under his command threatened Närke. A host of cavalry had to be sent against them, and a pitched battle had to be fought in north-west Värmland, in Jösse hundred, before the insurgents could be quelled. Cruel reprisals were then exacted from the Värmland countryside. In the late winter of 1438 the whole of the Fryksdal and Älvdal valleys were laid waste, and Torsten Ingelsson, together with another leading insurgent, Jösse Hansson, were burnt alive.

Both in Västmanland and in Värmland Karl Knutsson used fire to extirpate the evil dwelling in factious and disobedient peasants. Further on we shall see how this evil nevertheless survived and found its outlet in renewed risings.

One of the most widely read of Swedish historians, Carl Grimberg, sums up his older colleagues' erroneous assessment of the Engelbrekt rising: 'By their participation in the struggle for freedom the lower estates also freed themselves for all futurity from the threat of serfdom'. This statement would be good history if it said '*for the moment*' or '*for this time*', instead of '*for all futurity*'. Unfortunately, as it stands, the statement is false. The threat of servitude remained latent for centuries to come. It again became imminent a century after Engelbrekt, under Gustav Vasa's régime which was influenced by his German advisers, and again during the hegemony of the nobles in the mid-17th century, two hundred years after the 'little man's' revolt.

In the history of the Swedish people many dramatic events still await us.

The Myth

It is my belief that Engelbrekt, as a myth, achieved a good deal more than was ever achieved by the real Engelbrekt in the course of a mere two years.

After his martyrdom he became, as we have seen, a popular Swedish saint, hardly yielding pride of place even to Saint Erik at Uppsala. In the chroniclers' narratives his revolt was exploited to whip up hatred for the Danes; the suspected complicity of the national Swedish party's leader in his death was expunged from the records. During the latter part of the 15th century a regular cult grew up of the popular leader's memory. In the course of a dispute with his fellow-nobles Sten Sture the Elder* conjured up the bogey that the peasants might find a new Engelbrekt – 'cast up an Engelbrekt on to the neck of the realm'.

In the Reformation period the liberator was denigrated. The new Swedish Church accepted no Catholic saints. In his *Chronicle*, even Olaus Petri is critical of Engelbrekt; he exhorts the common people to be loyal to that authority which God has placed above mankind, and reproaches the Bergslagen miner for his rebelliousness 'against his rightful lords'. Olaus Petri's view was that from time to time men must 'suffer one tyrant, thereby to void themselves of many'. Even the strictly Lutheran Charles IX, who had himself revolted against Sigismund, the rightful King of Sweden, called Engelbrekt 'a

* See p. 86 et seq.

somewhat rebellious fellow'. But we cannot expect absolute monarchs to show understanding for any revolutions except their own.

But if Engelbrekt's name and deeds lived on down the centuries this was above all thanks to Bishop Thomas's *Song of Freedom*. Erik Lönnroth's admirable monograph of this poet (*Biskop Thomas av Strängnäs*, 1966) places him in his correct historical context and exhaustively explores his relation to the liberator.

Bishop Thomas of Strängnäs and Bishop Sigge of Skara had been staying with King Erik in his castle of Vordingborg, in Denmark, when the news of Engelbrekt's rising reached them. The two Swedish prelates were panic-stricken. In a still extant letter to their colleagues they give vent to their terror. For them this rising of the peasantry is 'a fire of evil and destruction' which had been lit by 'the blind commonalty of our realm'. In their letter both bishops pray to God Almighty that He of His gracious mercy will 'put out this perilous fire, that it grow not endlessly'. Clearly they had the long-standing Hussite Rebellion in mind.

A couple of months later Bishop Thomas was one of the lords spiritual who, at the Vadstena meeting, at first declined to despatch the letter rescinding their oath of fealty to King Erik. At this juncture Thomas was still opposed to the insurrectionary leader; as we have seen, he accuses him of plundering church property during the revolt. But before long Bishop Thomas joined the liberation movement and was sitting together with Engelbrekt in the Council of State. A few years after Engelbrekt's death it was he who wrote the remarkable song, which was to survive down the ages, acclaiming his memory. In 1434, Engelbrekt and his 'blind commonalty' had been, in the eyes of Bishop Thomas, the very personification of evil. Five years later, in 1439, in his *Song of Freedom*, he was lauding Engelbrekt to the skies as a saint and a worker of God's miracles, as God's instrument on earth.

'What sort of a man was this, who could make such an about-face?' Lönnroth wonders.

The sources do not suffice for a definite answer. We must seek purely psychological explanations, not to be found in the documents. It may be that his personal acquaintance with the popular leader caused Thomas's volte face. The bishop makes a somewhat

opportunist impression. But in the matter of Engelbrekt his conversion was probably sincere. Further, it should be borne in mind
that the *Song of Freedom* was written at a juncture when it had
become crucial at all costs to incite the Swedes to resist the king of
the Union, whom its verses depict as 'a tyrant and an enemy of
God'.

From the sources it is obvious that Bishop Thomas of Strängnäs
was a wealthy man, who had an eye to his worldly goods – a trait
by no means unusual among lords spiritual. Among other things
he owned smelting-huts in the very district of Bergslagen where the
great insurrection had begun. In the autumn of 1437 he complains
of not having received the mining monies due to him, because of the
troublous times. Bishop Thomas, according to what we know from
the sources (writes Kjell Kumlien, an expert on these problems),
'was deeply interested in matters to do with economy, and was
naturally concerned to exact the Bergslagen taxes due to his see and
whose collection was being seriously impeded by this rising centred
in the mining districts of Västmanland. This circumstance, hitherto
overlooked by research, should be taken into account in any study
of Bishop Thomas's attitude toward Puke's rebellion – perhaps also
to Engelbrekt's.'

That is to say, the bishop may have had purely personal and
financial reasons for his extreme anxiety on hearing of the rebellion.
From the outset, his attitude to Engelbrekt's war of liberation was
ambivalent. But however we choose to see his tergiversation, in
writing his *Song of Freedom* Thomas gave both Engelbrekt and
himself a permanent place in our annals. His work has survived its
first half-millenium, and whatever interpretation we place upon it
this timeless poem remains a living flame, burning in the darkness
of the Later Middle Ages: exciting words in the struggle to achieve
a state of affairs which has so far nowhere been permanently established in our world.

At Vadstena the little miner had seized the Bishop of Strängnäs
by the throat – an act of assault and battery against a church
dignitary which in normal times could have brought him to the
block – but by the irony of history it was just to this very Thomas
of Strängnäs that Engelbrekt was to owe his posthumous fame.

Underblown by the Gothic movement, by romanticism and by the nationalistic view of history taken by another of our Swedish poets, Geijer, the Engelbrekt cult reached its apogée in the mid-19th century. Now the mine-master is made to appear a liberal nationalist, and thus a personality very much in the spirit of that age.

Geijer and his epigones make Bishop Thomas appear to be deeply read in the ideological doctrines of 19th-century liberalism. At this time the liberator also conquers the Swedish theatre, where his star burns brilliantly. Engelbrekt also becomes the favourite hero for authors of historical novels. In 1865 'the king and people of Sweden' erect an imposing statue to 'that little man' in the market place at Örebro, where the 'faithful defender of Sweden's freedom' now stands. In his hand he holds an axe, and from his belt hangs a huge two-edged sword.

In the reign of Karl XV (1859–1872), this Engelbrekt-romanticism bursts into full flower. The mine-master becomes 'the first Swede', creator of Swedish nationalism. As for his Dalesmen, they are made out to be a sort of nobility among the commons, bolder, more courageous, more liberty-loving and in every way superior to other Swedish peasants. Yet Dalarna, we know for a fact, was colonized later than the provinces which lie to the south of it.

As recently as the beginning of this century when a wave of opinion in favour of strengthening the national defence swept the country, the term '*allmogefrälse*' – 'a nobility among the commons' – which sprung from this Engelbrekt myth of the dalesmen, was revived by the celebrated ultra-nationalistic politician and explorer Sven Hedin and exploited politically during the campaign for the so-called *bondetåget*, when thousands of peasants marched on Stockholm in February 1914. Even later, in the critical years of the Second World War, the Engelbrekt myth was invoked in word and print, for instance by the historian Nils Ahnlund to fight Nazi sympathisers. And earlier, when Natanael Berg's opera *Engelbrekt* had its première at the Royal Opera in Stockholm in 1929, it drew a big public.

But the 19th-century image of Engelbrekt is baseless. Even the great Harald Hjärne, the conservative historian, objected strongly to this theatrical apotheosis of the popular leader: 'If Engelbrekt and his Dalesmen loved their fatherland, which is by no means altogether certain, it was not to give vent to such feelings in gaudy boastful rhodomontades'.

Certainly not. And I should like to add: when, late in the evening, these peasants got home from a heavy day's work, they were surely so weary that they lost no time in stretching out their limbs to rest. They can hardly have had the energy to sing Bishop Thomas's *Song of Freedom* or other patriotic ditties. Still less, compared with Hjärne, am I convinced of their patriotism. To the commons, whose view of affairs was so strictly confined to their own province, the very word 'Swede' must have been a vague concept. Often the provinces' interests differed widely and any sense of common interests ended at the boundaries between them.

This is why I assume that Engelbrekt's folk primarily regarded themselves not as Swedes but as Dalesmen, Värmlanders, Västergötlanders or Smålanders. What united them, probably, was not any nationalistic feeling, but sheer hatred of the oppressor. And it was among these people that Engelbrekt's memory lived on silently, while the literary myth about him was being created by the educated upper classes.

I have shown how our national hero has been exploited for political, literary, dramatic and musical ends. In art, too, he assumes various guises. This rebel with the immense mediaeval battleaxe in his hand was a favourite motif with our Swedish 19th-century painters; but his destiny has also captivated some modern artists of consequence. The great sculptor Bror Hjorth (1894–1968) has depicted Engelbrekt as the genuine rugged popular leader he was, a powerful figure, a man capable of seizing dignitaries 'fast by the throat', a furious spokesman for the common man, a man who threatened to drag out the bailiffs 'by the hair' and who, when they refused to parley, burned their castles. Little or nothing is left, here, of the saint. In this sculpture Engelbrekt has been given the traits of character which I believe historically to have been his. I think that it is in Bror Hjorth's sculpture we come closest to Engelbrekt the man.

Sven Erixson (1899–1970), one of our best-known contemporary artists, has painted the murder of the liberator in oils. As far as I know it is his only work with a historical motif. Executed in naïvist style, it shows some resemblance to our old peasant paintings. Here the image, surviving in the imagination of the Swedish peasantry, is of the popular saint. Already felled by the first blow of Måns Bengtsson's axe, Engelbrekt has fallen to his knees. With one hand he steadies himself on his crutch, with the other – which has lost three of its fingers – he points at his assassin, who raises his axe for the *coup de grace*. Måns Bengtsson Natt och Dag is strikingly youthful, a mere stripling, wearing a red knightly garb with a lace collar and baggy breeches. In one corner we see Göksholm, his family seat. In the background a woman in black, the victim's wife, is falling on her knees, imploring mercy of the assassin. A great fire casts sparks across the whole painting, like stars gleaming in a night sky. As a painting it is a fascinating image of man's defenceless-ness in the face of overwhelming violence. Obviously Sven Erixson was deeply moved by the terrible event.

More statues, it should be added, have been raised to Engelbrekt than to any of our Swedish kings.

The achievement of the miner from Bergslagen can be re-evaluated and reconsidered and given another content than that given it by posterity. But in one crucial respect it can never be denigrated. Engelbrekt lit a flame of self-assurance in the people whom he led. Until he appeared on the scene they had been unconscious of their powers. Thanks to him they had begun to realise that they could defend themselves against the threat of serfdom. Not until Engel-brekt does the Swedish peasant appear as a powerful factor in mediaeval society, a factor which can no longer be ignored. From now on his rulers are obliged to take him seriously. The war of liberation's immediate gains were minimal. But its victories had awakened a will to resist, which legends about the popular leader were to keep alive for centuries. For the common people's future struggles for their own liberation the myth became an inestimable asset.

The work of Engelbrekt, dead, was to be more durable than his achievements when alive.

Our Daily Bark-Bread

BREAD IS THE SYMBOL of life's bare neccesities, of all that man needs in this earthly life. 'Give us this day our daily bread', says the Lord's Prayer. Elsewhere in the Bible it is called 'the bread of life'. One of the sacraments, through which the worshipper becomes a participant in the body of Christ, is a piece of bread. But the symbol is older than Christianity. Homer calls it the 'marrow of men'. An old Byzantine proverb says: 'He who has bread may have many troubles; he who lacks it has only one. But it is a great trouble'. One of our old Swedish laws agrees: 'Unhappy beyond all others is the breadless'.

Many other Swedish expressions use the same symbolism. That bread should have been held sacred seems only natural. He who showed it disrespect was punished – witness the story of the girl who, to protect her elegant shoes when crossing a bog, stepped on a piece of bread which she had brought with her. The earth swallowed her up. I have even seen farmers in the field carefully avoid treading on broken ears of wheat – instinctively fearing the desecration of that which is holy.

Our Swedish word for bread (bröd) was a 12th-century modification of the German Brot. But bread's earliest history is linked with the worship of the gods and their mysteries. To our forefathers the breaking of bread was a religious act. Mediaeval kneading troughs sometimes bore religious inscriptions, prayers to God to bless the dough. The women made the sign of the cross over the kneading trough and prayed for the loaves as they put them into the oven. The outcome could vary with the heat of the oven, both above and below. More especially, there was always a danger that the bread might separate itself from the crust.

Bread-making was exclusively women's work. At meals the

peasant's wife, known as *matmodern* (lit. 'the food-mother'), cut the bread up into slices and distributed it among her 'family': in smaller farms the servants and other employees always ate at table with their master and mistress.

Swedish peasants have cultivated four types of grain: barley, rye, wheat and oats. Depending upon the nature of the soil and the length of the growing season, which in Skåne is very different from what it is in Norrbotten, the type of crop varies from one province to another. Prehistoric remains show that the earliest bread known to us was corn-bread. Later came rye and oats, which, after the climate had deteriorated and the weather had become wetter and chillier, came into general cultivation. In *Egil's Saga* wheat is mentioned as being imported into Iceland. But long ages were to pass before wheat, which requires heavy soil, became a common sight on the fields of Sweden. Even as late as the 19th century it was still mainly being cultivated in the plains, our real agricultural districts.

But as early as the Middle Ages wheat bread formed part of the upper classes' diet, and after the triumph of Christianity it also came into general use for the new religion's chief ceremony – the Mass. No other flour except wheat flour was good enough for the oblation, the body of Christ, consumed at the Lord's Table. And our old provincial laws stipulate that bishops who are to consecrate a church shall be given wheat bread to eat: superior food, that is, suited to the solemnity of the occasion.

When I was growing up, wheat bread was chiefly known to me as the bread of the gentry. For other people, rolls of white bread were festive food, suited to weddings, christenings, funerals and the church festivals. It was never baked on ordinary days. Not until some way into the 20th century did white bread become the Swedish people's daily bread. And, indeed, one may ask whether this transition from rye to wheat has really been good for our health. Important elements are excluded from white bread, so we are told. Be that as it may – our Swedish white bread tastes dry and unappetizing in my mouth, and I always prefer rye bread as more succulent. As a boy there was no more wonderful smell in my nostrils than the odour of rye loaves, freshly baked and steaming hot from the oven.

Like all countrymen, I have grown up eating bread as the most important part of my diet; I am accustomed to it and do not really feel I have had enough to eat unless I have had some bread with my meal. Anyone who does hard physical work can hardly manage without it. During the last hungry years of the First World War, in 1917–18, when food was severely rationed in Sweden, the authorities realised this; they gave manual labourers an extra ration. At that time I was working as a lumberjack, felling trees. My 'extra bread card' gave me 50 grams more bread a day than a clerical worker received, altogether 250 grams.

In the Middle Ages a variety of breads were baked in Sweden. In the southern and eastern parts of the country and in Finland people chiefly ate a fermented and leavened rye bread, baked in an oven; whilst in Western and Northern Sweden they made a bread known as 'flat bread' or 'thin bread', made from corn and oats and baked on an iron slab over an open fire. Even up to our own day the Dalesmen have regarded rye bread as a special delicacy. In the brief summers of the far north, so-called 'ninety-day grain', corn and oats which ripened in three months, was cultivated.

In his *History of the Nordic Peoples* Olaus Magnus devotes several chapters to this crucial factor in their existence, which followed them from cradle to grave. He cites immemorial notions about the divine origin of bread. It was Ceres who invented the cultivation of grain, he says, and Pan who hit on the manner of grinding it and turning the flour into bread. Olaus Magnus had an encyclopaedic mind. He gives us detailed instructions in various ways of 'forming bread', indeed his account is so detailed that one forms a distinct impression that Sweden's last Catholic archbishop – because of Gustav Vasa's intervention, he was never permitted to take up his office – had himself kneaded dough and baked loaves with his own hands. Certainly he must have visited the women in the baking-huts and studied their way of going to work.

Olaus tells us how in the great farms of Västergötland the women folk baked rye-loaves 'large as warriors' shields, thick and round', a reference of course to the great roundels of 'crisp-bread' still made in Sweden. The men of Östergötland offered wayfarers – their honoured guests – saffron bread, which they also gave their departing guests, 'to refresh their spirits' on the way. Olaus Magnus describes a rare kind of bread which remained fresh and edible for more than 20 years: 'if baked at a child's birth, it can keep quite well without going mouldy until the day of that child's bethrothal'. But it had to be made according to certain instructions. The dough had to be made with water possessing certain qualities it only has in the month of March; and certain rules had to be observed when baking and storing it. But, providing all was done according to these rules, a bread is obtained which 'keeps for 16 to 20 years or even longer, if it be but kept under roof, against rain and snow.' The baking was done on their iron plates, round and wide as 'a warrior's shield'. A fire is lit under each such plate, and must be kept burning ceaselessly and slowly. In the hilly parts of Sweden women used to 'gather in the light spring days at a particular place and in particular numbers, to assist each other in the work'. Olaus' assertion that the bread will keep fresh for twenty years seems dubious. But it is true that in many peasant homesteads bread used to be baked which was afterwards buried in the rye and oat bins, where it would keep for several months without going mouldy. In this way the Christmas bake could be kept until Easter.

Olaus Magnus paints for us an idyllic and charming picture of the way in which the women collectively baked their bread. He stresses that it is 'a woman's art'.

One of women's great contributions to history.

Olaus Magnus, as far as I can see, makes no mention of the sort of bread which forms the main topic of this chapter – a bread which did not come from the field, but from the forest; which, not growing in the soil, was scaled off the trunks of trees: *bark bread*. For long periods at a time and at ever-recurring intervals bark bread has been the Scandinavians' famine bread. Food when the harvest failed, it is also part of our history, and therefore repays study.

In a country whose population consisted so largely of farmers, people helplessly exposed to the forces of nature, were utterly dependent on the weather. Each crop-failure – caused either by long drought or persistent rain – constituted a deadly threat. Each heavy spring thaw was followed by floods which delayed the spring-sowing. The crop would also be ruined by early autumn frosts. Every outbreak of cattle disease was followed by a shortage of milk, butter and meat. Nor was it possible for a province staggering under such disasters to obtain help from another which had escaped them. In our days a local catastrophe to the harvest in one part of the country can be offset by aid from another; but in the Middle Ages, and for centuries to come, any part of the country where the harvest had failed simply starved, abandoned by all the others. The population was sparse, roads were almost non-existent and effective means of transport lacking. To shift any significant quantities of grain from one province to another was simply impossible. Two or three sacks of corn could be loaded onto a crude ox-cart, or a bag of it slung across a horse's back – but what help was that?

In any isolated part of the country, therefore, a year of crop-failure meant outright catastrophe. We do not know just how many victims starved to death in such years, the source materials are too scanty. From the last famine years in Sweden, 1868–69, the parish books speak of parishioners who starved to death; but it is not until 1750 that we have any real parish registers, and the Middle Ages have left us no statistics of these tragedies. So we cannot even guess how many people died of hunger or its consequences. Representatives of a nameless suffering, they faded out of life, silent and unnoticed.

Not until the 18th century did the authorities seriously begin to do something about getting grain to districts where the grain-harvest had been inadequate: and even in the 1860's the problem was not properly solved. Where crop failure had been really serious, starvation still followed.

We know little about how people experienced those times of famine. The sort of help they begged for in times of prolonged drought or rainfall transpires from the psalms they sang in their churches. But here and there, too, a secular voice makes itself heard. The experiences of a peasant whose gleanings from his field had been minimal are ironically summed up in an old rhyme. I have written it down verbatim:

> Of corn I sow ten parts,
> And then I nine do reap;
> A tenth I give to the priest,
> And am happy the rest to keep.

In such years the peasant turned to the forest for his bread.

As far into the past as research can probe, bark bread formed part of our ancestors' diet, and for long periods at a time it was the daily bread on their tables. In his great work on everyday life in 16th-century Scandinavia, the Danish historian of culture, Troels-Lund, says of its consumption in Norway: 'In certain districts of northern Norway, where the grain often freezes before it can be reaped, bark bread was the finest nourishment'.

Certain years of Torgils Knutsson's regency, in the 1290's,* were among the most catastrophic in our mediaeval history. From 1291 we have contemporary records of 'hard times and great pestilentia'. The state of affairs was still further aggravated by the frequent coincidence of plague and famine. Semi-starvation greatly reduced people's resistance to disease.

One of our oldest reliable items of evidence on famine times in Scandinavia is to be found in a bishop's letter from 1232. It is Archbishop Uffe of Lund who, writing to the Pope, gives vent to his grief at the misery prevailing in his diocese. The previous year, cattle disease had destroyed the stocks of animals. In 1232 an even more terrible torment had befallen the province: 'a fierce famine which hath taken away the lives of a great part of the people.' Not knowing how many people lived in mediaeval Skåne, we cannot estimate what is meant by 'a great part'. The archbishop was writing to the Pope to explain why the Peter's Pence had not been despatched to Rome.

A severe winter, too, was another blight on the commons. Then icy temperatures joined forces with famine. In the harsh northern climate the winters were the testing-time of men. It was a question, quite simply, of keeping body and soul together until the spring. The coldest mediaeval winters have left certain traces in the sources. In 1296 and 1306 the Swedes had a 'severe winter'. In 1331 the word 'severe' (*svår*) is supplanted by 'hard'. That year five cubits of snow had fallen. In a country where distances between one cottage and another and from one village to the next were so great, so unique a winter, with snow covering the ground to a depth of three metres, must have been well-nigh intolerable.

* Moberg, *A History of the Swedish People*, Vol. I, pp. 95 et seq.

In some annals relating to January 1346, again, we are told that 'folk and cattle perished from the cold and bad weather'. During the Twelfth Night holiday in 1402 there was so great a fall of snow 'that one could hardly fetch needful firewood from the forest'. In 1405, it rained without ceasing from the feast of St Olof in July until Christmas, destroying all crops. In 1408, again, there was a famine winter. That year, among other catastrophes, 'much cattle died on Gotland'. (This information on times of famine has been supplied me by the distinguished historian Dr Ingvar Andersson.)

From Kristoffer of Bavaria's reign in the 1440's, too, we have repeated note of years of severe famine. His enemies sarcastically dubbed Kristoffer 'the Bark King'. Such a famished state of affairs, with people eating bark bread, was an admirable argument against his régime. But we also know of crop-failures and hungry times in the years when the Swedish nationalist Karl Knutsson was responsible for our Swedish weather, namely 1437 and 1438. In 1439, King Erik of Pomerania sharply accuses the Swedish Earl Marshal, maintaining that under his overlordship the peasants had been obliged to eat bark, 'like other soulless beasts'. And it is true, there were disturbances among the commons in the above-mentioned years, presumably because the peasants were starving.

In the first years of the 1440's, Finland was smitten by a dire catastrophe: the crops failed repeatedly. The rye, the Finns' main source of bread, was ruined by drought or frost. Dry weather in spring and summer reduced the sowing, and early frosts in the autumn hindered the harvest work. The documents bear witness to many deserted Finnish farms uncultivated as a result of 'these hard years'.

A century later, during the Dacke rising, 1542–43,* Småland suffered from an extended period of bark bread, long remembered by the population as a trial past enduring. The fact is, Gustav Vasa, in order to force them to their knees, had arranged an efficient blockade of all grain supplies to the rebellious Smålanders. No grain, no foodstuffs of any sort whatever, were allowed into Småland

* See pp. 42 et seq.
* See pp. 219 et seq.

from other provinces. People were obliged to resort to a diet of bark for their daily bread.

Fortunately Småland was a thickly wooded province.

During the three years 1596–98 our forefathers were plagued by what is perhaps the longest famine ever to befall them in historical times. It seems to have comprehended the entire realm and its neighbours, and is known to us from contemporary descriptions which give us a good idea of the state of affairs then prevailing. These accounts, written down in four different provinces, Väster-götland, Värmland, Dalarna and Hälsingland, are largely unanimous, and accounts from Finland, the eastern part of the kingdom, tell the same story.

In 1596, this people who lived wholly on the fruits of the soil had been overwhelmed by a general crop failure. Spring had come early that year, sowing could take place in favourable weather and everything pointed to a good harvest. But then came a tremendous delayed spring flood, drenching the fields and submerging them for so long that the seed was soon ruined. Summer and autumn brought what our hymnbooks call a 'lasting wetness'. Day after day the heavy rain went on falling. We are told how the clothes rotted on peasants' and labourers' bodies as they worked out of doors in the wet weather, under the open sky. No dry hay could be got in; it rotted and moulded in the barns. And the cattle, affected by the ruined fodder, sickened and died in their hundreds. The meat, we are told, 'could not even be used to feed dogs and cats.'

As autumn came and supplies from earlier harvests began to run out, no new grain could be harvested. The bins and pork barrels were empty. People looked for every thinkable or possible substitute for their normal diet. They consumed bark, buds, leaves off the hazel bushes, husks, nettles, hay, straw, and various sorts of roots. They ground up all bones for flour. Their bodies became weak. People became too limp to do heavy work. Lacking even the strength to turn the hand mills in which they were grinding bark for flour, they collapsed where they laboured.

During that winter and the spring that followed, innumerable victims starved to death. Unburied corpses could be found everywhere, both indoors and outdoors, in barns and sheds, under lofts, on roads and paths. Bodies lying out in the open were eaten by stray dogs who had no one to feed them. Corpses were found with fistfuls of hay and tufts of grass stuffed into their mouths.

Thefts occurred daily and hourly. People stole anything edible they could find. The punishment was always the gallows, or the branch of a tree. Everywhere the gallows were strung with corpses of those who had tried to feed themselves with others' food. In an attempt to check such criminality, many new gallows were erected outside the court houses.

The disaster seems to have been, if possible, even more ghastly in Finland than in the mother country. We possess written records of little children who, in their hunger, ate from their own bodies, chewing up their own fingers. On the table of every lower-class home, bark bread was daily bread. A disease, known as '*blodsot*' ('bleeding sickness'), presumably caused by malnutrition, brought many people to the grave. One court roll declares: 'Hunger made men so heavy as if their knees were sunk in the earth'.

Two more years of crop failure followed, though less severe. All parts of the country were affected.

During these years of failed harvests the authorities remitted certain taxes; evidently because they could not do otherwise. There was simply nothing left for them to take. Yet there were some royal bailiffs who still collected their levy – and kept it for themselves.

As always in times of great distress and misery, the countryfolk assembled in their churches to seek help and consolation. And the priests, as always, told their parishioners that it was to punish their sinful lives that God had sent on them these years of famine.

Our forefathers lived close to their animals, closer than anyone does today. They observed their beasts' ways and eating habits, and learnt from them. Instinct guides the beasts of field and forest to their nourishment: elks, deer and hares gnaw the bark off deciduous trees and chew saplings and plants. Horses eat the bark of young spruces, which contains vitamins, and they love the aspen's bark and leaves. A horse's belly can digest cellulose, i.e., wood sugar, indigestible by man.

It is my belief that it was originally the animals who showed humans which food in the forest is edible, and who taught them to flay the trunks of young trees.

For bark bread, only the membrane immediately under the rough bark – the layer which nourishes a tree's growth and forms the annual ring – was used. This inside layer would be scaled off with an iron scraper and collected, after which, before it could be baked, there came a long process of preparing the bark. First it was hung up to dry in the open air until friable; then beaten with a flail or crushed in some other way; then ground into a flour. The bark membrane is very thin, and many trees had to give up their skins before the kneading-trough was filled with dough. Time and patience were needed to collect and produce all this wood-flour; but these people who were seeking nourishment in the forest had time on their hands. Probably whole families, adults and children, went out with their scraping irons and flayed the trees.

Leksand Museum, in Dalarna, contains a remarkable flail, with sharp iron tags to it, once used for preparing bark flour. It is a monument to ancient Dalarna, a part of the country where bark bread was common fare.

The bark was collected in summer, before the end of July and the August mists. Thereafter the trees would be damaged by the scraping irons, and might dry up and wither away. Certain types of tree were chosen for bread, notably the pine which, found in every forest, was also the most plentifully available. Long before the spruce, which was another though lesser source of bread, the pine had spread over Sweden. Among deciduous trees, too, there were three species which yielded bark flour: elm, asp and silver birch. The elm was the greatest favourite of all. Besides being regarded as the most nutritious, its bark was also the easiest to prepare.

The elm family flourishes chiefly in Asia and North America, where there are no fewer than 130 species. Of these, only three grow naturally in Sweden. It was the so-called wood-elm, a tree common in south and central Sweden but very rare in Norrland, which yielded bread.

In his work, referred to above, Troels-Lund tells of the great importance of the elm during the famine years in Scandinavia

1596–98. 'Every man, both poor and rich,' he writes, 'had to nourish himself on bark bread, no grain being available.' People living in the agricultural districts of southern Norway and along the coast used the tasty bark of the elm, whilst those who lived in mountainous districts had to be content with pine. A contemporary chronicler describes the state of affairs: 'He who was then willing to give a poor man an elm in his wood did a deed of charity; but in the end everyone made free to an elm wherever he could find one, therewith to save his life.'

This was in Norway; but there is much to suggest that bark bread was more frequently eaten in Finland than in any other Nordic country. There the villages were even more isolated than in Sweden; help in time of famine was out of the question. In his poem on Pavo the peasant, who lived 'high among the sandy meads of Saarijärvi', the Finnish poet Runeberg [1804–1877] has raised a literary monument to his people, who had to live on bark bread. The poem has no counterpart in Swedish poetry. When he enjoins his wife to 'mix in half bark' into the bread she is to bake to help his neighbour, whose field has fallen victim to frost, Pavo appears to be the very embodiment of a noble soul: and as an image of truly neighbourly feeling within the old village community his helpfulness has a basis in reality. Yet I cannot regard the submissive, patient and contented Pavo as typical of the Finnish peasantry, among whom, I fancy, wrath, grumbling and impatience were not unknown. In Finland, too, peasant risings broke out. Pavo's patience is superhuman. It cannot possibly have been shared by his class as a whole. I see him as an individual portrait.

And indeed, as Runeberg was all too well aware, the history of the Finnish common people still remained to be written:

> What tongue has told the fearful tale,
> The strife this folk has sufferéd,
> When warfare roared from dale to dale
> And winter frosty came, with hunger pale?
> Who measured out the blood it shed
> And all its patient toil?

That the blood shed was immeasurable, we know. As for its patience, it was very likely not so great as Runeberg imagined.

The common man's outlets for his impatience, however, were too few to leave their impact on history.

Even during our 20th-century wars, when food has had to be rationed, the Finns have mingled bark with their bread. A Finnish engineer now living in Sweden has told me how, during the last war, he and his neighbours baked cakes of a flour, 30 per cent of which was the same substance as that used by Pavo's wife.

I have tasted bark bread, baked according to extant recipes. Somewhat sour to the tongue, it is otherwise insipid, i.e., tastes of nothing.

Our ancestors made use of many other ingredients besides bark for their famine bread. As late as in the 19th century the Norrland countryfolk chopped up husks and straw and ground the mixture into a flour, which thus consisted of the leavings otherwise given to horses, cows and pigs. As bread, to quote the expert judgement of those who ate it, it was 'hardly edible'. The sharp tags of straw and the acid husks exacerbated the throat, and were hard to swallow. Of those who ate such bread we are told from Dalarna that they had to drink a mouthful of water to each mouthful of bread even to get it down their gullets.

Mosses of various kinds, chiefly reindeer moss, were also used by the common people. The last time these plants were on the popular menu was in the hard years of the 1860's, Sweden's last great period of famine. In 1868, on instructions from the authorities in Kopparberg County, the country agronomist travelled around Dalarna to show the peasants 'how to bake certain species of moss and lichen.'

My mother told me how, in 1868, as a four-year-old, she went out with her mother into the countryside collecting hazel and heather buds to grind and knead into the dough. Cornflour, if any was left in the bin, would be mingled with this famine bread. Otherwise it consisted wholly of other ingredients. And even a hundred years ago bark bread was everyday fare in the homesteads of these parts of the Swedish countryside which most suffered from crop failure. I also remember my grandmother telling me how she had baked bread of pine bark. The greater admixture of ordinary flour in the dough, the more 'easily eaten' was her loaf.

What effect, then, did this bread, which so often appeared daily on our ancestors' tables, have on the health of the populace? If eaten for long periods at a time, was it harmful to the stomach? Could it make folk feel ill or cause sicknesses?

As far as I know, no one has researched these questions; so, to obtain a reliable and expert opinion, I have asked one of Sweden's leading specialists on diseases of the stomach. Before replying, he consulted experts on timber research, whose knowledge on the composition of wood bark is exhaustive. Whereafter he satisfied my curiosity:

The layer of the bark which was used for baking bread, he tells me, contains cane sugar, fruit and grape sugar. Further, it consists of hemicellulose, a little sebacic acid, and a certain quantity of protein. Of the components of the bark membrane only the cellulose and lignin, substances having no nutritional value whatever, cannot be digested. The irritation caused by bark on the mucous membranes, however, is quite insignificant and we have no reason to suppose it can have had any deleterious effect on the stomach functions, either in old people or in children. This famine bread was therefore perfectly harmless to those who consumed it.

My specialist on stomach disorders sums up: 'Bark bread was only in part worthless. Mainly it was a nourishing addition to people's food, and rich in minerals.'

This positive declaration by the experts surprised me. Like many others, I have always assumed that bark bread mostly served to fill the stomach, give the hungry a feeling of repletion; I have believed that it only temporarily relieved their hunger pangs. In reality this bread, taken from the trees of the forest, was a real source of popular nourishment. So we can assume on good grounds that, during the many famine years which have passed over this people, bark bread has saved numerous Swedes from starving to death.

Among the 'extraordinary destinies of the Swedish people,' as Carl Grimberg called them, none is more extraordinary than that it should have survived them.

Thrice King

T HE DECADES AROUND THE MID-15TH CENTURY are one of the most miserable epochs in the whole of our history. They were replete with conflicts within the Union, with civil war and struggles for power among the great families. Regents followed one another in swift succession. Between the death of Engelbrekt in 1436, and 1470, the year when Sten Sture the Elder became regent, the Swedish people had eight different régimes, two Union kings (Kristoffer of Bavaria and Christian I), three regents and, for three separate periods, Karl Knutsson Bonde as their king.

At times such confusion prevailed that the realm seems to have lacked any government at all. The Union party and the Nationalist party were constantly at war. Again and again the Union was renewed 'for all futurity'; and each time it broke up. The monarchy and the aristocracy disputed the right to grant fiefs, a matter of extreme importance. But the Swedish noble families, too, were locked in internecine strife over their estates. In these quarrels Sweden's oldest and most aristocratic families make their appearance, names which are to recur later in our history: the Oxenstiernas, the Vasas, the Bielkes, the Trolles, the Totts and the Axelssons. Of these, several believed themselves called to govern and take over responsibility for the entire kingdom. Such noble families, always at enmity with one another and disputing each other's estates, were often closely interrelated.

The history of this period, therefore, makes depressing reading. Is there any reason why a latter-day reader should devote time to it? I do not think so, and therefore I have decided to give only a summary account of this epoch, presenting some of its more intriguing personalities.

One of the families of magnates, the Bondes, produced a king of

Sweden. He was number eight among the Karls. Three times he
became head of state, a record not only among Swedish monarchs
but also (as far as I know) in world history.

Karl Knutsson Bonde must be viewed as a characteristic figure
of his age. Both temperamentally and intellectually he evinces
certain essential late mediaeval qualities. In Sweden he gave a last
spurt to the dying flame of chivalry. A hundred and fifty years had
passed since it had burned at its brightest. Most mediaeval personages appear to us as having had no inner life of their own; of being
carved in wood. Of their qualities as human beings we can form no
conception. But we know more about Karl Knutsson than we do
about any of his contemporaries. If Engelbrekt, the popular leader
of the commons, is an unknown man who in middle life suddenly
emerges from the anonymous masses, this man, thrice king, was
from the outset in a privileged position. Even as a young man he
achieved fame. And since he became the outstanding figure of his
age, he deserves a chapter to himself.

To be placed three times on a throne and twice deposed from it
suggests a dramatic lifetime amid ever shifting circumstances.
It resembles the destiny of that other mediaeval Swedish king,
Magnus Eriksson, who was also deposed and driven into exile.
The resemblance, however, is only superficial. Unlike Magnus
Eriksson, I cannot see Karl VIII as a tragic personality. It is not
here his fascination lies. To come by the crown was his goal, and
in his struggle to obtain it he was repeatedly frustrated. But there is
nothing tragic about the setbacks of the ambitious. A gambler
throws the dice and loses – what is there moving about that? Of
his own free will he stakes his money in order to win more; if he
loses he has no one to blame but himself.

There is a mediaeval rhyme about Karl Knutsson's mutable fate.

> While yet my barrel freely flowed
> Both man and woman friendship showed;
> But when at length it lost its store
> Not man nor woman knew me more.

Attributed to the king himself, the rhyme can hardly be historical.
Whoever its author, it bespeaks experience of human nature, an
experience which has lost none of its validity.

Karl Knutsson's lineage was the highest possible. After the Bielkes and the Natt och Dags, the Bondes are said to be our oldest extant Swedish aristocratic family. They were related to the Folkungs. Persistent research has even traced Karl's lineage back to Saint Erik, and further back than that no one in Sweden can trace the elegance or nobility of his origins – unless, of course, he can prove descent from Odin.

Karl VIII was without question the most brilliant nobleman of his epoch. An educated and travelled man, in his days of power he kept up a scintillating and stately court. Generous to his friends and supporters, for his relative Tord Bonde, according to the 18th-century historian Lagerbring, he paid for a sumptuous and costly wedding where the guests dined off 1,400 silver plates, a wedding present worth a large fortune.

Karl VIII was also our only mediaeval king of whom we possess a portrait. The great contemporary sculptor Bernt Notke, famous for his *St George and the Dragon* group in Stockholm Cathedral, made a statuette of Karl Knutsson in gilded oak. It is said to be a very good likeness. Anatomical examination of his bones has been thought to confirm this. The sculpture, in the gallery at Gripsholm Castle, shows the king on his knees at prayer. Coarsely sculpted, the figure gives an impression of great physical strength, and in fact the sources describe Karl VIII as a most stately knight, magnificent to behold on horseback. The face in Notke's statuette, however, is not notable for its beauty. The cheeks bulge as if he were blowing up a balloon, and the highly characteristic nose resembles a potato. Karl Knutsson's contemporaries' descriptions of him are therefore contradicted by this work of art. Perhaps the discrepancy can be explained by the changes which have taken place in ideals of manly beauty during the lapse of five hundred years.

To his contemporaries, at all events, the model was a manly and handsome man, notably so when compared with Kristoffer, King of the Union. His rival for the throne is described as of stunted stature, an ugly man with a poor posture. Nor did this advantage, possessed by the leader of the Swedish national party over his opponent, lack significance.

At the age of twenty-five Karl Knutsson left his family estate of Fågelvik in the Tjust district of Småland and joined forces with Engelbrekt. Not that he made any important contributions to the war of liberation. Militarily he was more successful in crushing the peasant revolts against him, after Engelbrekt's murder. The means he used to achieve this end have already been described.

Bishop Thomas characterizes the Earl Marshal, as he then was, as follows:

> Many a stiff neck bent he
> That would not suffer his rule . . .

Perhaps when he wrote these words the author of the *Song of Freedom* was thinking of the four captured peasants, 'the worst', whom the Earl Marshal had had burnt outside Västerås Castle, in December 1436. The *Karl Chronicle* fleetingly depicts this event in six lines:

> . . . and the worst of them all
> forth from the mob he did call,
> whom folk declared
> worst blame had dared.
> These bade he confession make,
> and burnt forthwith at the stake.

Having sent the ringleaders to their fiery death Karl Knutsson granted the rest of the insubordinate peasants their lives. According to the *Karl Chronicle*, they thanked him for 'his mercy and great honour', and swore never again to repeat their act of lunacy. The same effective deterrent was applied to the two leaders of the Värmland rising, as the *Karl Chronicle* says in a single line:

> Both were burnt in one fire.

As has already been suggested, Karl Knutsson intended to reign over an obedient and submissive commons.

In the *Chronicle* the man who thrice became king of Sweden is likened to the greatest of all heroes, the Archangel Michael himself, prototype of all crusaders, original ideologist of chivalry. Even so, after King Erik's deposition, the Earl Marshal reached in vain for the crown. In 1441, Kristoffer of Bavaria was elevated to the throne, and Karl had to content himself with the fief of Finland. The *Chronicle*'s comparison between the two candidates is crushing for the Union monarch. At his coronation, the populace, seeing the two men together, cannot comprehend the choice which has been made. In their eyes Kristoffer, small and squat, looks completely insignificant beside the tall and imposing Karl. It is he who bears himself like a king.

This unnatural choice instantly brought its own punishment, in the form of a severe crop-failure. In the last years of the 1430's when the Earl Marshal was governing Sweden, the weather had always been fine and what it should be, alleges his chronicler; but as soon as the Union king had taken over, the weather changed and became dreadful. Each year turned out worse than the last, and famine ensued. It was Kristoffer's sinful and vicious life which was bringing these hard times on the people. The ancient belief in a causal connection between fertility and the lives led by kings was still strong. The king was still held to be responsible for the weather, part of a deeply rooted monarchic superstitition which has survived the millennia.

According to the *Karl Chroncile*, the commons hated Kristoffer:

> peasants and husbandmen all
> him bark-king call.

It was said that, though the people were living on bark bread, the king's train, when he passed through the countryside, was so enormous that five 'lasts' of corn had to be brought together merely to feed his horses. The evils imputed to Kristoffer were too many for the author of the *Chronicle* to enumerate: 'it were too long to write'. The king is depicted as a thoroughly rotten individual, a rake, a gambler and a whoremaster. He drank 'almost every night', and was much given to lechery. He was also a perjurer, whose word could not be trusted. In brief, he was a spirit from hell, for whose sake the people had to bear these sufferings.

In 1448, when Kristoffer lay on his deathbed, Sweden was swept by a monstrous hurricane which laid low the forests. In the Blackfriars at Skänninge, Östergötland, the roof of the choir collapsed in the gale and two monks were crushed to death during Mass – so

violently did Nature react at the moment when this devil went back
to hell where he belonged.

Like Queen Margareta, Kristoffer, the Union king, was persistently denigrated by the Swedish nationalist party; and for a long
while this pitch-black image of King Kristoffer was accepted by
Swedish historians as true to fact. But modern research has seen
him in a considerably kinder light. A Swedish historian, Gottfrid
Carlsson, and a Danish, Kristian Elster, are agreed in assessing
Kristoffer's reign, though no more than a seven-year interlude, as
mainly beneficial.

He made some important judicial reforms. Magnus Eriksson's
corpus of laws for the whole realm were reviewed and revised,
improving certain aspects of the judiciary; the new version was
given Kristoffer's name. Henceforth, in each assize, a general
enquiry was to be held every year. Further, an important regulation
was introduced into the rules governing the institution of kingship.
From now on the king was to take only the advice of indigenous
counsellors: foreigners (*utföddan män*) were no longer to sit in the
Council of State. Actually this was merely a reversion to a paragraph in the original Union Agreement, whose flouting by King
Erik of Pomerania had been one of the causes of the insurrection.

In the 1430's the realm had seen a great increase in deeds of
violence. Unable to maintain law and order, the central authority
had failed to protect citizens' lives and property. Under a new royal
edict subjects were forbidden to take the law into their own hands,
to wreak personal revenge or settle their affairs by force of arms. The
Strängnäs Decree's ban on bearing weapons, in 1437, had referred
only to peasants. Now, in the name of the rule of law, it was extended
to apply to noblemen and magnates as well, indeed to all citizens
except the king's Council and his officials. In yet another decree
– the fifth, if my count is right, within a century – the old ban on
exacting 'hospitality' from the commons was once again renewed.
Presumably it had no more practical effect than its forerunners.

So Kristoffer, that ugly little fellow, would appear to have done
his Swedish subjects a certain amount of good, after all. Here is a
final verdict on his reign, as passed by Gottfrid Carlsson, that
eminent connoisseur of our later Middle Ages:

'It is hardly going too far to say that no greater misfortune ever befell the idea of a Nordic Union than King Kristoffer's sudden death at the age of only thirty-two.'

No bad passing out mark for the Bavarian! It should also be added that, as far as we know, he never burnt any insubordinate peasant at the stake.

Sweden was an electoral monarchy. In 1448 a new king was to be elected. Karl Knutsson's most dangerous rivals were the Oxenstierna clan, but its representatives, Bengt and Nils, together only received eight votes, as against Karl's sixty-three. And 'then the people cried out aloud that they would have no other king,' writes the 19th-century historian Fryxell. Various portents had also foreshadowed Karl's elevation to the throne – the election took place in the spring, after a long period of severe drought, and fears were entertained for the year's sowing. But on the very day of Karl Knutsson's arrival in Stockholm as a candidate for the throne, it rained cats and dogs and the downpour refreshed the torrid earth: 'the common folk, recognizing therein Karl's accustomed good fortune, believed they saw God to be well pleased, and their devotion to him became all the greater.'

So now Sweden had a wholly Swedish king. The first reign of Karl VIII lasted until 1457. His subjects' devotion to him, however, seems to have grown cooler with every year that passed and after nine, in the provinces of Central Sweden, it had run out altogether. The Uppland peasants revolted and he was overthrown.

This rising was led by no lesser a personage than the Archbishop of Sweden, Jöns Bengtsson Oxenstierna, a prominent figure of the age. If this history were mainly concerned not with the Swedes but with their chieftains, Jöns Bengtsson at this point would deserve a great many of its pages to himself. A highly cultivated man, he had been rector of Leipzig University, one of the most famous seats of European learning. But his interests were extensive. He was also a soldier, as able to wield sword and lance as missal and chalice. Our mediaeval bishops were men of many parts.

As archbishop of Uppsala, Oxenstierna had found cause for grievous displeasure with Karl Knutsson's policies toward the

Church and the nobles' estates. Now he decided to drive out this unchristian king and reinstate the Kalmar Union. For the Church these conflicts between Swedes and Danes were no more than deplorable civil wars within European Christendom. If the commons were displeased with Karl's régime it was mainly because of his fiscal methods, which had become sheer fleecing and extortion 'to bone and marrow'. The peasantry, too, were crying out for a new king, whether Dane or Swede made little odds. All they demanded was some relief from their heavy burdens.

Cleverly exploiting Karl's unpopularity, Jöns Bengtsson, standing before the high altar of Uppsala Cathedral, divested himself of his pontificals, his bishop's mitre and all the rest of his ecclesiastical insignia, and swearing he would not don them again until he had set the country to rights, put on his armour and buckled on his sword, as if arming for a crusade. At the head of a troop of knights this cleric and amateur soldier defeated the king's men-at-arms in a snowstorm on the ice of Lake Mälaren, routing a professional general, experienced in many wars. The duties of Archbishops of Uppsala have subsequently been restricted, but such a combination of bishop with cavalry commander was by no means unique in the Middle Ages.

Chased from his throne, Karl Knutsson fled to Danzig, where he remained for seven years. Taking with him into exile quantities of valuable possessions as well as considerable sums of money – taxes levied from his Swedish subjects – he was spared the exile's usual indigence.

On July 2, 1457, at Mora Stones in Uppland, a new Union monarch, Christian I of Oldenburg, was acclaimed. Before long it became obvious that this Danish king stood in as great need of his subjects' taxes as the Swede had done. Historians are unanimous in finding little difference between Christian's fiscal policies and Karl's. Great though the new king's exactions were, they were always inadequate to his expenses, and his constant financial straits gave him the popular nickname 'Christian-bottomless-empty-pocket'. The commons' written complaints against him also bear witness to his total mendacity. 'At times he lied to the sack', we read in one such document. To 'lie the sack full' is an old popular expression.

After six years of such rule the commons of Sweden had had more than enough of Christian I. Again the Uppland peasants rose, and marching on Stockholm, partly occupied it. An armistice was concluded, but the king broke it and subjected the peasants to a regular bloodbath. E. Hildebrand states that about one thousand men were slain on August 21, 1463; even those who had sought sanctuary in the chapel of a monastery were cut down.

Archbishop Oxenstierna, who had called in the Union king, now became the leader of the opposition against him. Finally he was flung into prison and taken off to Denmark. This triggered off a general Swedish insurrection. Its leader was another cleric of military endowments, Bishop Kettil Karlsson Vasa of Linköping, an ancestor of Gustav Vasa. Christian's army of legionaries was decisively defeated by the Swedish peasant army in battle at Haraker, north of Västerås, in April 1464. In this battle a young squire, Sten Gustavsson Sture, son of King Karl's sister, distinguished himself for his courage and presence of mind. Later he was to become known as Sten Sture the Elder.

'Now,' writes Olaus Petri in his chronicle, 'was made a general outcry among the peasants throughout the land that they would have back King Karl.' The exile was therefore recalled and at an assembly of the whole realm in Stockholm, in August 1464, acclaimed as king for the second time. At this meeting all estates are said to have been represented, which is why Erik Lönnroth is of the opinion that this assembly, more than any other, is entitled to be called the first Swedish parliament.

But Karl VIII's second reign was to be brief: a mere five months, the shortest in Swedish history. His sworn enemy Oxenstierna, released from his Danish prison, came home, and, in alliance with his episcopal colleague Kettil Karlsson, soon succeeded in rendering Karl's position untenable. By January 1465 he was obliged to abdicate, laying down the crown of Sweden before the high altar in Stockholm Cathedral and solemnly undertaking never again to hanker after it.

On this condition Karl was to receive Raseborg and Korsholm in Finland in fief. By way of consolation he was also allowed to retain his royal title.

This time Karl's place of exile lay within the realm. Tradition says he lamented his fate at Raseborg Castle:

> When I was lord of Fågelvik
> No man could call me poor or weak;
> But when of Sweden I was king,
> Unhappy, I owned not anything.

The following years of the 1460's were a period of extremely confused government, and the state of affairs almost more than I can describe. Regents succeeded each other at brief intervals, all presumably aspirants to the crown. First, Kettil Karlsson seized power, but as early as August 1465 was relieved of it by Jöns Bengtsson Oxenstierna. Oxenstierna in his turn was succeeded by Erik Axelsson Tott, a new star in the political firmament. The Oxenstiernas belonged to the Union party and enjoyed the support of the Danes; the Totts were opposed to the Union. As so often happens in history when two parties are at odds, victory goes to a third. And that was what happened now, the third party being of course Karl Knutsson Bonde. Recalled from his exile in Finland in November 1467, his promise never more to reach for the crown forgotten, he entered the capital as king for the third time. Oxenstierna attempted one last rising against him, but failed.

This was the fifth change of régime within three years. Those who like to see power changing hands had their fill of such spectacles in the Sweden of the 1460's.

King for the third time, Karl was allowed to retain his throne up to his death, on May 15, 1470. On his death bed he married his concubine in order to legitimize an infant son. He lived to be sixty-two, a ripe old age in mediaeval times. Altogether, between 1448 and 1470, he had only reigned for twelve years.

In his lifetime Karl Knutsson Bonde had taken care to arrange for his posthumous reputation. He was the first Swedish king to appreciate clearly how important propaganda is to those in power. It is the duty of those who govern to enlighten the governed as to the excellence of their régime and their own admirable qualities, and explain to them how catastrophic any other government would be. The *Karl Chronicle* has all the necessary ingredients of such a stroke of propaganda.

As propagandist and demagogue Karl VIII was a precursor of Gustav Vasa and, like his more famous successor, a successful one. Posterity believed the *Karl Chronicle*. Our nationalist historians, almost without exception, have represented Karl Knutsson as the country's bulwark against malevolent and intriguing Swedish prelates. (His propaganda of hatred against the Danes will be studied in my next chapter.) The men who opposed him are represented as faithless, treacherous and unpatriotic.

But in his chronicle, Ericus Olai, one of Karl VIII's contemporaries, is more discriminating. While he presents Engelbrekt as the good and noble leader of his people, of Karl Knutsson even though he was in power at the time when his chronicle was written – Ericus Olai avoids painting too flattering a portrait. Indeed, carefully though he chooses his words, he even dares to insinuate that Karl was an intriguer, at times a timid and even downright cowardly one.

We have seen what cruel treatment Karl Knutsson was capable of meting out to his rebellious subjects. Karl obviously had neither scruples nor inhibitions; but this has always been taken for granted in persons who lust after power, and he was certainly neither as cruel nor as tyrannous as many other mediaeval princes. Approving his political goals – a free and independent Swedish kingdom – our historians have been indulgent toward his methods. Karl Knutsson's patriotic sentiments would appear to have been sincere. It was also his policy to extend the powers of the monarch as against those of the nobility and the Church. But time and time again the Swedes revolted to depose him; obviously they did not regard his régime as beneficial to the people he ruled. In his mediaeval history E. Hildebrand opines that the words on Karl's memorial stone at Mora, *natione suecus* ('born Swedish'), are no empty phrase; but he adds: 'His misfortune was that he did not know how to put his country's interests first'. To a nationalistic historian, of course, to be Swedish is in itself a virtue.

The sources generally describe Karl Knutsson as a charming fellow, who made an agreeable impression on his entourage and who knew how to win friends and influence people. He also behaved in a manner befitting a king, in his subjects' eyes a great point in his favour. It is required of a king that he shall look stately on horseback; and Karl VIII filled the bill perfectly. It has always been a popular requirement that anyone who by the Grace of God occupies a throne shall look the part. Even so latter-day a poet as Verner von Heidenstam [1859–1940] insisted on this; on one occasion he expressed his scorn for kings who walk about in overcoats. Presumably he had been deeply ashamed to see his own king, Oscar II, demean himself by wearing so humiliating and vulgar an article of apparel. Heidenstam would have taken great pleasure in the sight of Karl Knutsson, that truly royal personage, entering Stockholm – several times over – on horseback.

In the *Chronicle* which bears his name, Karl VIII embodies every ideal of kingship; and it is in this light Swedes have been taught to see him in their history books. One might even ask whether even today the last vestiges of the *Chronicle*'s propaganda is not to be found in our school curriculum. The three authors of a school history book published in 1969 make Karl Knutsson out to be neither more nor less than the great liberator of his country. They sum up his achievements as follows: 'At the same time there were many who wanted Sweden to be a free country. The leader of these freedom-loving Swedes was Karl Knutsson'.

From the facts adduced above we can estimate the exact degree of freedom enjoyed by the Swedish commons under the rule of Karl the Liberator.

The epitaph of the man who was thrice king of Sweden is written in the first person singular. That he should posthumously continue the apotheosis of the *Karl Chronicle* is perfectly in style. Amiably he characterizes himself:

> Gladly I did that which was pleasing to God;
> in Stockholm Castle I died. God command
> my soul to eternal rest.

How Swedes Learned to
hate Danes

Swedish men,
Be watchful then;
The Dane by nature
Is a cruel creature.

(From Hyltén – Cavallius – Stephens:
Sveriges historiska och politiska visor, 1853)

SWEDEN HAS FOUGHT MORE WARS against Denmark than against any other country. Up to the formation of the Kalmar Union a state of war between the neighbouring peoples had virtually been the norm. During the first Union period, it is true, there had been a long period of peace; but in the 1430's armed conflicts, interrupted by armistices, of which the longest was under Sten Sture the Elder, began again; and the last decades of the Union were one continuous war. Afterwards, between the final break-up of the Union and 1814, Sweden and Denmark fought no fewer than eleven wars: 1563–70, 1611–13, 1644–45, 1657–58, 1659–61, 1674–78, 1700, 1710–21, 1788, 1808–09 and 1814. If we had statistics of the numbers of people, Swedes and Danes, who lost their lives in these eleven wars, they would add up to a horrifying figure.

Century after century the two peoples have been each other's curse and hereditary enemies. How can such a thing have been possible? What was the reason – or reasons – for all these wars?

The answer is to be found, I believe, in the popular hatred of Danes for Swedes, and vice versa, in the Late Middle Ages. It was a hatred, always smouldering, which burst into flame again at every

61

renewed outbreak of hostilities. A hatred which persisted for nearly 400 years. The phenomenon is by no means unique; it has many parallels in world history, for instance in the mutual hatred between the Germans and the French which has flared up again during two wars in our own century.

But such collective feelings of enmity, loathing, rage and resentment, involving whole peoples, cannot be strictly speaking hereditary; are not a fact of nature. Nor are they spontaneous and self-generating. The Swedish peasant had done the Danish peasant no harm, nor had the Danish peasant harmed the Swede; therefore they felt no personal enmity. Not knowing each other they could hardly either love or hate each other. Probably they were wholly indifferent. What is certain is that both wished to be left in peace, had such a thing only been possible. In both kingdoms the peasantry's lot was a hard one – the Danes' being the harder – and this lot was not enhanced by going out to slaughter each other and burn down one another's homesteads. For the peasant, war was above all a recurrent torment.

It has been stated that even as late as the Engelbrekt rising the feelings of the Swedes 'were remarkably free from any hatred for the Danes'. Such hatred can therefore only have come into being at some later date – as a result of extraneous influences. It was the ruling caste which, in the 15th century, during the struggles within the Union, implanted and exploited it as an instrument of policy. It was artificially nourished; the fruit of propaganda.

The Late Middle Ages saw the birth of the political song in Sweden. Most of our 15th-century poetry is anonymous political propaganda. Usually such songs were supposed to be creations of the populace, sprung from its honourable and instinctive loathing for its neighbours to the south. Actually they were commissioned by the authorities, by kings and regents, who salaried their authors. Modern research has established that many of these ditties originated in Karl Knutsson's chancellery.

In these poems the Danes are invariably described as an inherently bad lot. Treacherous, cruel and bestial monsters, they had been fashioned that way by God, and therefore could not help it. The gravest charge against them was that of breaking faith.

From these contemporary writings it is obvious, on the other hand, that the Swedes were invariably true to their word; a virtue most highly esteemed, as we see in the *Gotland Song*, from the mid-century:

> What Swedish men declare,
> that do they stand by;
> no man beguile
> nor rich nor poor;
> this ever was their way.

Against the Swede's unshakeable habit of keeping his word, the Dane's constitutional treachery was contrasted as night to day. This sub-human image of their neighbours was held up to the gaze of an unenlightened and gullible commons, who were in no position to check its truth. The subjects of the Swedish crown had to be incited against the Danes, and the surest instrument for swaying an illiterate peasantry was by easily memorized ditties. As they toiled in the fields and meadows, they passed the time of day humming these songs which were rooting in their minds the myth of the diabolical Dane.

Naturally, both at this time and later, in the 16th century, a corresponding hatred for the Swedes was being implanted in Denmark and exploited in various ways by the powerful, for their own ends. A number of Danish chronicles, too, appeared in print; in them the Swedes, in their turn, were depicted either as monsters of guile and cruelty or else as comically conceited peacocks, strutting about and showing off their gaudy plumage. Such writings no doubt appealed to the famous Danish sense of humour.

Professor Sven Ulric Palme has written an essay on the origins of anti-Danish feeling in Sweden. Whether any corresponding Danish study has appeared on the violently anti-Swedish feeling which flourished in Denmark from the 15th century onwards I do not know.

Hatred for the Danes is one of the leitmotifs of the *Karl Chronicle*. The *Erik Chronicle* has obviously been the author's – or authors' – stylistic model. But whilst the *Erik Chronicle* has great artistic qualities and is on the whole polite and courtly in tone, at points even capable of human sympathy, the *Karl Chronicle* is crude, clumsy and coarse throughout. Saturated with a nasty sadism, it evinces a rabid hatred for Karl's enemies. In it Danes are described as devils from hell, veritable angels of Darkness, whom it is quite simply the duty of every Christian man, and most pleasing in the sight of God, to plague, kill and exterminate.

Its account of how Bishop Arnold Klemedsson met his violent death, in 1434, exemplifies its contents. Arnold, being Danish-born, was of course a damned spirit, whom King Erik against the will of the Swedes had tried to place on the archiepiscopal throne at Uppsala, an action which seems to have precipitated a life-and-death struggle. With sadistic glee the *Chronicle* describes Arnold's wretched and deeply deserved end in his castle:

> At Arnö full fearsomely fared he;
> And there this spurious bishop died.
> In slivers sliced his servants him
> And salted into barrels three.
> To Denmark then they took away
> This damned, accurséd man.

By the last two lines the *Chronicle* presumably means that the bishop, having been righteously treated in Sweden, was now restored to his own proper origins in the underworld.

The seed scattered from the *Karl Chronicle* contained many fertile grains of anti-Danish hatred; falling on fertile soil, they brought forth a hundredfold.

Besides being spread abroad in songs and ballads, this devilish image of the Danes was disseminated orally, in documents and in the manifestos read out to the laity at their outdoor gatherings, their assemblies and markets. As an institution the Catholic Church, which controlled everyone's beliefs and modes of thought, favoured peace and the Union; but certain clerics placed themselves in the service of this nationalistic agitation and their sermons on that admirable theme – the noble character of Swedes and the rascality of all Danes – proved a considerable asset.

From his archiepiscopal throne at Uppsala, Johannes Magnus, archbishop and historian, together with Hemming Gadh,* the

* See pp. 94 et seq.

greatest Dane-eater of the age, preached this gospel of hatred. As the most eminent spiritual authority in the realm his position was unique, and he used it to attack Sweden's nearest neighbour. In the ears of this prelate the Danish language sounded extremely funny; it tickled his sense of humour. The Danes, he declared, haven't even the sense to talk like ordinary folk; they cough and splutter out their words, turning and twisting them deep down in their throats, so that they can hardly get them out. Even to speak at all, they are obliged to distort and wrest their mouths, the upper lip to the right and nether lip to the left. This deformation of their features, the archbishop was sure, was sheer vanity. They were so conceited they imagined it became them.

The most important of these 15th-century political propaganda poems are to be found in the collection of songs from which I have taken the quotation at the head of this chapter. Typical of the genre, this Gotland song, probably dating from 1449, is one long orgy of hatred for the Danes. It runs to 28 verses, every one of which ends with the stern warning: 'Swedish men, be watchful still!'

In this poem two characteristics are seen as above all typical of the Danes: cruelty and guile. Danes never keep promises or agreements, and in this they resemble the most poisonous and treacherous of arachnids:

> The scorpion useth to play,
> embraceth with his mouth alway;
> with his tail stingeth;
> so do the Danes
> when they parley.

In a document from the period we are told how the Danes treat the crew of a captured Swedish ship: not content with cutting off their ears and noses, they even chop off their hands and feet, after which they fling them, maimed and limbless, into the sea.

Malicious ridicule of wounded enemies is rife. In *A song of the Battle of Brunkeberg, A.D. 1471* (*En vijsa om Brunchaberg Slagh Anno 1471*) Christian I is held up to cruel mockery, and his name is spat upon. He is ridiculed for having received a ball in his nose – a comic place to be wounded – and also bleeding from the mouth.

With arquebus lead
Four front teeth fled
One after another,
In blood him smother.

Here we are light-years away from any chivalry or gallantry toward a beaten foe. This disdainful poem has been made out to be a genuine soldier's song, composed by one of the combatants at the Battle of Brunkeberg. In point of fact it is a product of Sten Sture the Elder's chancellery.

Of the three Stures, Sten Sture the Younger was the cleverest at propaganda. He travelled through the country inciting the commons against the Danes and all who favoured the Union. At council meetings and in market places he caused manifestos to be read out, accusing members of the Union party of various grave crimes.

These polemics between the two kingdoms, unexcelled in crudity and ferocity, continued during the 16th century, the Vasa period, when, instead of abating, these expressions of an undying hatred grew even more virulent. The Danes for their part disseminated a chronicle libelling the Swedes; and Gustaf Vasa riposted by having one of his henchmen, Bishop Peder Svart, pen a piece which, in crudity and the number of its insults, was fully a match for the enemy's. In the well-known song about King Gustav and his Dalesmen, bucketsful of high-grade calumny are poured over the Danes. Particularly nasty are the wretchedly ineffectual attempts at humourous jibes at the enemy.

During Gustav Vasa's reign the last traces of the tolerant and humane Union spirit, earlier found in both peoples, were finally stifled. A raucous nationalism, always sensitive to questions of prestige, took over.

On either side national feeling, at the least dissension, was easily hurt; even over events from the distant past. Learned men, Swedish and Danish, became involved in long disputes over the numbers of the fallen at the Battle of Lena, in 1208, three and a half centuries earlier. Had it been 5,000 men, or 6,000? This wrangle, though it did not actually lead to war, had other and most tragic consequences. In the 1560's the dispute over the right to use the Union arms, the

Three Crowns, was one of the causes of the Seven Years War. One wonders how deeply the common man in Sweden and Denmark can really have been attached to this national symbol, whose origins were anyway not specifically Scandinavian but European. If anyone had asked him to lay down his life for this emblem, I do not believe he would have been prepared to.

It was during the reign of Gustav Vasa that the fuel for this nationalistic megalomania, which was afterwards to burst out into complete lunacy in the 17th century, was gathered. The chief contributor was Johannes Magnus. In his history of the prehistoric kings of the Swedes and Goths he claimed that the Swedish kingdom had been founded immediately after the earth had dried out after the Flood. As for the antediluvian epoch, even the sharp-eyed Johannes Magnus could not discover any Swedish kings.

That the Swedes should gradually have come to accept this rabid view of the Danes as cruel, treacherous and devilish, implanted in them century after century, is therefore not surprising. 'Even in the lower ranks of society the conception of the Danes as the hereditary enemy became deeply rooted' (E. Hildebrand). And thus it was that a popular hatred, which the enemies of the Union could draw on whenever they needed a war-psychosis, was artificially created. Each successive war heaped new fuel on the flames, which were kept burning down the centuries.

During the wars of the 16th and 17th centuries manifold cruelties and atrocities were committed against the populations of the border provinces. Naturally this provided fresh stuff for propaganda which, exploited to the utmost by either party, renewed the two peoples' mutual hatred. The means used were old and well-proven. Each people was told all about the *enemy's* murders, his acts of pillage, rape and arson, and was given detailed accounts of the *other side's* violent deeds. Afterwards all this lopsided information was mirrored in histories enjoying official sanction in schools as factual and objective. Swedish schoolchildren were told all about what the Danes had done; and what the Swedes had done was duly brought to the knowledge of Danish schoolchildren.

I can speak to the point. Swedish soldiers, as far as I could discover from my history books, both in elementary school and higher institutes of education, have in all our wars never been anything but kindly and humane, or behaved otherwise than decently and correctly. After all, these wars were all justifiable wars, fought in defence of their fatherland. Even when they fought in such distant lands as Denmark, Norway, Germany, Poland and Russia, they were doing no more than defending Sweden. And always they fought honourably, decently, with shining weapons. Never did they commit atrocities, kill their prisoners, commit rape or take the lives of women and children.

By contrast, these history books taught me all about the Danes' monstrous behaviour in Småland, my own part of the country, during border wars. Certainly there was no lack of materials. On the other hand, I was kept in ignorance of my own countrymen's activities on the other side of the border. If they had not committed the same outrages as their enemies, they would have been showing an elevation of spirit utterly unnatural to their age – but it is in Danish, not in Swedish schoolbooks, you can read about these atrocities.

The Kalmar War of 1611–13 is famous for the barbarous cruelties committed by either side – witness a letter written by the 17-year-old Gustavus Adolphus dated February 13, 1612, to his cousin Duke Johan and extant in the State Archives.

With triumphant delight the royal youth describes a successful punitive raid – what we should today call an act of reprisal – which he had just carried out against Skåne. Within a single fortnight he had laid waste and levelled to the ground no fewer than 24 large Skanian parishes. Gustavus Adolfus reports to his cousin how he and his troops had 'rampaged, destroyed, burnt and killed, utterly at our own will.'

Royal words and therefore not to be doubted.

In this letter the king expressly declares that the Swedes 'had met with no resistance' from the 'enemy' – explicitly, the 'enemy' being a defenceless civilian population, including its women and children. How many people, we may ask ourselves, escaped alive from this Skanian Song My of 1612, – in which Gustavus Adolphus's soldiery were allowed to kill 'utterly at their will', 356 years before the Song My in Vietnam?

I first came across this authentic letter in a Danish work on the Kalmar War, and it has somewhat modified the image idea of our great hero-king I was presented with at school. Deeply impressed by our history books' accounts of his deeds I had accepted Gustavus Adolphus as one of my childhood idols, fully on a par with Sitting Bull, Buffalo Bill and Texas Jack. With his noble spirit, his courage, his scorn for death, he had utterly seduced my schoolboy heart. In my games I did my best to emulate Gustavus Adolphus, as I did all our other great warrior kings. In an autobiographical novel I have related how my alter ego tried to tread in the hero-king's footsteps:

'As Gustavus Adolphus he was up in the loft struggling with sheaves of straw which were Tilly's black cavalry, the damned catholics, locked in struggle with Wallenstein's host until, wounded by nine bullets, he lay exhausted. One dark and murky February night Karl X Gustaf storms the icy ramparts of Copenhagen, but after a bloody fray is repulsed – in a frenzy of rage he runs up the roof of the ice-cellar, and though clinging desperately to its roof shingles again and again comes tumbling down.'

How deeply I resented Karl X Gustaf's failure to storm the Danish capital in 1658! He had so nearly captured it. If he had, it would have put paid for ever to our treacherous and untrustworthy neighbours and incorporated their country in our own. Scandinavia, once and for all, would have become one great Swedish kingdom.

Enough of this hatred which had originated in the Middle Ages, and had even survived in 20th-century schoolbooks for a Swedish boy still to think of the Danes as treacherous cowardly people whose word was never to be relied on. Every time Sweden had been involved in some war in other lands the Danes had seized their chance to attack us in the rear. They had done so when we were busy with Poland in 1657; and they had repeated the same treacherous attack in 1788 and 1809, when we had our hands full defending Sweden against the Russians. What the national schoolbooks omitted to mention, however, was that the Danes' attacks on these occasions were paying us out in kind for Field Marshal Lennart Torstensson's attack on Jutland in 1644 and for Karl X Gustaf's unquestionable breach of the Peace of Roskilde in 1658.

Earlier generations of illiterates, I imagine, found it even easier than a 20th-century schoolboy to swallow this propaganda image of the Danes which helped to make possible no fewer than eleven wars between the two peoples. Generation after generation, century after century, such feelings of collective hatred were a heavy legacy on the backs of two neighbouring peoples, racially akin. Many hereditary enemies are known to world history besides the Swedes and the Danes. Indeed, I have never read of two neighbouring peoples who have been hereditary friends. It seems as if only hostility between peoples is hereditary and abiding on this earth.

But at the point of transition between the Middle Ages and the modern era there was a man of immense authority living in Sweden who did not preach this gospel of hatred: Olaus Petri. He took no part in this frenzy against the accursed Danes, which Gustav Vasa during his reign only intensified. Olaus Petri writes of these conflicts between Denmark and his own fatherland with an objectivity remarkable for his time. His judgments on the conflicts of the Union period are nuanced, free from all hatred. Unlike the official propaganda, he drew no distinction between Swedes and Danes. For him the one folk was not made up of good, noble and faithful people, and the other of beasts and turncoats. His history assesses events ethically. It is grounded in Christian morals.

With Olaus Petri viewing history so utterly differently from Gustav Vasa, it is only logical that the king should have discounted the reformer's history of Sweden, regarded it as 'of little worth'. He also had the power to suppress it, and did everything he could to prevent its dissemination. Even in the 16th century Olaus Petri's *Swedish Chronicle* could have been multiplied a thousandfold by Gutenberg's invention; but for more than two and a half centuries it was only available in handwritten copies. Not until 1818 was his work, which opened a new epoch in Swedish history-writing, printed and published in Sweden.

When he writes: 'Full oft hath truth had to stand aside in history', the reformer states an eternal truth. For his part he made an honest attempt to seek it out. No dupe of the hue and cry against our neighbours to the south, he realised the magnitude of the disaster to both peoples inherent in this novel nationalism. Nothing but fresh wars could spring from such a soil. As for the patriotic claptrap of Swedes and Danes – and the Danes were certainly not behind us in boastfulness – he writes in his chronicle:

'Wherefore little doth it behove the Swedes to laud themselves for all they have won in Denmark, no more behoveth it the Danes to boast of what they have gained in Sweden: great dam and ruin hath befallen both parties.'

Words written about the year 1540. Naturally Olaus Petri could form no idea of the 'dam and ruin' or of the sufferings which would be inflicted on both peoples in the course of the eleven wars they would have to fight against each other, up to 1814. But his words about truth which 'full oft hath had to stand aside in history' were confirmed by the fate which befell his own *History*. Not until four years after the commencement of a lasting peace in Scandinavia, in 1818, would the peoples of whom his work treated be able to read it in print.

From age to age, from generation to generation, war has been mankind's ever faithful companion and its most dangerous enemy. Christians have sought its cause in the congenital and inextirpable evil in human nature, that evil whose first-fruit was Cain's murder of his brother Abel, and in their parents' original sin, passed down to ensuing generations. To the Marxist, with his materialistic view of history, no war, in any society, is anything but a class war; an eternal struggle for possession of the land and its natural resources, and one which will continue as long as the economics of capitalism persist in our world. Apparently the Marxist does not even exempt the wars of religion, which cost millions of Europeans their lives in the 16th and 17th centuries. By concrete examples I have tried to demonstrate a third cause of war: nationalistic feeling, inciting the peoples to hate each other.

Compared with our 20th-century instruments the medieval means for fostering such hatred were primitive. The mass media, press, radio, TV are many times more effective than Karl Knutsson's propagandist poems, disseminated in handwritten copies. In the hands of unscrupulous overlords bereft of all conscience our new instruments of propaganda constitute an imminent threat to peace among the peoples of this earth.

Whatever the ultimate causes of war – and they differ from case to case – there appears to be a general consensus as to the truth of a fact so true as to be trivial, indeed banal: if mankind does not abolish war, war will abolish mankind.

The Forests and Popular Liberties

'—where are great forests, wherein is all their consolation.'—Gustav Vasa.
Where the plough cannot go,
nor the scythe make its blow,
standeth the forest——.

Old saying.

IN A LETTER to the poet Atterbom, of September 13, 1837,
C. J. L. Almquist, poet, novelist, social critic and dramatist, wrote:
'You know I am a declared friend of the peasantry.' Almquist had
tried a peasant existence himself, and even if he idealized it in his
stories he probably knew better than any other member of the
educated classes in his day and age what life was like for the common
people. On page 595 of his *Monografi* he lays express emphasis on
the peculiar status of the Nordic – Swedish and Norwegian –
peasantry in Europe, calling it a unique social phenomenon, which
had stirred the amazement of foreign visitors. 'Alone among all the
countries of Europe, Scandinavia . . . possesses in its *peasants* a class
at the very base of its population who, as long ago as anyone can
remember, already enjoyed political rights ... We who live in
Scandinavia and have been accustomed to these peculiarities from
our childhood up, perhaps see in them nothing remarkable; but the
surprising fact of it appears to the eye of an observer, the more he
compares other European peoples with those of Scandinavia.'

In his comparisons between peoples, as in so much else, Almquist
is himself a keen observer, superior both in learning and in knowledge. As long as he was able to remain in Sweden he was regarded
as possessing the cleverest head in it; but finally to save it from
falling on the scaffold, this brilliant author had to emigrate to the
United States, accused of poisoning a money-lender.

Almquist overestimated the political freedom enjoyed by the Swedish peasantry, by the commons. Nevertheless it is true that mediaeval feudalism subjected Europe's peasantry to a general serfdom, and this serfdom included the peasants of one Scandinavian country: Denmark. Almquist could also have observed the 'surprising fact of it' in a people whom he does not mention, namely the Swiss. Only in three continental countries – England's position was exceptional – in Sweden, Norway and Switzerland, did the common people escape the full weight of feudal oppression. A crucial reason for this, it seems to me, was the physical nature of these three lands.

In 1291 the original Swiss cantons, Schwyz, Uri and Unterwalden, founded the Swiss League and therewith the Swiss peasant republic, which the Habsburg princes' armies of knights found it impossible to conquer. Already, in the Early Middle Ages, the fresh breezes of liberty were blowing in this Alpine country. The little state was surrounded by mighty powers who time and again sought to conquer it by superior military strength; but behind the magnificent ramparts of their mountains its people defended themselves successfully and preserved their freedom. That this little peasant republic should have come into being in the very midst of these rapacious mediaeval principalities and thereafter survived for almost seven centuries seems utterly miraculous.

In Norway's mountains and deep valleys the Norwegian peasants, too, had dwellings inaccessible to outside interference. Mounted men-at-arms found no roads to advance by. Nor had the country any indigenous nobility; and the Danish nobles were few in number, and thereto extremely remote from their own capital in Copenhagen. To keep the Norwegians under effective surveillance was beyond the power of their Danish overlords.

Sweden, lastly, was a vast, almost uninhabited country, whose forests served her population as Alps the Swiss, and the mountains the Norwegians. The 'surprising fact' noted by Almquist thus comprehends the mountain peasants of Norway and Switzerland and the sylvan Swedes.

Our earliest evidence for the topic now to be discussed dates from the great Roman historians. In his narratives of his own campaigns against the Germans, Caesar refers at several points to the severe obstacles presented by the forests to his troops' advance. Tacitus, too, speaks of the forests as being the breastwork of the Germanic peoples. Caesar writes: 'It is the greatest pride of the German tribes to surround themselves with broad desolate frontier regions. They regard it as evidence of their own strength that their neighbours should have been driven out of their lands and gone away, without anyone daring to settle in their proximity. This makes them, in their own opinion, safe and free from all fear of sudden assaults'. (Caesar: *De Bello Gallico*, IV). Pomponius Mela, too, writes how the Germans did not wage war to gain an empire or to extend their territories, but in order that the countryside all around them should lie untilled and uninhabited. In those days the great forest regions along the frontiers of their realm had constituted part of their defences.

Our first historian to write in the Swedish language, Olaus Petri, is also the first Swede to lay stress in his chronicle on the enormous importance of the forest to the popular liberties of his fatherland: 'Sweden is such a land as swamps, mountains and forests do fortify, on such wise that the commons cannot long be forcibly oppressed, forasmuch as they have great means to oppose their lords'. And they exploited these means. In his history of the Nordic peoples Olaus Magnus describes how a peasant rising begins: 'The manner in which this is done, is that the population or peasantry, to the number of several thousand from the same part of the country, assemble at an agreed time in the forest.'

On many points the views of Gustav Vasa and Olaus Petri differed sharply: but that the Swedish forests were the bulwark of peasant freedom was one on which they were entirely agreed, as we can see from the king's letters during the Dacke rising. Gustav is resentful at the defeats which his troops of noblemen and German men-at-arms are repeatedly suffering at the hands of the rebellious Smålanders. But he finds something to which he can attribute these reverses: the forest. He writes: 'Little could we molest them up there, where are great forests, wherein is all their consolation.'

Not only has the forest been a 'consolation' to the people by affording a refuge in time of war; it has also been a vital condition of their existence, and this long before it became the Swedes' most important source of exports. We have seen how the bark of its tree trunks contributed to their daily bread. Ever since men settled here the forests have also provided them with game for their meat, with grazing and fodder for their cattle, with timber for their dwellings, with fuel to warm them, with tapers to light them, with bark for preparing their leather, and with tar and charcoal.

Quite literally, the products of the forest have accompanied the Swede from cradle to grave. Tools and utensils were all made of wood: the men's harrows and primitive ploughs, the women's spindles, spinning wheels and looms. Wood became the wheels under their wagons and the oars for their boats and skiffs. The first boat which ever floated on the water was hollowed out of the trunk of an oak. From the trunk of the alder were fashioned the wooden clogs which were people's everyday footwear. The trough in which their dough was kneaded and the table from which it was eaten were likewise of wood, and so were all their eating utensils, spoons, ladles, bowls and plates. From the forest, too, came the bench where a man sat in the daytime and the bed he slept in at nights. Of wood was fashioned a cradle for the new-born babe, and a coffin for the old man who had just died. A human being's first resting place, it was also his last.

In this way, from birth to death, the forest followed a man. And of old the forest was everyman's property – and no one's. 'The forest grows as well for the poor as for the rich,' is an old Swedish saw. Our ancestors called the forest 'The poor man's garden'. They also used it as their fortress and bulwark. Olaus Magnus writes that the Norsemen considered it 'right and just to take nature to their aid in crushing cruel enemies'. He devotes a whole chapter of his history to *On Fights in the Forests*, showing how the local population exploited their natural bulwarks offered by the terrain: 'They make deep notches in the trees along the road where the enemy is expected, bind the trees together at their crowns and so arrange their ropes and tackle as easily to pull them down and overthrow the enemy while yet he is afar off; with the outcome that horsemen and footmen, as if stricken by lightning, are slain in heaps on the spot, or else, if by chance they have entered some wretched narrow path, are overwhelmed with stones which are hurled down [on them] as if from the high walls of a fortress.'

There was another simple but effective means of barring an enemy's advance through wooded country. Impassable log-jams were constructed of trees felled criss-cross over roads and paths. These fellings served as forts, from behind which a Fabian defence could be kept up. During the Middle Ages these were primitive frontier fortresses; I have seen traces of them along the old national boundary between Småland and Blekinge.

In a country of deep forests like Sweden foreigners could hardly take a step without going astray. In such a terrain foreign legionaries could not find their way. But the natives knew every inch of it. The foreigners had to contend with an enemy who knew how to make use of natural obstacles and how at any moment to become invisible. The men of the forests, the peasants, struck when it suited them, and hid when it did not. In his letters Gustav Vasa himself bears witness to how his German legionaries, whom he had brought into the kingdom as his indispensable allies against his own Swedish peasants, could not do service in the depths of the great Småland forests. In such terrain they could not fight. Every bush terrified them out of their wits: behind it might be lying a man with a crossbow, ready to let fly a lethal bolt. At home on the plains of Germany, during Thomas Münzer's insurrection of a decade and a half before, these legionaries had had no difficulty at all in cutting his peasants to pieces. But the fighting methods of the inhabitants of Sweden, this land of forests, were strange to them, took them aback.

Here an unsought contrast presents itself with a Danish peasant rising in the 1530's. During the so-called Counts' Civil War, King Christian III suppressed his subjects' insurrection with the aid of German legionaries specially called in for the purpose. The decisive battles were fought on the plainlands of Skåne and Själland, in the open fields, where several thousands of peasants were cut down by the swords and lances of well-equipped corps of mounted cuirassiers. Slaughtered like cattle, they had no chance of escape. Whereafter the impotent Danish peasants were forcibly suppressed, deprived of their liberties. Not until the mid-19th century did they achieve a position comparable to that of their Swedish and Norwegian brothers.

My theory, then, is that the difference between plainlands and forest has deeply affected the liberties of the Scandanavian peoples.

Nowadays we should call this medieval forest warfare 'guerilla warfare'. The term was first used during the Spaniards' revolt against Napoleon, which contributed so much to his fall, and it has been the usual word for resistance and freedom-movements all over over the world ever since. Guerilla warfare is waged by irregulars, without a regular military organization and who observe no conventions of war. Such fighters are sometimes called partisans, sometimes '*franc-tireurs*'.

The Second World War saw resistance movements against the Nazi empire in a number of occupied countries. The most successful were the Jugoslavs, whose mountains and forests were a great asset. Otherwise the partisans consisted partly of regular military forces, hundreds of thousands of undefeated troops hiding in the great forests, where they took a heavy toll of the intruders. During the Winter War of 1939-40 the Finns, too, were greatly assisted by their immense desolate forests, where the Russian invaders could find no roads and, like Gustav Vasa's legionaries, all too easily went astray.

Anyone interested in the subject will find many books on it. Its topicality is obvious. For more than a decade now the wole world has been following the guerilla war being waged in the jungles and swamps of South-East Asia. Nor are forests the partisan's only recourse. There are other parts of the globe which the Creator seems to have designed specially for guerillas.

But the forests not only provided a hiding place for insurgents, where they could gather and prepare their actions undisturbed; whenever war broke out it was also a reliable place of refuge for the fleeing population. As soon as the 'fiery cross' was sent out to sound the alarm at an enemy's approach, the villagers and their families had recourse to the depths of the most impenetrable parts of the forest, taking with them as many of their indispensable belongings as they could. Homes and farmsteads were left to their fate, in most cases a fiery one. When, in due course, the refugees returned, they found only the ashes of their dwellings, in which they began to search for such objects as had escaped the flames.

The marching troops brought violence, robbery and conflagration into the land. The old court rolls contain any amount of incontrovertible evidence of such rapine. They record the peasantry's unending complaints of their sufferings at the hands of troops passing through the countryside. Sometimes such events are called *Durchzug* or *Durch-Marsch*, German words which witness clearly to the nationality of these unbidden guests, speaking their own country's language. From the border wars the provinces of Southern Sweden have preserved numerous accounts of peasant families, men, women and children, who had fled from the legionaries and taken refuge in the forest. They have been passed on from one generation to another, both in local histories and by oral tradition. *When war came to the farmstead* could be their common rubric.

'The blessed forest saved our lives,' writes the rector of Markaryd, a border village, in his notes of the Danish rapine in 1611. Many people, we may assume, owed their lives to the forest, our forefathers' bulwark in time of war.

But in another respect too the forest afforded protection to the individual. For anyone who could not satisfy his need of freedom within the village community it afforded a refuge from society's obligations, laws, rules and customs. Earlier I have stressed the conformism of the old Scandinavian community, and how little elbow-room it left for its deviants. Anyone who differed temperamentally from the majority moved within a narrow framework of tolerance. The peasant liberties inherited from heathen times and from the Early Middle Ages, severely reduced after the introduction of the class society, also imposed their own limits; and these might not be exceeded. Fixed by the interests of family and clan, they were formulated in the interests of the community. Our own age's reasons of state afford a comparison. The general advantage curtailed personal freedom; common interests were opposed to individual ones. If, as we are inclined to believe nowadays, each person's life is a goal in itself, we are here involved in an insoluble contradiction.

Peasant society had originally been based on blood-relationships, on natural family ties. And from this it had developed into an association for mutual peace and protection, opposed to other families and clans, similarly allied. But it was *entirely voluntary in character*. It was based on a social contract, to which the members of that society had acceded of their own free will, and this contract could be annulled by anyone who did not feel disposed to comply with its requirements and statutory duties. The individual was free to leave society and live his own life outside the village community; but thereafter, no longer enjoying society's protection, did so entirely at his own risk. No modern society permits the individual to make such an exit. Against reasons of state he is powerless. But in ancient peasant society this was by no means the case. If displeased with the community, or no longer at home in it, an alternative, not offered by modern society, was always open to him: *the forest*.

All round the inhabited parts of the countryside were immense wildernesses, where as yet no organized community existed. In documents from the village courts these wild tracts are referred to comprehensively as *the forest*. They became an asylum for all who had unilaterally annulled their contract with society. Juridic notions permitted a form of exile, referred to in ancient court rolls as '*skoggång*' ('gone to the forest'), where such voluntary exiles are called '*skogsmän*' ('woodsmen'). Vis-à-vis society they were equal legal entities, with whom it could negotiate.

The subject has been studied in depth in a classic work by G. O. Hyltén-Cavallius, called by Strindberg 'the cornerstone of Swedish ethnography'. On the basis of the 17th-century court rolls this author demonstrates that by no means all these woodsmen were criminals who had fled from justice. To a great extent they were people whom we should today call political refugees. 'That is to say, the Småland woodsmen, notorious in the history of Gustav Vasa, so far from being ordinary border thieves, were often men from the most powerful clans in the country, who had fled to the forest for political reasons. In so doing they were following an immemorial custom of the Gothic peoples, and to this extent were wholly within their rights.'

We can ignore the 'ordinary border thieves'. What has captured my imagination is this other sort of woodsman's motives for abandoning society. In one instance my reasons are purely personal: family reasons, which have also had a bearing on two of my novels.

In the work I quote from above we read the following excerpt from the court rolls:

In 1620, in Algutsboda parish, a certain woodsman by name Åke Duvemåla, together with his mistress, had 'far out in the wilds of the forest, among a heap of fallen timber whither none could well come, dug a hole in the earth, and then away under the earth a goodly way, large as a fair-sized cellar, and before all made a door. Thereafter he had built therein a stove of clay and stone, and dug the chimney up through the soil, with a damper in it. Within he had a bed, benches and all his belongings, pots, dishes and whatever [else] he needed. Some way from the lair was a spring where throughout the winter he had his watering place, on such wise that he rarely went out of his lair for food; but his whore not at all. And those who have seen this lair in the earth, they have said upon oath that they could never have deemed it possible to find such a thieves' hiding place. Item, the neighbours thereabouts do complain that they each year have lost fearfully many small beasts, sheep, goats and other creatures. Many hides too have been found, in sign and evidence that he is guilty of such thieving'.

Duvemåla is a little village in my own native parish, and consists only of three farmsteads. In 1833, my grandmother was born on one of these farms, which has been in the possession of the same family since the 17th century. I ask myself: did this woodsman, Åke of Duvemåla, derive from this homestead? If he did, he may be one of my maternal ancestors. It is this possibility which has aroused my interest in him.

Åke had left his village and was living in a lair in the earth with his 'mistress'. This last expression does not accord with the parlance of those days and must therefore be the editor's circumlocution. In the direct quotation from the court rolls some sentences, further on, call the woman the 'whore'. Åke's motive's for 'going to the forest' cannot be in doubt. Not being legally married, he and his woman could not live together in the village, and therefore had had to take to the woods.

It was this excerpt from the court rolls which gave me my idea for my novel *Mans kvinna*, in which an unmarried peasant falls in love with a married woman, wife of another peasant, and flees with her into the forest. The book ends with their flight. The same motif is revived in another of my novels *Ride To-Night*, in which the peasant Ragnar Svedje takes to the forest to continue the resistance to 'the German lord of Ubbetorp Manor'. This novel describes the life of the woodsmen after they have left the village. For housing I have taken the lair which Åke of Duvemåla furnished for himself and his 'whore' in the oak-clearing. In his lair, though he refuses to join him in his thievery, Svedje lives together with the forest thief Ygge. The court rolls bear witness that Åke of Duvemåla stole small farm animals, sheep and pigs, etc. Short of such thefts he and his woman would not have been able to keep body and soul together.

A number of other judicial cases, in which a man and a woman had sought refuge in the forest because of illicit love, are to be found in 17th-century legal documents. In certain circumstances 'double whoredom', so called, where both parties were guilty of adultery, was – under the harsh laws of those days – punishable by death, The guilty parties are referred to in the court documents as 'runaway fornicators' or as 'runaways from the land, male and female'. At the assize in Allbo hundred, on June 28, 1627, the court dealt with a case of adultery, where an 'old man ready to drop, more than 80 years old, had in his old age escaped across the frontier with his mistress'. Any old man who committed such a mighty deed today would certainly make the headlines.

The flight of lovers to the forest was an understandable reaction to peasant society's inhuman laws against their cohabitation. Otherwise, voluntary flight from society was due, as Hyltén-Cavallius puts it, to 'personal dissatisfaction with the general state of affairs'. Such conflicts between the individual and society which, even as late as the 17th century, found outlet in flight to the woods, are immemorial, timeless.

As a rule tents made of branches seem to have provided the woodsman's dwelling. As for nourishment, the larder of the wilderness was still not exhausted, and much of his food he could take direct from nature. The forests were replete with game, and in the lakes streams and rivers the fish were plentiful. If he need something more tasty to put on his bread, the peasants' farm animals had to be slaughtered where they grazed. Originally an honest man, he necessarily became a robber and a thief. In summer and autumn the wild berries of the forest supplemented his diet. Bread must have been an acute problem, that is if the woodsman was not prepared to content himself with what he could bake from tree bark.

This free life of the woodsman was no romantic or idyllic existence. Dependent on the forest for his board and lodging, he was forced to wage an even harder struggle against hunger and cold. When hurt, or stricken down by some serious disease, he was left to die alone and helpless in his forest lair, like a sick animal.

He must have had strong reasons for putting up with such a life. Defiance was basic to his temperament, and freedom so highly prized that for its sake he renounced the safer existence within the community and all the advantages enjoyed by persons of fixed abode. Words cost nothing; it is actions which have to be paid for, and the woodsman's cost him dear. As Hyltén-Cavallius puts it: 'He lives undefeated and indomitable, still fighting society, and when finally he goes under, still defiant to the last, he dies fearless as he has lived.'

Who can but respect so passionate a love of freedom?

I was born in the middle of a forest, and it has set its stamp on me. All my life I have carried with me my origins. I understand what the forest has meant to the people who have had their home there, and to us who have grown up within its confines.

When I was a child, its spirits of nature were still an everyday reality for many older people. I heard men say how, with their own eyes, they had seen the wood goblin. Once upon a time the forest lands had been densely populated with giants and trolls; but nowadays these were dying out, either struck by lightning or else run over and killed by the trains which had begun to run through the forests on their gleaming rails. For a long time I believed what the older people told me. The tall tree-stumps, with their claw-like branches, were dead and atrophied trolls. But gradually I began to doubt the existence of the beings whom so many people had talked to me about, but which I myself, neither by daylight nor in the dark, had ever seen in real life.

In the daytime, as soon as ever I could I ran out into the paddock, penetrated deep into the gloom among the tree-trunks, but never, though I often got lost during these childhood excursions into the wilds, do I remember being anxious or scared. On the contrary: from those memories of the forest I retain only a sense of security and freedom.

My best hiding places were the densest thickets. There no one could see me. When I was not in the forest, at home and at school, I was exposed to the eyes of others. Always I was being observed and, as often as not, being told off. I was surrounded by adults who wanted to decide over my behaviour. But as long as I was out of everyone's sight I was free to behave as I liked. I could shout at the top of my voice, throw myself down on the mosses, kick my legs and turn somersaults, and no one cared. No matter what I was up to, there was no one there to reprimand me. All round were only trees and bushes, and no matter how crazy my behaviour these did not curse me. Overhead, like a caress, was only the gentle hush of the pines and spruces. The tall trees seemed to be protecting me, to defend my right to autonomy and to behave however I liked. At home and at school there was something known as good or bad behaviour. This was nowhere to be found in the forest.

For all these reasons I was happier as a child in the forest than anywhere else. For me the forest represented security. The child's dawning need for freedom found an outlet in a life close to it; a need which became ever more insistent as I grew older.

Afterwards, when I was still older and became a lumberjack I experienced the forest differently. When I was ten I used to go with my father to his clearings, and from the age of fifteen onwards worked for several winters in my parish's great crown forest. Of all physical work I have ever done, forestry is the hardest and most demanding. But it was also the sort of work I found most to my taste and which gave me real pleasure – work in the fresh air, an air redolent of pine-gum and pine needles, work carried out in utter privacy, free of the foremen who disturb factory work or the farmer's supervision on a farm. In my days felling was done by two-man teams. Each such team chopped away in its own particular tract of the crown forest; piecework, with which one's employer could not interfere. Just two men, working together in the solitude and freedom of the forest, their own masters.

In times past the forest used to be called 'the poor man's winter shirt'. Diffusing warmth from his stove, it also warms men's shivering bodies in other ways. No surer way exists of driving the cold out of one's limbs than to take an axe and fell some great tree. Before many minutes have gone by, great beads of sweat are dropping from one's brow. Though the lumber-jack, quartered in some wretched shack, may sometimes shiver at nights, he need never feel cold by day.

In my autobiographical novel *When I was a Child** I have described how a lumberman experienced the forest while at work:

'Walter was back in the forest where he had started life as a seven-year-old. The vast forest which in winter provided cover from the gale and in summer shade from the sun. The lumberman's work was free. He does not have to keep pace with a team or fit in with them. Here he worked at his own speed, quickly or slowly and rested when he liked.

'Walter attacked the old spruce. His axe bounced off the frozen tree, which flew out in little chips, hard as pebbles. The conifer forest grew lighter or darker as the shadows of clouds flitted over crowns and branches. The trees sighed, cracked and with a last long soughing sigh, the sigh of the dying, fell.'

For me the Swedish countryside means above all the forest. Unchanging it stands there at all times of year, whatever the weather, waiting for me. In winter all waters lie frozen hard under their icy lid. But the forest is always just as open and accessible. In winter its greens are even more vivid than in summer and its scent, for me, even fresher and healthier. The forest, whether I've been working in it or just strolling about, has given me the strength for my never-ending grind at the typewriter, to which I've mostly sat chained like a galley-slave at his oar. Whenever the writer of this history has been utterly weary the forest has been his remedy, his cure. And still is. Which is why he has devoted these pages to it.

Always, from my childhood and youth up, I have associated the forest with *freedom*.

* Orig: *Soldat med brutet gevär*. 1944. Transl. G. Lennestock, Knopf, N.Y. 1956. Heinemann, London.

The Three Stures

NOT UNTIL AFTER HIS DEATH was the first Sture called 'the Elder'. While he was still alive, of course, no one could know that two more regents of the same name would come after him. When he first took over the government it was under the name of Sten Gustavsson Sture. A nephew of Karl Knutsson, he was keeping the reins of power inside the family.

The tradition which ascribes to Karl the philosophical reflection that, as king, he had 'been a wretched and unhappy man' also avers that on his deathbed he warned his nephew against accepting a crown which brought to its wearer only grief and misery. It is possible that Sten Sture followed his uncle's advice when he accepted and always retained the title of regent (*riksföreståndare*). But his action may also have been based on psychological insight. Sweden was an elective kingdom. Herr Sten was familiar with the mentality of its great men. He knew how hotly they aspired to a royal crown. Many human lives had been sacrificed in the struggle to obtain it and all who could not attain to it were envious of the glory it conferred. In remaining content with the status of regent Sten Sture not only wielded the same real powers as if he had been king, but also protected himself against the envy of his aristocratic brethren.

The Sture family is long ago extinct. Originally it consisted of five different branches, each with its own coat of arms. One branch sported a bull; another a sturgeon; a third an ox's head, between whose horns was a star. It was this branch which was eventually to become the Oxenstierna (Oxe-star) family, perhaps the most famous aristocratic dynasty in Swedish history. Sten Sture the Elder's shield was charged with three water-lily leaves.

A genealogical enquiry into the Stures is without interest to my history; but one indisputable historical fact must nevertheless be discussed here. For half a century after 1470, members of this clan dominated Swedish politics and were largely responsible for the destinies of the Swedes.

On Walpurgis Eve, 1471, a meeting was held at Arboga, to which, Olaus Petri tells us in his *Chronicle*, both burghers and peasants were summoned. At Arboga the Swedish people were to agree on the election of a governor for the whole realm. A 'last' of German beer was 'prepared' for the peasants, after which they gave their votes to 'him who had given the beer they desired'. The outcome of the voting was that those who supported Sten Sture gained the upper hand. He was 'chosen governor'.

Olaus Petri does not mince matters. Herr Sten was elected because he had stood them all that beer. German beer was regarded as a good deal stronger than the Swedish, and a 'last' contains around 290 litres, which means that something in the region of five thousand pints of good strong beer were drunk at the Arboga assembly which appointed Sten Sture the Elder regent. One of the passages in Olaus Petri's history which made Gustav Vasa, Herr Sten's descendant, 'no little wroth' was this tale of the Arboga beer, which he found derogatory to his ancestor's memory. The king was a grandson of the regent's sister.

'It turns sour like Arboga beer' is an old Swedish saying, presumably originating in those barrels which flowed so freely at Arboga on Walpurgis Eve, 1471. Studying the matter on the spot, just five hundred years later, I am able to confirm that a good beer is indeed brewed at Arboga. One, furthermore, which has no disagreeable after-effects.

Herr Sten had gained most votes at the assembly but as regent he did not command the support of a united people, not even of a united peasantry. Before his power could be consolidated, there had to be a military confrontation with Christian I and the Swedish Union party. It took place on October 10, 1471, at Brunkeberg, just outside the gates of Stockholm. After five centuries there is every reason to lay great stress on the true implications of this battle, which actually exemplified a deep split in the nation usually glossed over by historians. A large host of Uppland peasantry together with smaller bodies of Sörmlanders and possibly Västmanlanders, whose leaders were afterwards treated as traitors, fought on the Danish side. That October day, some Swedes fell fighting for the regent, Sten Sture; others for the Danish Union king, Christian I.

Nor did the regent's total victory at Brunkeberg lead to the unification of the Swedish provinces in a national state, as we today understand the term. That day was still far off. In certain parts of the country, such as Dalarna and Småland, a separatist movement survived for another seventy years or so.

In the contemporary *Sture Chronicles*, we read that the three Stures' régime was mild and just, and that for this they were much loved. Under their government, by and large, times were good in Sweden. When, once in a while, the peace was disturbed, it was only because of the infidelity of the Danes, 'false treaties' and the dastardly tricks with which they succeeded in pulling the wool over the eyes of the honest gullible Swedes. These chronicles give a picture of the Sture period which is as lop-sided and touched up as the one the *Karl Chronicle* gives of the immediately preceding epoch.

Historians have drunk deep from the Sture chronicles, and there is little more to be got out of them. Many passages are devoted to the aristocracy's internecine strife. They relate how lords struggled over castles, fortresses, fiefs and estates and the power which goes with property. Somehow I seem to have read all this before. The Sture clan had managed to lay its hands on a sizeable slice of the Swedish soil; but in the Axelssons, the Karlssons, the Trolles and the Vasas they had powerful rivals. The Axelssons, more especially, were landowners of the first order, and up to his fall in 1487 were Herr Sten's most dangerous opponents. Ivar Axelsson, their leader, was son-in-law to Karl Knutsson and therefore related to the regent.

Economic developments in Europe always had implications for Sweden and play a large rôle in our history. During the Later Middle Ages the city burghers had grown much more numerous and important. Capitalists were steadily converting land values into money values. In Sweden, nevertheless, the bourgeoisie's path to power through the money bag was travelled a good deal more slowly than in commercial centres of the continent. In Sweden, arable land still constituted the most important component of wealth or capital. Wealth, indeed, was identical with its possession. Together with the Church it was the aristocracy who were the great landowners and their wealth was retained, secured and increased by continual intermarriage among their families.

Property gives power over men. Throughout history this has been its great, often decisive rôle. But these conflicts between the mediaeval magnate families, sprung from their insatiable greed for power, become trivial and wearisome by eternal repetition, and I hardly think I do my reader a disservice by not going into them in detail. But that they were always going on and exercised an important influence on the course of events must nevertheless be pointed out.

Not that the conditions under which the tillers of the soil, more than nine-tenths of the population, were altered by these changes in land-ownership. Bergkvara, for example, an estate belonging to the Trolles in the heart of Värend (Småland), was one of the largest and most valuable of all south Swedish estates. Even today it comprises 1200 acres of arable soil – and on its domain it had hundreds of peasants and labourers. To these people it mattered not a jot whether the Trolles or some other aristocratic clan were the owners of this immense domain. Either way, they had to put in just as many days of compulsory labour at Bergkvara, days as wearisomely long and as strictly supervised, no matter who lorded it over this noble estate. In their lives nothing ever happened which has been regarded as worthy of note; their lords' struggles for possession of the land, on the other hand, have been extensively recorded for posterity.

But the reading they make is as tedious as it is distasteful.

As a monument to the victory at Brunkeberg the great *Saint George and the Dragon* group was erected in Stockholm Cathedral. This massive oak and elk-horn sculpture is the work of the German artist Bernt Notke, who had already immortalized Karl Knutsson. For Notke's superb young knight, the victor, Herr Sten Sture himself, is supposed to have stood model. His long sword upraised, he is shown in the very act of slaying the dragon, a terrifying and loathsome monster, whom we must suppose to represent King Christian I.

Of Herr Sten the *Rhymed Chronicle* tells us that 'in his time no man was his peer'. Panegyric can hardly go further. Yet comparison between Sten Sture the Elder and other mediaeval Swedish rulers undeniably falls out in his favour. He did not take his enemies' lives; nor did he burn peasants at the stake. Above all, he seems to have been a restorer and preserver of the peace. After four decades of incessant warfare and internecine strife, with Herr Sten's government the realm enters on a period of peace without counterpart since the days of Queen Margareta. Across the Baltic, along the eastern frontier, there were a few disturbances; but in Sweden itself a period of quietude began which lasted for about twenty-five years, a whole quarter of a century, and for this the credit must first and foremost go to the regent.

The people, who were crying out for peace, appreciated the new régime. In 1484, an eloquent Latin inscription was set up over the sacristy door of Kalmar Church, outside Uppsala. It reads: 'Peace flourisheth in Sweden, because Herr Sten ruleth.'

He also made an important contribution to Sweden's national independence, by abrogating the power of the German residents in Sweden's trading cities, in whose councils they had hitherto occupied half the seats. Thereafter the Swedish interests dominated. In cultural matters, too, important progress was made in the first Sture's days. In 1477 Scandinavia's first university was opened at Uppsala and a few months afterwards Copenhagen followed suit with its own seat of learning. In 1483, an immigrant German printer published, in Latin, the first printed book ever to appear in Sweden: an edifying work called *Dialogus creaturarum optime moralisatus*. It was a historic event. Gutenberg's invention had at last made its appearance in a remote, culturally indigent land. The man who was primarily responsible for these cultural developments was Jakob Ulfsson, Archbishop of Uppsala.

As for Herr Sten himself, he has gone down to posterity as the dragon-slaying knight astride his horse in Stockholm Cathedral. On its haunches can be seen the arms of the Sture clan. As a man, however, he is less accessible to us than his uncle, Karl Knutsson. Almost no personal letters can with certainty be attributed to him; no diaries; nor have we a single jotting demonstrably from his hand.

To the 19th-century historian C. T. Odhner, Sten Sture the Elder is 'a man who enjoyed the unreserved confidence of the people, whose rights he protected and who associated familiarly with common men, consulted them in their councils and visited them in their homes.' These verdicts I cite mostly as curiosities of the nationalist school of history-writing. Nevertheless, I believe they do have some basis in reality.

A modern expert, on the other hand, Professor Sven Ulric Palme, has tried to denigrate the traditional dragon-slayer and national hero in a biography which dwells on a hitherto overlooked aspect of the first Sture's activities; namely, his private business affairs.

Palme carefully documents his account. He has dug up deeds, wills, contracts of purchase, papers dealing with matters of inheritance and other incontrovertible documents, and the portrait which transpires from these sources is that of a leading representative of what we should call his day's high finance: a ruthless businessman, an unscrupulous land-speculator and a collector of other men's estates. After the death of Karl Knutsson, he omits to implement the terms of his will, by dishonest transactions acquiring for himself parts of his uncle's property which he withholds from their rightful legatees. Although he already owns many estates and farms, he is always acquiring more. Estate after estate falls into his hands. He speculates in fields and meadows, in mills, in waterfalls and eel-fisheries, at times using methods dubious or even illegal to come by them. In some cases he even seems to have cheated widows out of their husbands' inheritances. On one occasion he even extended his ruthlessness as a businessman to his political activities. He falsified, so it seems, the so-called Treaty of Nöteberg, 1323, which fixed the kingdom's eastern frontier with Russia.

In Palme's work Sten Sture the Elder stands exposed. The *Sture Chronicles* gilded the picture but the gilt has rubbed off. Yet so far from reducing his fascination for us it rather augments it, brings him closer to our own age. In Sten Sture the Elder, certainly one of the most remarkable personalities of 15th-century Sweden, we discover a timeless trait: insatiable acquisitiveness. As a business-man he is seen to have belonged to an undying and most disagreeable race of men: the robber baron and exploiter of landed property, a species which in our own day has proliferated all over Sweden – the lot-jobbers and real-estate sharks who speculate in the rising land-values of our Swedish soil, buying up and parcelling out ancient peasant holdings and selling them off at two hundred per cent profit.

If Palme's work is to be believed, the national interests meant nothing at all to the elder Sten Sture. It was not in the kingdom's interest he was working, but in his own. Palme gives him a place in a rogue's gallery 'of the great popular seducers in our history'.

On the other hand it is obvious to me that Sten Sture enjoyed the commons' confidence, and that it was here, throughout his long reign, that his régime found its abiding support. If, according to Palme, he did not deserve it, but had come by it by demagogy and guile, why – I cannot help asking myself – didn't the people in the course of twenty years see through his blandishments? As far as I can see, it was under the first of their line that the Stures became popular with the commons, a popularity from which his two successors benefited and which lasted far into the 16th century. There must have been some reason for this. As I look for patterns of cause and effect in Swedish history, I cannot help believing there must have been some connection between the first Sture's regency and his clan's abiding reputation with the commons.

One comes closest to the truth, I think, if one describes Sten Sture the Elder as a master of *realpolitik*, with all that this implies of opportunism and time-serving mingled with ruthlessness. Cir-cumstances, he found, altered cases. 'Probably he thought he could best promote the interests of the land and realm', opines Gottfrid Carlson, 'by serving his own'. This is no unique faith among those who yield power. 'Politics is the art of the possible', declared Bismarck. One great and popular 20th-century Swedish statesman, Per Albin Hansson, has agreed with him. Five centuries earlier than our social-democratic prime minister, Herr Sten seems to have reached the same insight – *pari passu* – as he.

Constantly in conflict with his Council of State and other powerful nobles, Herr Sten managed to remain regent for a period of twenty-seven years.

In 1497, however, the Council finally evicted him from office. He was defeated by the Unionist King Hans of Denmark, who the same year made his entry into Stockholm and was there crowned king, his son Christian being simultaneously crowned heir apparent to the Swedish throne – a coronation which was to have fateful consequences two decades later.

After a few years Herr Sten again succeeded in becoming regent. But already in 1503 he departed this life. His death is associated with some curious circumstances which speak volumes about the political state of affairs prevailing in the Sweden of those days. The succession was secured by a bold coup. It is an occurrence from the Swedish Middle Ages that could have been taken from the pages of *The Three Musketeers*.

For a long while King Hans's queen, Kristina, had been courageously defending Stockholm against the Sture party. When the capital finally fell, she was taken prisoner. By and by Sten Sture released her and personally accompanied that great lady on her journey southwards to the Danish frontier. On his way back he suddenly fell dangerously ill.

Immediately, poison – an all too normal cause of sudden death in fashionable circles during the Renaissance – was suspected, the Danish queen's physician being regarded as the culprit. But other suspicions fell on Svante Nilsson's betrothed, a certain Fru Märta, who, it was assumed, had wished to get the regent out of the way in favour of her husband to be, a member of the Sture family. If nothing else, these rumours and suspicions are an index of the confidence placed in one another by the rivals for power.

As he journeyed northwards towards Stockholm the regent grew weaker and had to halt at Jönköping. And there, on December 13, 1503, the first of the Stures died. He was about sixty – his exact age is not known – but still in the prime of life. His death was wholly unexpected.

By its very suddenness it created an extremely serious situation for the Sture party. No one seemed to be left in Sweden to stand in the path of King Hans. who now had an excellent opportunity to make a comeback.

It is at this juncture that Hemming Gadh, one of the most remarkable Swedes of the Later Middle Ages, appears. He was one of the regent's attendants. For twenty years he had been Herr Sten's ambassador in Rome, and thereafter, with the regent's support, had been elected to the Linköping see. Here was another military prelate, who knew as well how to wield a soldier's sword as the sword of the spirit; a reincarnation, it seemed, of Jöns Bengtsson Oxenstierna, who had also lived as intensively in the material world as in the immaterial. To all three Stures Hemming Gadh became an influential adviser, and in this capacity probably contributed more to Swedish history than has ever been appreciated. One of the most virulent anti-Danish partisans of the Sture epoch, he was afterwards imprisoned in Denmark, in company with Gustav Eriksson (the future Gustav Vasa), by Christian II but afterwards went over to the Union king, who rewarded him by cutting his head off. This Swedish nationalist who became a traitor is an enigmatic personality. We shall meet him again in due course.

Doctor Hemming, as he was called, was Herr Sten's faithful friend and supporter, and at his master's sudden demise proved himself to be the man to avert the perils of the situation that had arisen in Jönköping.

What was to be done? Obviously, the regent's death had to be concealed from the Danes and from the Union party. So to gain time and give the Sture party a breathing space in which they could arrange for the election of a successor, the regent's corpse, too, had to be concealed. Doctor Hemming exacted a strict oath of secrecy from all in the dead regent's party who knew what had occurred. After which – it was the depth of winter – Herr Sten's corpse, wrapped and covered in 'a multitude of skins' was laid on a sledge. But Gadh realised, too, that the party could not arrive in the capital without a living regent. Therefore a double had to be found. As it happened, the dead man had a faithful old servant, Lasse Birgersson, Deeply devoted to his master, he also by great good fortune strongly resembled him.

Wearing the deceased's clothes, rings and chain of chivalry,

Lasse Birgersson was placed on his easily recognizable horse. Since there was nevertheless a risk of detection whenever the party halted, the double's eyes were blindfolded, on the pretext that some eye-trouble from which Herr Sten had long been suffering had taken a turn for the worse, and with it his eyesight, so that he was unable to recognize people. All who desired speech with the regent en route were referred to Doctor Hemming Gadh, who had been given plenary powers during his master's unfortunate illness.

In this way the unique funeral procession wound its way to Stockholm with one regent, dead, under a heap of hides, and a living one, blindfolded and on horseback. Since the company was travelling by sleigh, the journey was necessarily a slow one; and Doctor Hemming sent on outriders ahead to Stockholm to inform Svante Nilsson that Sweden temporarily lacked a regent. In this way Svante gained a breathing space in which to summon his supporters to the capital.

On the company's arrival with Herr Sten's corpse an assembly was summoned. Before it met, it was announced that the old regent had suddenly died. Whereupon a successor was elected. Not un-expectedly, he turned out to be Herr Svante Nilsson, who at once began to busy himself with consolidating his own position, im-mediately occupying Stockholm Castle and other major fortresses throughout the realm.

This political coup, which would make an exhilarating chapter in any adventure story, took place in Stockholm in December, 1503. The man behind it had been the most learned Doctor Hemming Gadh. For two decades he had lived in Rome, no doubt learning such lessons from Pope Alexander VI Borgia's and Machiavelli's Renaissance Italy as were now to come in very handy.

If I have given a brief account of these events it is because they are so typical of that age; a tangible example of events taking a decisive turn as a result of a clever utilization of circumstance. Power was transferred in a fashion which was made to appear wholly fortuitous. Yet events could have turned out quite differently. Power could have gone to some quite different person. It seems to me I have rarely come across any historical event of which I can say with conviction that it happened as it necessarily had to, or that things could not have turned out otherwise. Historiographers may one day discover a law which governs events. Such insight is altogether beyond a layman. To me history seems often both irrational and unpredictable, which is precisely why I find it so fascinating and am consumed with curiosity about it. If history were fated, or followed eternal laws, or were predictable or automatic, I should lose all taste for it.

Number Two

Svante Nilsson is less well-known than the other Stures, and less space has been devoted to him in our history books. He came from another branch of the family than his predecessor, and in his own lifetime is said never to have used the Sture name. At one time an adherent of the Union party, who had been attached to King Hans, he had afterwards gone over to Herr Sten and the Swedish party.

The second Sture does not seem to have been a colourful figure. Compared with his predecessor he makes a faded impression as regent. Nor was it easy for him to assume office. The legacy of the first Sture – the everlasting war against the Danes – was burdensome, and in 1503 the Swedes looked as though they were likely to lose it. The people whom he now had to govern had every reason to ask whether it was ever going to end. The Union dispute was originally to have been decided by force of arms; but almost a century had now gone by and the method had proved fruitless.

In the southern border provinces people were so weary of the war that the peasants were concluding their own peace treaties, as we shall see in my next chapter. In this part of the country the inhabitants were refusing to bear arms against the populations of Blekinge and Skåne, in a solemn letter even going so far, on one occasion, as to inform Svante Nilsson to that effect. What did the regent do about these traitorous subjects? As far as we know, nothing. It was beyond his power.

Such things could happen during that part of the Middle Ages when separatism flourished among the Swedish provinces. The commons were going through one of their active periods, asserting their own independence through the provincial assemblies. When the popular assemblies made difficulties and declined to support the levies against Denmark, the central authorities' military resources were insufficient to exact obedience.

Unable to raise the troops he needed within Sweden, Svante Sture recruited German cavalry and infantry. For we are in the great age of the legionaries, and Herr Svante appears to have been the first national regent to have called in Germans. It is true, they had earlier been employed by King Albrekt; but then, he was a German himself. In recruiting foreign armies the regent was a forerunner of Gustav Vasa, whose national Swedish state could never have been founded without German aid. These professional military men, who killed for pay, came to be hated and detested all over the country for their unruly behaviour and outrages against the population. Whenever their pay was not forthcoming, they plundered the villages. All this foreign soldiery was but one more stone added to the burdens borne by the commons. Since the King of Denmark, too, employed German legionaries, Germans went abroad to kill other Germans on Swedish soil in a war between Swedes and Danes. No better illustration could be found of this utter meaninglessness of the Union wars.

In Svante Sture's time Kalmar, the key to the realm of Sweden on the south-eastern coast and regarded as Scandinavia's strongest fortress, virtually impregnable, was the great bone of contention. At this time Kalmar Castle was being held by the Danes, who defended it against Swedish besiegers for six years, 1503–1509. The commander-in-chief of the besieging army was Doctor Hemming Gadh, now a bishop. He had military capacity but no diocese, the Pope having refused to ratify his appointment to the see of Linköping. Although a man in the autumn of his years – he was sixty – Gadh was more disposed to warfare and affairs of state than episcopal matters. Unquestionably he was adept at the art of siege warfare. Though his attempts to capture Kalmar Castle were not successful, he did the Danes much damage there.

Generally speaking, the second of the Stures tried to continue the policies of his forerunner. In his attempts to play off the commons against the powerful lords of the Council he was less successful than Sten Sture the Elder. Chiefly this was because of the Union war. The Danes had allied themselves with the Hanseatic League. All-puissant in Scandinavian commerce, the League blockaded Swedish harbours, and prevented all salt imports. To the population salt, which was basic to the preservation of meat, butter and fish, was indispensable. Everything else necessary to human life a peasant household could provide for itself. Only salt had to be brought from overseas. It is impossible to exaggerate the crucial importance of salt to the economy in those days. Christian II knew what he was doing in 1520 when, wishing to regain his hereditary Swedish dominions, he gained the goodwill of the peasantry of certain Småland hundreds by giving a bushel – or in some instances a gallon – of salt to each homestead.

This salt shortage, threatening the population with starvation and cunningly exploited by Herr Svante's opponents, became one of his greatest problems of domestic policy. In foreign affairs he achieved ultimate success by signing a treaty with Russia and putting an end to the disturbances along the eastern frontier. But the state of war with Denmark persisted, and as long as he remained regent became the norm.

Svante Sture's régime, however, only lasted eight years (1504–1512) and ended with his death, which was as unexpected as his predecessor's.

A rich silver mine had just been discovered in the Sala district in Bergslagen, and the Västmanland miners had been summoned to a meeting at Västerås to discuss whether the new find might not be of great benefit to the realm. At their assembly on January 2, 1512, the regent was present. But during the meeting 'he fell straitway down and was dead', probably from a stroke. For a few days his death, too, was kept secret, while preparations were being made for the election of his son. To some extent the events which had followed the death of the first Sture at Jönköping were repeated after the death of the second at Västerås.

Number Three

Sten Sture the Younger is a more interesting personage than his father. With him a notably gifted ruler enters the stage. Our older historians have acclaimed him as one of Sweden's greatest heroes, one of the standard-bearers of its liberties; one of those whom the poet acclaims as

> ... noble shades, revered fathers,
> Sweden's heroes and knightly men*

Geijer calls him the 'most noble and chivalrous of the Stures', and *The Last Knight* is the title of Strindberg's play about him. This pride of place derives from the circumstance of his falling in battle, still a young man, at Lake Åsunden, a classical death for any hero.

Sten Sture's chivalrous career had begun at a remarkably early age. At the coronation of King Hans in St Nicholas Church, Stockholm, he had been dubbed a knight at the age of four. The peace treaty between the Swedes and the Union monarch, namely, contained a paragraph under which a certain number of Swedes were to be knighted. Sten Sture's father, Svante Nilsson, who had had a hand in Hans becoming King of Sweden, was one of those to be knighted – so it was only natural that the son, too, should benefit from the king's gracious pleasure. For twenty-seven long years the Swedish throne had lacked an occupant, and the Swedes, for lack of a king, had had no one who could elevate them to the order of knighthood. Naturally, many admirable and highly deserving Swedes had suffered from this long period of kingless government, and had found it a grave shortcoming that they could not be knighted. Now, after so long a period of deprivation and vacuity, they grasped their opportunity. Vanity, that timeless attribute of the human race, was at long last to be gratified.

The sources inform us that many aristocratic ladies, too, were eager for their husbands to become knights. Feminine vanity on a husband's behalf was not peculiar to 15th-century Sweden – even today any Swedish wife whose husband can sport an order on his chest can count on honorable placement at the royal dinner table, and no year goes by without birthday honours in the form of 6,000 orders to Swedish men and women being handed out; a tradition

* Poem by J. H. Kellgren (1751–1795).

going back to our mediaeval coronations, of which one of the most notable was this coronation in 1497. We Swedes need kings for our own vainglory. The need is as immemorial as it is inextirpable.

Concerning the knighting of Sten Sture at the 1497 coronation, Fabian Månsson writes: 'But no knightly dubbing caused so much annoyance as the sight of a four-year-old child being led forward to stammer out his oath of chivalry. The commons, however, laughed at it, and sung ditties, the gist of which was that aristocratic females were crying out to be dubbed knights, inasmuch as they had boy-babies growing in their bellies.'

Svante Nilsson's little son must have been about half as tall as the sword which dubbed him. Whether the four-year-old compre-hended anything at all of the important oath he then swore may also be doubted. But in his early years he is supposed to have played with swords and trained himself in warlike arts. For these, during his brief lifetime, he was to find ample use.

At the time of his father's demise Sten Sture the Younger can hardly have reached the age of twenty – his exact date of birth is not certainly known. But he was already married to the 17-year-old Kristina Gyllenstierna, one of the few Swedish women to find a place in our mediaeval history. Sten Sture was a mature, even precocious youth, who knew what he wanted; and that was to succeed his father as the first man in the country. From the outset he showed the will and power for action, not to say the ruthlessness, of a man of ambition. Now he made haste to steal a march on his rivals for the regency.

His father had not used the Sture name, but the younger man, obviously well aware of the weight it carried with the commons, immediately assumed it. In all haste he took over the castles and fortresses commanded by his father's bailiffs and made them his own. Having done this, he travelled round the realm to win the favours of the lower orders on the eve of the election of a new regent. In a word, the third Sture, like the leaders of our modern political parties on the eve of a parliamentary election, went canvassing. In their assemblies, outside their parish churches, in their market places, he spoke to the assembled commons, caused manifestations to be read out, putting the fear of the Dane into them likewise a fear of traitors within the Council of State and the nobility. In short, he spared no efforts to convince the populace that there was only one man fit to defend their liberties and their welfare, namely himself.

The magnates fought young Herr Sten 'with life and power' (*med liv och makt*). Few members of the Council wished to see Svante Nilsson's son succeed him. 'For the council of the realm rarely had the same wishes as the clergy, miners and peasants', writes Fabian Månsson.

But the lords of the Council, for once, did not get their own way. With most of Sweden's fortresses in his hands and a 'benevolent commons' on his side, the younger Sture was altogether too strong for his adversaries. In July, 1512, the Council had to accept him as regent.

But once in power, he fell foul of the Church, a fateful dispute which he tried to resolve by force of arms. Against Archbishop Gustav Trolle, the representative of the Holy See in Sweden, he committed an act of violence which was to have important consequences.

Professor Gottfrid Carlsson has revised the fair image of the 'last of the knights' painted by tradition, and condemns his action against the archbishop. As he sees the matter, Sture's destruction of the archbishop's residence at Stäket near Uppsala and the capture of its occupant was an action almost beyond condoning. Sten Stures' men not only mishandled Gustav Trolle's servants but also the primate himself. As that age saw these things, such an outrage might have been regarded as the most banal of political arguments. But it should also be mentioned that the decision to commit it had been taken at a parliamentary meeting in Stockholm, in 1517.

This dramatic conflict between Sten Sture the Younger and Gustav Trolle was to be bloodily resolved by the infamous Stockholm Bloodbath of November 1520. Our annalists have regarded the regent as the noble hero of the drama and the archbishop as a despicable and treacherous, not to say diabolical, figure, 'the Judas Iscariot of Swedish history'. If Trolle was the instigator of the Stockholm Bloodbath – a point on which historians disagree sharply – he certainly must be regarded as a scoundrel of the first order. Unquestionably he was a hard-hearted man. But after the gross injustice which the Sture party had inflicted on him one can understand his thirst for revenge.

For his attack on the archbishop, Sten Sture was excommunicated by the Pope. In practical politics he had set in motion the schism with Rome which Gustav Vasa was to complete.

The chivalrous young Sture shows a less agreeable face to research when one considers his behaviour toward his stepmother Märta Ivarsdotter, widow of Svante Nilsson. From extant letters it transpires that he stripped her 'without mercy of the entailed estates and fiefs which the regent had given her, and which were her only means of subsistence.'

In the days when I was an admirer of warrior kings and Indian chieftains, 'the last of the knights', too, was one of my boyhood idols. In his *Song of Athens*, Viktor Rydberg* had represented to me what a glorious death would be mine if I fell 'fighting for your land, for your fatherland'. And I was deeply moved by the same exhortation, placed by another poet in the mouth of the young Sture as he parades his peasant army before the Battle of Duvnäs Forest:

> Ye honest Dalesmen,
> break shields and helmets asunder;
> we fear no men . . .

That was the way! That was how brave men should act! And who could scorn death more completely than young Herr Sten? As a hero he has been immortalized by Edvard Bäckström in his ballad in the play *The Prisoner of Kalö* from the late romantic period of the 19th century, when the heroic poetry practised mainly by writers who had proved unfit for military service was still in flower. The first time I remember hearing this ballad sung was by a fine singer around the year 1910, at a volunteer riflemen's celebration. The last verse, more especially, about the hero's death on a sledge on the Mälaren ice, sent thrills of emotion up and down my youthful spine:

> When fallen he lay on his bier
> And the snowflakes played in his wounds,
> Mildly he looked on his own:

* Swedish poet 1828–1895.

'Why pale, ye men, at death?
Fresh courage! when greatest your need
Then God will find his man'.

National romanticism needed to acclaim masters of the craft of war. And in young Sture it made a find. His victories over the Danes at Brännkyrka and Duvnäs revealed his military capacities. He must have been the most consummate Swedish military commander of his day. And Doctor Hemming Gadh supported him in word and deed. Of Herr Sten's courage there can be no doubt. No one knows how the battle on Lake Åsunden might have turned out had he not been wounded at the outset – 'a hand's breadth above the knee' – and had to be carried from the battlefield. The Swedes might well have been victorious. Usually soldiers survive a bullet in the leg, and one wonders what went wrong with his wound. But the art of medicine, as exercised by the surgeon-barbers of those days, was extremely primitive. During his return to Stockholm the wound was probably not looked after properly and infection must have set in. The third Sture died of blood-poisoning.

Some of our chroniclers see in Sten Sture the Younger a statesman. His ambition was probably boundless. We have evidence that in his last years he even aspired to the kingship. Presumably he regarded his victories over the Danes as having amply earned him the crown of Sweden; and indeed no one can begrudge him his ambition. There is much evidence that he had made himself popular among the commons, and doubtless they would have been glad to see him on the throne as King Sten Sture I. Still in the full flush of his youth, only three or four years older than Gustav Eriksson Vasa, he seemed to have the greater part of his life before him.

But a Danish bullet put paid to the twenty-seven-year-old regent's career. We may speculate as to what would have happened in Sweden had he continued to govern it. In liberating the country from the Union and crushing the power of the Church, if not in other respects, Gustav Vasa carried out the young Sture's policies. Nor was Gustav's personality cast in the same mould as his predecessor's. In my view there is a discernible and crucial difference between these two men. Sten Sture was more a man of the people. Gustav was – or afterwards mostly became – the ally of the aristocracy. Nor did the young regent ever have to combat any peasant risings against his régime. Gustav, by contrast, had to suppress five great popular revolts; and to do it accepted the help of the nobility.

What sort of reign might have been King Sten's? So often history seems the sport of chance. It is my belief that if that bullet at Åsunden had had another trajectory or spared the young regent's life, our history from 1520 onwards would have been quite different.

According to Olaus Petri, when King Hans had occupied Stockholm Castle, in 1497, he said to his defeated opponent Sten Sture the Elder; 'Ye have made an evil testament in Sweden, inasmuch as ye have made the peasants, whom God hath created slaves, into masters; and those who should be lords ye have made slaves.'

An effective line for a play. But who can believe there is a word of truth in it? Who can suppose that, in the 1490's, the peasantry of Sweden were the real lords of the realm or were trying to enslave its upper classes? What this remark – if it was ever really made – certainly expresses, concisely and to the point, is the feudal view of a peasant. The king was also indicating the difference between the status of the Swedish commons and of the Danish. The Swedish peasantry enjoyed a considerably greater measure of freedom than their Danish brethren, who lived in a state of feudal servitude which was a relic of their ancient thraldom.

Historians differ widely in their view of the Swedish commons' status during the Sture period. Without summarizing all their views, let me touch on the more extreme. I leave it to my reader to form his own intermediate view. My own will transpire presently.

In a major modern work by E. Ingers, the peasantry under the Stures are made out to have almost become a ruling class. Ingers thinks that, by and large, the Stures realized the programme summed up in the words 'a well-disposed commons'. Ingers heads his chapter on the Sture epoch 'The Great Age of the Swedish Commons'. According to him, all three Stures were concerned with the interests and welfare of the common people, and their policies satisfied its demands. They associated on a familiar and equal footing with the common man, and listened to what he had to say. This work makes out that for the Swedes the Sture epoch was a golden age. After their national state had come into being they bitterly regretted the change, and always hankered after its return.

The state of affairs during this allegedly great age of the commons finds expression in a mural, dated 1482, one among the many which cover the walls and vaults of our Uppland churches. On either side of the arms of Sweden stand a knight and a peasant, together holding up the shield. The knight is wearing his steel helmet; the peasant has taken off his soft round hat and supports the shield on his shoulder. All classes of society are united in striving for the common good. A piece of pictorial propaganda, it is slanted in the same way as the words of the *Sture Chronicles*.

Fabian Månsson,* who had a profounder knowledge of the Sture and early Vasa epochs than any of his contemporaries, was of the opposite opinion. He takes quite a different view of their history. Altogether he wrote six volumes on the subject, 2,640 pages of print. None of our other historians have devoted so much time, so much energy or so many pages of manuscript to this era. Having several times re-read his six books, I am sure no living historian knows more about this subject than Fabian Månsson did. Not, of course, that I uncritically accept all his conclusions.

Though I knew Fabian Månsson personally, our meeting did not take place until 1937–1938, the last year of his life. By then he was a sick and weary man, who knew his days were numbered. By the year of his death, 1938, five of his six historical works had been published. Two parts of his great work on Gustav Vasa and Nils Dacke were already in print, and the third, unfinished, came out in 1948, ten years after his death. He knew very well his remaining strength would not suffice to carry through this demanding work in the short time he had left. I remember how tired his voice sounded, as he said: 'So much work still needs to be done on this period. I can only hope that younger men will come after me to continue my research.'

Fabian Månsson was the son of a poor fisherman and small farmer in the south of Sweden. He was a historian of the people, who

* Fabian Månsson (1872–1938), member of the Swedish Parliament from 1912 to his death, was one of the pioneers of the Swedish labour movement, famous as an orator and for his remarkable achievements as a writer of history.

wrote about the people, for the people – an original blend of historical science and imaginative literature. His works are as stuffed with dialogue as a historical novel; but they also contain great quantities of historical facts, which the author's endless energy and patience has assembled from innumerable sources. Since Fabian did his own research and went direct to the original sources, he is usually to be relied on. Passionately addicted to documented truth, he had a highly developed historical sense. But in the end he had collected so much material that it overwhelmed him. His books overflow with a wealth of detail, are therefore difficult to survey and, as epics, burst at the seams. Fabian Månsson was no master of the art of self-limitation. And this is why his history of the Sture and early Vasa epoch did not gain the popularity it deserved.

Yet no professional Swedish historian, in my opinion, can match his insight into the past, nor his ability to recreate long-vanished times and environments. He had a sixth sense for people's way of seeing their own existence and for the conditions under which they had lived. No one else has given us so graphic or lively a picture, couched in such pithy and powerful language, of the dramatic transition from the Middle Ages to that later epoch to which the Stures and Gustav Vasa have lent their names.

Fabian Månsson's trilogy *Sancte Eriks gård* (Saint Erik's Estate) treats of social and political developments in Sweden between the Engelbrekt rising and the end of the Sture period. The estate in question is none other than Stäket, the archbishop's residence, which Sten Sture the Younger, in 1517, demolished into a heap of ruins and rubble. Månsson's great work has an eloquent sub-title: *The birth pangs of national unity*. Simple and congenial, it exactly fits the contents. Only after an enormously difficult and protracted parturition did the national state of Sweden come into being. This process, so infinitely costly and painful to the Swedish people, took a hundred years. Much blood was shed in its course. And it was the common man, above all the peasant, the tiller of the soil who had to bear these birth pangs and torments, all the miseries of that age when Swedes were becoming one nation.

When at long last it was born, however, the child turned out to be a monarchy, an administrative apparatus which mostly stifled the little freedom and independence as the commons had hitherto enjoyed.

For Fabian Månsson the Sture epoch was far from being the great age of the commons. Rather it was a time of endless trials and tribulations. His thesis is that the great families tried – and indeed often managed – to involve the various provinces' peasantry in their own internecine quarrels, ensnaring the lower classes of the population into a conflict in whose outcome they had no stake whatever. No matter which side won, their lot remained the same. In Fabian Månsson's view, even the three Stures exploited the commons in precisely the same fashion as all the other aristocratic parties, using them as tools for their own power politics. Apart from the Stures, the next most important factor was the Council of State, which was made up of the leading men of the high nobility and the Church. Their cultural attainments have already been limned: several of these lords of the council could neither read nor write.

The historian also attributes the Union wars, the greatest popular burden of all, to the crassly egoistic policies of the upper classes. If one group of magnates wished to preserve the Union, it was merely because they thought it lay in their own private interests. Owning estates in all three Scandinavian countries they could best administer them if the north was at peace. The Sture party, on the other hand, the nationalist nobles, did not want to be subordinate to any Union king. They were opposed to the Union because they desired a free hand to rule their own country as they saw fit. If the commons, the peasantry, all the lower classes of society, were in favour of retaining the Union, it was because they wanted *peace*.

At one point Fabian Månsson defines their motives:

'The peasants thought they would gain greater advantage from the Union, from peace and quiet, than from the endless vendettas and arson which occurred in times of war. This was why, from generation to generation, they sat still and, in their hearts, tacitly acclaimed the Union.'

Both these sentences, in my view, express the basic desires and longings of the Swedish people during the Late Middle Ages. Not that the Swedes were the only people who had to go through the 'birthpangs of national unity' during this epoch. Developments in Sweden must be viewed against the dramatic revolution then taking place everywhere in Europe, a revolution characterized by the dissolution of feudalism and the growth of powerful monarchies. The new rulers who sat on the thrones of Europe were despots. It was a process which, when it reached Sweden in the first decades of the 16th century and was finally implemented by Gustav Vasa, had long been going on in other lands.

Only one continental people had succeeded in defending themselves againt the Hapsburg's armies of mounted knights: the inhabitants of Alpine Switzerland. In their free peasant republic, founded by the Oath of 1291, popular liberties had been preserved; but only by arming the entire population. Fabian Månsson strongly underlines the incontrovertible fact that it had only been by force of arms that the Swiss had escaped princely oppression and serfdom. A historic personage, Didrik Petri, rector of Söderåkra, is obviously the author's own mouthpiece when he declares:

'Only by arming all the commons can a good society be founded. The Swiss Republic shows us that'.

On the other hand, when Didrik Petri goes on to explain the miseries of the Swedish commons as the consequence of their having 'left themselves undefended' he can hardly be a mouthpiece for the author. Fabian Månsson knew very well that the Swedish peasantry, as a whole, had never been disarmed. The many attempts to deprive them of their weapons had only met with temporary and partial success. They had always retained their hunting weapons; and these they also used in war. Furthermore, these arms were home-made; if forced to hand over their crossbows, they immediately made themselves new ones.

The reference to the Swiss Confederation is crucial to Fabian Månsson's view of society and of history. His ideal society was a community of interests, a country of small peasants, subject to no superior state authority or bureaucracy, and one which placed no restrictions on personal freedom – a community which in reality was an ancient form of communism, with its roots in the early Christian Church, whose members had held all things in common.

Obviously his ideal society, with its freedom of the individual and its decentralized popular self-government – which he fancied he saw realised in mediaeval Switzerland – had little in common with the communist states of today.

In Sweden, events took quite another turn and, to my mind, a most regrettable one. The outcome of national unity and all its birthpangs was a royal despotism; a state in which, after Nils Dacke's insurrection, no further revolts were possible. The question of whether such a development was necessary – indeed the whole question of historical necessity – is worthy of close analysis. At this point I for one am assailed by grave doubts as to that mystical law of event known as 'historical necessity'.

On the whole I accept Fabian Månsson's version of the Sture and Vasa epochs. The essence of his interpretation cannot here be detailed in all its amplitude; but in all essentials it seems to hold water. On one point, however, I regard his conclusions as erroneous. His theory that the Stures, too, ruthlessly exploited the commons for power politics and for their own ends, is based on insufficient evidence. Their government, as no one can deny, was less severe and more popular than either that of their forerunner (Karl Knutsson) or of their successor (Gustav Vasa). Unless this is conceded, how explain the Stures' popularity with the commons, to which so many sources bear witness? Some writers represent the Stures as demagogues, seducers of the commons. Is it not strange that the people, thus seduced, should have given them its confidence, and that in certain provinces they were even loved? Surely, in the course of fifty years, it would have occurred to the common man that he had been thoroughly duped and exploited by these three regents – if he really had? Would it not have resulted in an insurrection? Yet, there was no insurrection against them, as far as we know. Why not? The question remains unanswered.

Viewing our history integrally down the centuries, the following can be said: Compared with the two centuries immediately preceding – the two hundred years which had passed since a class society had first come into being in the 13th century – the Sture period, for the Swedish people, represented an improvement. By and large the first Sture, unlike his two successors, succeeded in his pacific policies. And what the common people wanted more than anything else was peace: 'Thus, from generation to generation, they sat still, and in their hearts tacitly acclaimed the Union.'

This movement of the popular mind is the subject of my next chapter.

A Warrior People's Dream of Peace

IN HIS HISTORY of the Nordic peoples Olaus Magnas describes the 'terrible struggles' which they had 'ever been obliged to fight'. In words and images he depicts their wars on land, at sea, in valleys and on the hills, in forests and in the fields, in the mountains and on frozen lakes, in every conceivable theatre of war. 'From the very outset hath wars and disturbances ever been on the increase and, sobeit God interveneth not, will never cease in this world, as long as man's nature remaineth that which it now is.'

More than four centuries have passed since these words were written; but as yet, as everyone knows, there has been no sign of any divine intervention.

Olaus Magnus calls the Scandinavian kingdoms the 'abode of the war god'. The Swedes, more especially, had gained a steady European reputation for their bellicosity, a reputation which reached its climax in the 17th century, when Sweden became a great power and Swedes were fighting on most European battlefields. In his letters and despatches, Pierre Chanut, the French ambassador to the court of Queen Christina, describes the Swedes as a notably warlike people. They cannot live without wars, he writes. Without wars Sweden, within a few years, would again become a poor country: 'Sweden needs to keep her people on the move and not let them rest.' When the Peace of Westphalia is signed, in 1648, Chanut is dubious whether this lack of a war will really be to Sweden's advantage.

To me the century when Sweden was a great European power seems to have been our most unhappy and miserable in modern times. Pierre Chanut, too, that clever diplomat, regarded Sweden's political grandeur as transient. 'It had been won with German soldiers and French money'. Concerning this remark, so shocking to all Swedes who may still today entertain fanciful notions of their own greatness, Professor Curt Weibull, in a recently published work, observes: 'Chanut might have added: together with able commanders and a carefully organized and implemented plunder of the countries in which the war was being waged.'

Today no one of unclouded judgment really believes that any people's predestined scene of activity on this earth is a battlefield. Presumably there have at all times been certain individuals born to be soldiers, who have only been able to realize their own destinies by killing their fellow men. But no one will ever convince me that whole nations have been made up of this particular species of brute. As for us Swedes, we have of course been just as well- or ill-suited, just as much or as little destined to warfare, as any other people.

In this history I have only dwelt on those of our wars which appear to have been major calamities. Historically, the Swedes were always regarded as a militant nation. Therefore I shall now devote some space to the pacific nature of this same people.

For six hundred years the inhabitants of what today are the five Swedish provinces of Västergötland, Småland, Halland, Skåne and Blekinge lived along a frontier which, to them, was nothing but a curse and a nuisance. This frontier is supposed to have first been drawn up in 1054. It remained in force, with brief intervals, until 1658. As long as it existed, the outbreak of each successive war between Sweden and Denmark turned the countryside on either side of it into a theatre of hostilities. From the wars of our own time in various parts of the world we know how tragic is the lot of border populations. In the past the men of Västergötland, Småland, Halland, Skåne and Blekinge were all subject to a similarly monstrous fate. The liberal 19th-century historian Fryxell sums it up in a single sentence of his Swedish history. In the end, he says, the poor people along the frontier hid themselves in the depths of the forests, 'in their hearts cursing both Swedes and Danes.'

An original source, witnessing to the manner in which the frontier between Sweden and Denmark was drawn up in 1054, is to be found in the Older Västergötland Law, where we are told that this de-marcation of the two kingdoms was done by the King of the Svear,

Emund Slemme, in Uppsala, and by Sven Tjugoskägg ('Twenty Beard') of the Danes, a monarch who is thought to be identical with Sven Estridsson. From the point of junction between Västergötland and Halland in the north, to Brömsebro, on the Blekinge coast in the south, the kings, accompanied by twelve men from either kingdom, erected six frontier stones. Professor Gerhard Hafström has published a remarkable study of the old boundary: in 1934, almost nine hundred years after it had first been erected, he excavated the sixth and last frontier stone at Brömsebro. Today it is protected as a historical monument the local people are proud to show off to visitors. The probable sites of the other stones were also discovered by the same historian.

The *Rhymed Chronicle* immortalizes this event of 1054:

> Twixt Sweden and Denmark these XII men
> Six stones set up, and [they] stand there yet.

Long stretches of the frontier were utterly unnatural. They took no account whatever of the countryside as such, nor of the habitations of those who lived in it. Usually the boundary coincides with lakes and rivers, but in the great forests it is simply the shortest line between two points. In places this frontier between the two realms bisected villages and separated adjacent farms, thereby also separating members of the same family and clan.

Yet no frontier stones could expunge what they had in common, or the friendships existing between their clans and families. They were, and remained, close relatives. Against their will the authorities had drawn up a frontier which they had never desired; and they continued to associate in despite of it. As before, they intermarried, they traded, they bought and sold cattle, bartered services and commodities. In the countryside along the frontier the community of interests remained undisturbed. The border folk needed each other.

Though formally either Swedes or Danes, these were extraneous labels, arbitrarily imposed from without. In their own view of themselves the border folk seem to have remained the same people as they had always been down the centuries, down the millennia. It was quite simply impossible, all of a sudden, to expunge so immemorial a community of interests. The Smålanders had more in common with the Skånians and men of Blekinge than they had with such remote peoples as the Upplanders or Dalesmen.

But the outbreak of each new war turned the border peasantry into enemies. Nothing seems more natural than that they should have opposed such a forcible transformation, nothing more humanly explicable than their reluctance to go over the border and kill their relatives, friends and neighbours. All the border folk desired was to be left in peace and quiet. What advantage could they derive from troubling their neighbours?

In one of my novels (*Förräddarland* 1967) I have written of the commons' predicament along the border in wartime. The action takes place in my own part of the country, on the frontiers of Blekinge and Småland. For many years before I began to write that book I had been preoccupied with this motif, so deeply embedded in the lives of my ancestors and preserved orally in popular tradition. And in my description of the separate peace signed by the peasantry along the frontier in 1522 I drew on material of which I shall now give an account.

These frontiersmen, in my opinion, are among those whom history has overlooked. Little mention is made, in our academic histories, of their separate peace treaties. Nor have I been able to find more than a single study of the subject, an essay by Professor Folke Lindberg in *The Swedish Historical Review* 1928. It has been my main source of information.

This paucity of source materials is explicable. These treaties among the peasantry, being unsanctioned by the central authorities, were not included among official documents. But two documents of importance have nevertheless been preserved for posterity. They relate to the peaces contracted on the border in 1505 and 1525.

Though historians describe these separatist treaties comprehensively as 'peasant peaces' (*bondefreder*) the word is somewhat adventitious, inasmuch as in a number of instances they were signed by both nobles and burghers, and sometimes drawn up by parish priests. The size and kind of the contracting parties, too, varied widely. Treaties of peace were concluded between whole provinces, between hundreds and even between parishes. These last, of course, were strictly local affairs. Usually they have left no documentary trace; may even have been purely oral, in which case they have left posterity in the dark.

As early as the 11th century we know of separate peace treaties being signed between Scandinavian provinces in time of war. The phenomenon is referred to in the history of Snorre. King Olof Skötkonung of Sweden was waging war against St Olaf of Norway, but Ragvald Jarl, on behalf of the Västergötlanders, concluded his own peace with the Norwegians. The king at Uppsala may have disapproved of the Västergötland peasantry's high-handed action, but without the salt they imported from Norway they could not live, and in such straits the province had simply been obliged to sue for peace. Again, during the war of 1381 between Sweden and Denmark, the province of Skåne, independently of Denmark, signed a separate peace with the Swedes. As we have seen, this happened again in 1434 and 1436, when they concluded an armistice with Engelbrekt without asking King Erik of Pomerania's permission. The declaration of neutrality by the five Värend hundreds during the Danish invasion of 1520 was of the same order.

But the great age of peasant peace treaties was the two last decades of the Middle Ages, 1505–1525, a time when Sweden and Denmark were almost continuously at war. Half a score of peace treaties between the frontiersmen are known to history from this time, and two are documented beyond all doubt in extant texts.

Most of these peace treaties were concluded between the Smålanders and the men of Blekinge, who were dependent on their mutual trade across the frontier. The Smålanders could not do without the salt, herring and spices which came from Ronneby, and the men of Blekinge needed meat and butter from the cattle-raising district of Värend. 'The oxen were the peacemakers', is an old popular saying from the borderlands. Gentle and pacific indeed is the ox.

In the history of these peasant peace treaties, Furs Bridge, across the Lyckeby River, a waterway which for six hundred years constituted the boundary between Sweden and Denmark, occupies a prominent position. At Fur, today a railway halt on the Karlskrona-Växjö line, the Lyckeby River crosses an immemorially ancient road leading to Ronneby in Blekinge. The pine forest grows dense along the river banks, whence the bridge's name (*furu*=pine). Down the centuries travellers have halted here to rest at an inn or tavern. In the Middle Ages, Furs Bridge was an important meeting place for the border folk, who assembled here to consult on their common affairs. Originally built of logs, it has been supplanted in our own day by a modern road bridge. But remains of the oaken timbers which used to support the span of the older bridge can still be discerned in the waters of the Lyckeby River.

This old bridge over the waterway which constituted the frontier was neutral territory and therefore a natural venue for meetings and peaceful negotiations. In these timbers which once formed part of the bridge and which five centuries have hardly sufficed to rot away completely, I read a genuine fragment of the history of the Swedish people. Questions of the welfare or otherwise of human beings, matters of life and death, have been decided on them. On Furs Bridge were concluded a number of parish treaties between Vissefjärda parish, on the Swedish side, and Fridlevstad on the Danish. For me these oaken timbers are original documents, the sort which historians call relics, and to which they assign a primary source-value. They are tangible evidence of past occurrences. In them the peace treaties concluded on this bridge come to life and bring me closer to history than any written document.

In 1505, war broke out again between the regent Svante Sture and King Hans of the Union. Once again the borderlands were exposed to all the horrors with which they were so familiar; to passages of men-at-arms and all that this implied of plunder and rapine, fire, devastation and death. But immediately the inhabitants on either side of the border sent representatives to a provincial assembly at Hjortsberga, in Blekinge, to avert this threat by mutual agreement. In August 1505 this meeting bore fruit in a peace treaty between Värend, Möre, Sunnerbo and Västbo hundreds, on the Swedish side, and the province of Blekinge and the Skånian hundred of Göinge, on the Danish. The treaty was put into writing, and its crucial points, modernized, read as follows:

'Notwithstanding that a state of war exists between the crowns of Sweden and Denmark, a state of unbroken peace shall be maintained as hitherto between the parties who are signatories to this treaty.

'The commons shall not follow their lords further than to the boundary of the realm.

'If the lords should prepare raids across the border, the people on that side which is threatened shall receive advance warning.

'Free trade and traffic shall prevail across the frontier, as hitherto.

'The parties shall together combat the bands of robbers in the forests along the border, and he who gives these criminals protection or assistance shall be branded a traitor.'

The treaty was confirmed by the Värend provincial assembly at Växjö, on August 15, 1505. A copy was sent to the regent Svante Sture and duly entered into his copy book, where the document has been preserved for posterity. Clearly and unmistakably it tells us how in times past the common people, on both sides of the border, made a mutual attempt to keep the peace.

Overtly and in writing the men of Skåne, Blekinge and Småland, in thus refusing to cross the border on a violent errand or under arms, had opted out of the war; had become deserters. On either side the signing of this agreement made them guilty of associating with the enemy in time of war. The most remarkable paragraph of all is that in which they undertake to give each other warning of impending attacks across the frontier. To warn the enemy – that is obviously treason, and the penalty for it is death. Even today, if Sweden should go to war, a special law can be brought into force to this effect.

We do not know how the regent reacted or whether he reacted at all. Any reply he may have despatched to the provincial assembly at Växjö has been lost. Probably he resigned himself to a state of affairs beyond his control. As we have already seen in considering his reign, he lacked the military resources to force a recalcitrant peasantry to take the field against the Danes. This being so, the provincial assembly was in a position so strong that the central authorities were no match for it. Nor is it likely that this separate peace treaty, signed at Hjortsberga in August 1505, came as a surprise to Svante Sture. It was by no means unique, as can clearly be seen from the commentary appended to the treaty, according to which the commons 'had made a pact between themselves, now as in the past'. This is a very important item of information: *their peace treaty was in accordance with ancient tradition.* So we have every reason to suppose that other treaties of a similar nature must have been concluded, even though they have left no trace in history.

The other extant document bears witness to a separate peace treaty, concluded between Värend and Blekinge, at Kolshult in Blekinge, on May 18, 1525, and confirmed by Hjortsberga provincial assembly on the 22nd of that month.

In the spring of 1525, the situation was as follows: With forces based on Gotland, the Danish Commander-in-Chief Sören Norrby was fighting energetically for King Christian II of the Union, whom still remained to be finally defeated. Now Norrby was on the point of invading Blekinge. But the men of Blekinge made haste to renew their ancient pact with the inhabitants on the other side of the border, and on St Erik's Day the two neighbouring peoples met at Kolshult. What occurred then is to be seen on a piece of parchment still extant in the Danish archives.

Lengthy quotations from historical documents are likely only to bring a yawn to my reader and cause him to skip my pages; so I refrain from them. But this old fragment of parchment from Kolshult bears such eloquent witness to the pacific nature of these Swedes, that it deserves to be reproduced without abbreviation.

Slightly modernized, it reads as follows:

'We, the common peasantry who build and live in the land of Blekinge, do by this our open letter make it known to all and sundry that in fifteen hundred and twenty-five after the birth of God, on Saint Erik's Day (May 18) we were assembled at Kolshult, together with our good friends who build and live in the land of Värend, concerning the bond and undertaking to which the countries long ago agreed and bound themselves, with letters duly sealed and signed. Now we do promise and aver upon our honour and manhood, that if (the which God forbid) any would anger or do hurt or dam to the land of Värend, then will we follow after to help and console you and stand manly by you to the utmost of our power, as good sworn men of the peasantry should do.

Item, dear friends, should it so be that any rascality or footloose men of the forest make so bold as to cause damage or hurt in the land of Blekinge and then enter your land, then do we request that ye shall capture and seize all such and send them to us. The same are we willing to do unto you, if any should force his way in to the land of Värend.

Item, when we receive sure tidings from you that any danger threatens, then will we come to your rescue and spare neither night nor day, and hope to God you will do the same again for us.

That thus it shall be, and on both sides be kept without breach, and that thus in truth it hath been decided: thereto append we our province's seal beneath this our open letter, written and given at Hjortsberga provincial assembly, Monday next after *Rogacionum for ascensionem Domini*, in this year which is written (May 22, 1525).'

The document, in the Danish archives, still bears the broken seal of the province of Blekinge.

This peace meeting was held on the feast of Erik the Holy, an important date in the peasants' calendar: if this saint granted ears of rye, another, Saint Olov, would grant them rye loaves. That year it fell on a Thursday, and the agreement was already ratified at Hjortsberga assembly on the following Monday. The danger was imminent, and people made haste to protect their own countryside. The document confirms their pacific traditions when it says that 'over a long time past' there had been treaties between the provinces in the form of 'good sealed letters', confirming them. Again we find the promise of mutual assistance 'to the utmost of our power' against all who intend 'hurt or damage' in the countryside. Special mention is made of individual men of violence; but most important of all is the paragraph stipulating messages concerning danger, 'then will we come to your rescue and spare neither night nor day'; a sentence which can only mean that the danger in question lay in Sören Norrby's advancing and pillaging legionaries.

This original document shows, incontrovertibly, how deeply the allied folk along the frontier detested these national wars.

How important to the kingdom as a whole was this provincial separatism, which found expression in these treaties of peace among the peasantry? Whether they had any effect on state policy is hard to say, though in certain instances they obviously bore political fruit. In 1523, a provincial peace treaty between Västergötland and the Skånian provinces obliged Gustav Vasa to cancel an invasion of Skåne.

In January of that year his two commanders, Lars Siggesson Sparre and Bernt von Melen, invaded Skåne in considerable strength. The campaign was 'carefully prepared and extremely costly'. At this time von Melen, a German, was Gustav Vasa's favourite. On his master's account he had enlisted 3,000 German men-at-arms. The rest of his army consisted of a forced levy of Swedish peasants. The attacking troops outnumbered the defenders of Skåne several times over.

Swedes and Germans crossed the Lagan River, the national boundary, but had not advanced very far into Skanian territory before the whole enterprise ground to a halt. After only six weeks in the field, Lars Siggesson and von Melen had to commence their withdrawal, and recrossed the frontier. Notwithstanding the great superiority of the invading army, the whole attempt to conquer Skåne became, from the outset, an inglorious failure.

Von Melen's post facto explanation of his military fiasco was that he had been frustrated by the early spring floods. Overflowing their banks, the rivers in Skåne had become so swollen, he claimed, that his soldiers had been unable to cross them. Actually, his men-at-arms had never even got as far as any Skanian river. They had halted at Markaryd, just inside the frontier. If his army had been able to cross the Lagan, which is broader than any other Skanian river, how can these lesser waters have presented so formidable an obstacle? Von Melen's explanation was nothing but an excuse, as even his contemporaries realised.

The real fate of the campaign transpires in a document still to be found in the archives of the Hanseatic League. It is a report dated February 11, 1523, from one of the League's observers in Sweden to the council at Stralsund. The German observer writes:

'Further, Gustav Eriksson, the leader in Sweden, possesseth upwards of a thousand cavalry, German and Danish, and he hath upwards of 3,000 men-at-arms and innumerable peasants. Further, that he wished this winter to invade Skåne with them and lay it waste by fire; but the peasants of Västergötland, which lieth nearby, would not follow [him], inasmuch as they are leagued with the peasants of Halland and Blekinge, on the Skanian border, so that the one peasant should not harm the other. When His Danish Majesty wished to invade Västergötland and Sweden, plunder and burn, then would the Skanian peasants not support him, but hindered and fought against the royal troops; the same would the Västergötland and Swedish peasants even abide by, according to their treaty.'

So it was not the flooded rivers, after all, which prevented Gustav Vasa from invading Skåne! What had put paid to the invasion was the peace treaty between the commons of the border provinces. On both sides of the frontier hordes of peasants sabotaged the campaign. The peasants of Västergötland refused to follow the German legionaries – what business could they have in Skåne? – and the Danish king's plan for an invasion of Västergötland, too, had to be called off: 'that would the Skanian peasants not support'.

In 1523, an ancient peace treaty between the peasantry on either side came into force and proved effective 'so that the one peasant should not harm the other'. Ten simple words which sum up the sense of these separatist peaces.

'So at all events we have no reason to doubt the existence of a peace treaty between the peasants of Skåne and of Sweden at this time', writes Folke Lindberg; and goes on: 'If, furthermore, we take into account the fact that, at the time in question, the ancient pact between Blekinge and Värend must have been in full force, the picture becomes complete. We gain the impression that what faces us is a gigantic association of the commons in the Skanian provinces and the whole of Southern Sweden.'

Another aspect of the story of the peaceful strivings of the border peasantry was the attempts of the population of Värend in Småland to stay outside the last wars of the Union. In the Sture epoch, indeed, Värend almost seems to have been an independent republic only loosely attached to the rest of the realm. The province had no desire to involve itself in these national wars between Swedes and Danes, and during Christian II's successful invasion of Sweden, a kingdom to which he had a titular right, the Värend peasants lay low. But in 1520 they were alarmed by a letter from the King of the Union demanding that they should recognise him as King of Sweden and swear him fealty.

This put them on the spot. The war's outcome was still uncertain – Stockholm was still holding out against the Danes, who might not be victorious. In opting for the Union king the Värend peasants would have taken sides. On the other hand, it they refused Christian his oath of fealty they would have the Danes to reckon with, and be lumped with the other side. Apparently they could not care less who won, Swedes or Danes, as long as they did not themselves have to join in the struggle. Although in favour of the Union, which had brought their province great blessings, they were loth to recognise Christian as their king. They had no desire at all to become the subjects of so tyrannous a ruler. Later that year their suspicions of the Union king turned out to have been justified: in the summer of 1520 he decreed that the Smålanders should hand over their weapons and this led to a peasant rising against him, centred on the Kalmar district. But neither did the province accept a Swedish tyrant, as later became plain in Nils Dacke's insurrections.

But the king's alarming letter demanded an answer, and a meeting of the provincial assembly was summoned for March 25, 1520. I should give a great deal to see the minutes of that meeting, which had to arrive at so excruciating a decision. As it is, no one knows whether their reply to the king was unanimous. At all events, the people of Värend decided to play for time; before reaching a decision they wanted to wait and see how 'matters and negotiations' fell out in other parts of the country. In their letter to the king, therefore, they declare themselves temporarily neutral. Värend would continue to lie low until Saint Olov's Day, July 29. If by that day Christian had brought the rest of the country under his dominion, Värend too would recognise him.

The Smålanders' opportunist and unheroic attitude is reminiscent of Sweden's neutral policies during the Second World War. But its purpose – the preservation of peace – was as valid and as humanly understandable in the 16th century as it was four hundred years later.

For Gustav Vasa these peasants along the frontier of his state who concluded independent peace treaties were nothing but a pack of traitors; self-opinionated folk who, if he was to feel safe on his throne, would have to be extirpated. Against this powerful Renaissance monarch the provinces could no longer assert their individual autonomy. Though it fought him to the bitter end, after the failure of Dacke's insurrection even Småland was finally incorporated in the realm. And this was the end, once and for all, of the separatism of the so-called 'folk lands'.

Yet even after Gustav Vasa, even, surprisingly enough, far into the 17th century, the commons continued to make peace along the frontier. Gerhard Hafström's book on the old Swedish-Danish frontier (1934) mentions three parish treaties concluded in the 17th century on the historic Furs Bridge, the immemorial meeting place between Smålanders and the men of Blekinge. In 1611, 1644 and 1657, as in the Middle Ages, representatives of the neighbouring parishes of Vissefjärda and Fridlevstad met on the bridge – in each case to sign their own peace treaty in time of war between Sweden and Denmark. At the 1644 and 1657 meetings the Smålanders' spokesman was the Vissefjärda clergyman, Nicolaus Petri, known as Master Bock ('goat'), and the sheriff, Per of Bockabo. At times it seems to have been the custom for parish priests to take the lead at these meetings.

Even later, during Karl XI's 1674–78 war, we have evidence that a parochial peace treaty was concluded on Furs Bridge. The document, drawn up on that occasion by the peasants themselves, is dated 1675 and partially extant. By that time Blekinge had been part of Sweden for almost twenty years, yet some of her population were not prepared to help Denmark recover her lost province. It would have meant the reestablishment of the detested national frontier. In this document we are told that a 'sure and strong peasant peace' has been concluded.

This is the last such treaty on the southern border to be found in the sources.

But several peace treaties were also concluded between the peasantry on either side along the Swedish-Norwegian border, from the Middle Ages up to the mid-17th century. On the Swedish side it was the Värmlanders above all who put out peace feelers to the peasantry across the border in war-time. During the Kalmar War of 1611, for instance, the Värmland peasants invited their Norwegian brethren to a peace meeting, and this led to a pact between them.

A Norwegian history contains an eloquent anecdote from a war between Sweden and Norway, showing the neighbouring peoples' feelings when conscripted to fight each other. Two peasants, musket in hand, met at the border. Amazed, the two men just stood and gaped at each other. Then the Norwegian threw down his weapon and burst out:

'Well I never! If it isn't Ola from Kattbo!'

It *was* Ola from Kattbo. He too also threw down his musket, and the two peasants fell into each others' arms.

The common man's reluctance to go to war extended even to conscripted troops. We know of a great many cases of desertion, evasion and flight, particularly during the century when Sweden was a great European power. During the 1620's, when the men were to be stacked aboard transports and shipped overseas to Poland and Germany, there was a notable increase in such acts of desertion. Not a few conscripts objected to being despatched abroad like so many parcels – the whole transport had been organized by Gustavus Adolphus in person. There were even attempts at mutiny. But our nationalistic historians are extremely gingerly in their treatment of these events.

This right to make peace independently across the frontiers was deeply entrenched in the popular mind, and in the border country the memories of these peasant treaties survived from generation to generation. Remarkable evidence of this is a private member's bill mooted in the Lower Chamber of the Riksdag on January 22, 1869, by a certain Jonas Jonasson, M.P. for Gullaboås in Södra Möre. Objecting to the armaments race in Europe, this M.P. expresses his indignation at 'the enormous sums of money used every year to acquire and maintain materials for the mass-mutilation and destruction of our fellow human beings. Not only do the peoples have to raise these monies by their sweat and toil, they are also forced to sacrifice their very lives and blood.' It is not the peoples who are the cause of wars, asserts this peasant from Gullaboås; on the contrary, they have often resisted them by concluding peace treaties of their own. His bill goes on:

'Within the hundred which I have the honour to represent, mention is often made of how, during the wars between Sweden and Denmark, the commons in this place situated on what was then the frontier concluded a so-called *peasant peace* with their neighbours in Blekinge, leaving it to others to destroy one another, something for which they, for their part, had as little wish as reason; and whilst among the peoples today the idea on which such a peasant peace reposed seems to be steadily developing, those who rule them pay less and less heed to it.'

The idea of peasant peaces, he suggests, could be implemented by all states, thus realizing the dream of universal peace. Since one people must take the first step, and the Swedes, for the past fifty-five years, had been enjoying the blessings of peace and it would be an action worthy of them to be that people. His bill culminates in the proposal 'that the Riksdag shall submit to His Majesty's Government a humble petition that His Majesty's Government will be so gracious as to extend the hand [of friendship] to all the regents and parliaments of Europe in favour of a general disarmament and with the aim to conclude with Sweden an everlasting peace.'

Even two centuries after the cessation of the border treaties with the disappearance of the border, their memory was still very much alive among the commons of Södra Möre.

The traditional image of the Swedes as a notably warlike nation stands in need of revision. Generation after generation, there were these other Swedes. Swedes who nourished an inextirpable love of peace. The border peasantry were the pioneers of peace in Scandinavia – such is my contention; which is why I have devoted so much space to this 'warrior people's' dream of peace.

Tyrant I: Christian II

IN SWEDISH HISTORY Christian II of Denmark, Norway and Sweden, the last king of the Union, appears mainly as the chief butcher of the Stockholm Bloodbath, the wholesale executions with which he tried to secure his position after he had crushed the Swedish resistance. Horrific descriptions of those November days in 1520 have fastened in the minds of Swedes. Christian the Tyrant has lived down the ages as a bloodthirsty sadist. Some chroniclers even seem ashamed of the fact that such a blood-sullied monarch should ever have sat on the Swedish throne at all. Nevertheless, Christian II had been duly crowned in Stockholm on September 7, 1520 and properly acknowledged by the Council and the Estates. A few days after the Stockholm Bloodbath the surviving city burghers even staged a great feast in his honour. It was only after his final defeat that he came to be called Christian the Tyrant, and that was about all there was to be said about him. His features have been limned once and for all. In Swedish history Christian II has been made to stand in the corner – and there he has stood ever since.

But this image of the last king of the Union, whom we see there so clearly standing in the corner, is altogether too summary. The portrait can be complemented from sources which add many lights and shades and show Christian II to have been a most complex and richly endowed personality; an astonishing figure; a man of contradictions. The tyrant who was responsible for the Bloodbath, of course, remains. He is beyond rehabilitation. But he also becomes a tempting subject for psychological study. Christian's reign appears to have been one long series of paradoxical and inexplicable actions, both good and bad. How they can all have been the work of one and the same man is an enigma. Poets, dramatists and novelists, always attracted to history's enigmatic personalities, have found in

Christian II a fascinating theme. In one instance at least he has given rise to a literary masterpiece: Johannes V. Jensen's *Kongens Fald* (1913).

As a human story the life of Christian II, oscillating between greatness and abasement, is without counterpart among our Swedish kings. At the age of six he was crowned heir to the throne in Denmark and Norway. At the age of eighteen he was crowned in Sweden, where, in 1499, we even find him acting as stand-in for his father, King Hans. In 1513, at the age of thirty-two, he is King of Denmark and Norway and, seven years later, of all three Scandinavian countries. He marries a sister of the Emperor Charles V and thus becomes the brother-in-law of the most powerful of all European potentates. Being himself absolute monarch over the three kingdoms of the Nordic Empire, he is himself virtually the Emperor's peer. Christian II's position in fact was more powerful than that of any later Scandinavian monarch. But only three years were to pass before he was stripped of every vestige of authority and driven into a humiliating exile. After an unsuccessful attempt to regain his throne, Christian is flung into prison. There, for twenty-seven long years, he spends the rest of his life as a prisoner of the Danish State; and dies in captivity.

One of his successors on the Swedish throne, Karl XIV Johan* declared proudly on his deathbed: 'No one ever had a career like mine'. Christian II could have said the same, but not as a matter of any pride. Where Karl XIV Johan succeeded, Christian II failed. And the loser who falls on evil days – particularly if he is a highly gifted personality whose every undertaking, however grandiose, ends in disaster – is always a more interesting human figure than the man of success and good fortune. How did it come about?

Even a ruler who has earned the sobriquet 'The Tyrant' has the right to as fair a trial as possible. Usually it has been considered adequate to explain the last Union monarch's evil deeds as being typical of a Renaissance prince. Any ruler who gave vent to violent passions is liable to be saddled with this cliché. Christian, we are told, was a product of his time and place. I am not satisfied with such

* Marshal Bernadotte, summoned by the Estates to be Crown Prince of Sweden in 1810.—*Transl.*

an explanation. I do not believe that people are only the children of the time and environment in which they grow up. Widely differing individuals, leading very different lives, spring from the same age and environment. An epoch is a tree which bears various fruits. The 16th century shows us both good and evil people. It gave birth to tyrants, but also to saints. Christian II and Gustav Vasa were equally 16th-century rulers, and as tyrants they had many peers in Europe. But it was also the century of such great men of the spirit and humanists as Erasmus of Rotterdam, Thomas More and Olaus Petri. They, too, were children of their age and milieu.

Christian II, eldest son of King Hans of Oldenburg, was born on March 8, 1481. The founder of this dynasty had been Christian I, celebrated in Sweden as king of the Union. He was also famous for his unusual stature. Formerly he was supposed to have been well over six-foot tall, though the Danes have measured his skeleton and found it to be less. His father King Hans, we are told, though noted for his firm grasp of practical affairs and eye for realities, suffered from periods of acute melancholy, suggestive of a manic-depressive temperament. He was musical, loved feasts and gaiety, but also evinced a weakness for the fair sex. This king kept a titular mistress, a married woman, Fru Edele Jernskegg.

Christian's mother, Queen Christina, was sister of the Elector of Saxony, Frederik the Wise, who ruled over Luther's native country and therefore has his place in the history of the Reformation. She is described as a God-fearing and pious woman.

Before she gave birth to Christian, her first-born, strange natural phenomena, signs and portents occurred, foreboding the boy's remarkable and dramatic destiny. The 16th-century Danish historian Huitfeldt repeats a contemporary anecdote from the birth. The boy was heard to be weeping aloud in his mother's womb: 'He could clearly be heard'. A natural conclusion: the child was loth to come into the world. And 'at the hour of his birth' the boy came out of his mother's womb with one hand open and the other clasped. When his closed fist was opened by the midwife, it was found to be full of blood and mucous. Whence another conclusion: 'He was to be a bloodthirsty person'.

This anecdote about Christian's birth, however, is posthumous and therefore coloured by what was then known about his life. There is nothing remarkable about a baby being born with blood in his hand, as every doctor and midwife knows. Luckily, not all newborn infants who have blood in their fists at birth turn into bloodthirsty people.

King Hans' and Queen Christina's first-born showed hardly any of the family traits characteristic of his father, grandfather or other relatives. Nor did he outwardly resemble any members of his typically blond and Nordic-looking dynasty. Christian wore the aspect of a dark-haired southerner. In a contemporary portrait now in the Copenhagen Museum of Art, his features are altogether southern. First and foremost an observer cannot help being struck by the dark, strangely veiled eyes. In this painting Christian the Tyrant has the gaze of a dreamer and a seer. He seems absent, lost in thought, withdrawn, unaware of place and moment. Far away in the distance he beholds something which holds him in thrall. But deep in the darkness of his eyes is a dangerous glint. At any moment one imagines it can burst into flame.

Altogether, Christian does not seem really at home in his Danish environment, and various attempts have been made to explain his southern physiognomy. He is supposed to have been a royal bastard, fruit of a liaison between the queen and a Roman aristocrat, a papal legate who had been staying in Copenhagen the year before his birth. Such an Italian father would explain his 'hot blood' and violent temperament. This theory is attractive, but must be rejected as a romantic fancy, and no Danish historian has ever taken it seriously. For the newly married Queen Christina to have had sexual relations with anyone except her husband or borne the king a bastard successor to the throne is a patent absurdity, the more so as she is known to have been a woman who satisfied every requirement of honour and virtue.

For the son of a king, Christian's education was most unusual, As a little boy he was placed in the charge of Hans Meisenheim Bogbinder – 'book-binder' – and his wife. These merchant burghers of Copenhagen, respected and reliable middleclass people, accepted him as if he had been their own son. The king's confidence in them must have been complete to have put them in charge of his son. And

presumably the task of bringing up the crown prince of Denmark
was accepted by them as a signal honour.

Nothing could have been better for the future ruler than to escape
the confines of the royal castle and live among the ordinary run of
mankind. He gets to know his future subjects from the inside. In the
house of Hans the bookbinder, Christian, during his childhood's
impressionable years, gained insight into the conditions under which
the popular classes lived. We do not know how long he stayed with
his foster-parents, but his stay in the burgher home was to have
important consequences for his reign. In this new environment he
must have become aware of the great difference which obtained
between the various Estates; during his years there he gained
experiences which he later exploited as king. As a social reformer
and radical legislator he was in a position to base his ideas on a
realistic knowledge of the common people.

In works on Christian II we are told that he 'was educated wholly
in the principles of humanism' – a remarkable description of the
education of a pupil who later became known as The Tyrant.
Historical facts prove that the last Union monarch did in fact enjoy
an all-round education unusual in those days among the sons of
princes. His childhood years in the burgher home, when he
associated on an equal footing with craftsmen and their like, were
certainly a fruitful part of his apprenticeship.

On reaching the age of twenty-five years, Christian was regarded
as mature enough to govern a kingdom. King Hans appointed his
son governor of Norway.

That was in 1506. The following year, at Bergen, came the great
experience of his life. He met Dyveke.

Sigbrit Willumsdotter, widow of a Dutch merchant, had emigrated to Norway with her young daughter. In Holland both women
had been living in extreme poverty, and in their new country were
seeking a less intolerable existence. In Bergen, Sigbrit Willumsdotter opened a bakery, selling its products, waffles, various cakes
and pastries in the city's market places. Though the mother went
unnoticed, the daughter, Dyveke, who was unusually pretty,
attracted all the more attention. The young Dutchwoman was a
'wonderfully beautiful girl, of handsome proportions, slim and

slender as a reed, with refined features and a mild expression; she was shy and gentle, and her deportment and whole nature were characterized by an extraordinary charm'.

In his book about Christian II, the Danish historian C. F. Allen describes the prince's first meeting with Dyveke. The governor's chancellor, Erik Valkendorf, had seen the girl out with her mother selling cakes in the market. Struck by her extraordinary beauty, he had mentioned her to Christian. This had awakened the young prince's curiosity, with the result that Mother Sigbrit and her daughter were among the guests invited to a banquet given by the city of Bergen for the governor in its Town Hall. During the dancing Christian, 'out of respect for the convenances', had asked one of the city's own daughters for the first dance, but then asked Dyveke to dance with him, and thereafter had neither thoughts nor eyes for any other. She had captivated him utterly, at first sight. The banquet over, Christian resolutely opened negotiations with Mother Sigbrit, and she offered no objections. Her daughter became the twenty-six-year-old governor's mistress.'

In those days a man in Christian's elevated station, a king's son, had little trouble in getting any woman he desired as a sexual partner. He could simply pick and choose. The sequel to that banquet at Bergen in 1507, therefore, was in no way unusual. The governor of Norway took young Dyveke to his bed. What is remarkable is that this was not the prelude to a transient affair, no mere princely caprice; it led to a relationship which has rightly taken its place in history. Here we have the only royal romance in the annals of Scandinavia to have political consequences – because of its effects on the despot's psyche. Christian's love for Dyveke and its tragic ending are thought to have been decisive for his actions on a number of crucial occasions.

Of Dyveke we know little more than that she possessed unusual feminine charm. When she first went to the prince's bed it was probably as Mother Sigbrit's obedient and well brought up daughter. Dyveke herself can hardly have had any say in the matter. But there is evidence to suggest that she came to love her lover. At all events, for her the relationship lasted as long as life itself – i.e. for ten years, until her mysterious death in 1517.

What is certain is that Dyveke was before all others the woman in Christian's life. As long as she lived he was 'wildly passionate' in his devotion to her. That it was not only lust on his part, but true love, is beyond question. As his actions were to prove.

Mother Sigbrit and Dyveke went with the governor of Norway to Oslo, where he had a house built for them in the immediate proximity of his own palace. Later, when Christian succeeded to his father's throne in 1513, both women moved with the new king to Copenhagen, where he also furnished a dwelling for them, hard by his castle.

Dyveke was the king's lover, mistress or concubine – whichever word we use to describe her position, it was no secret. She was his titular mistress, and to keep mistresses was a privilege of princes. Christian was merely following his father's example and the custom in royal houses in those days. An unwritten law, however, required that royal mistresses should preferably be of noble birth; and Christian had had the impudence to choose one from among the lower orders, a woman, furthermore, of foreign birth and of unknown origins. His overt relationship with Dyveke was regarded as a challenge to the Danish nobility, and by the highest circles of Copenhagen society she was ill-seen, even hated.

After Christian's political marriage to Elizabeth, sister of Charles V, Dyveke became an insult to the Emperor himself, and Charles demanded that his brother-in-law should send his concubine away. Christian refused. Resolutely flouting all objections to his love-affair, no matter what their source, he kept his mistress close to him.

Mother Sigbrit's presence at court still further augmented the scandal and it was through the titular mistress's mother that the affair came to assume political proportions. Sigbrit Willumsdotter was a strong-willed, fearless and ambitious woman, a woman to reckon with, who came to exert a great influence over the king. Her flair for business was so great that Christian entrusted her with the realm's affairs, elevating an unknown foreign woman of low birth, a mere bakeress, who had stood selling bread in the public market-places, to a key position in finance and politics. The action was utterly unique in European history. For the blue-blooded arrogant aristocracy it was, of course, a scandal of stupendous proportions. But Mother Sigbrit knew what she was about. Troels-Lund writes of her that she was one of the best finance ministers Denmark has ever had!

Not only was Dyveke's mother a foreigner and an outsider; she also came to be regarded as a witch, who had gained her ascendency over Christian by magic. In her house she was believed to have installed a laboratory and there, experimenting with alchemical pumps and retorts, manufactured gold. The mind of that age was in thrall to an obsession with magic and witchcraft, and there were those who regarded Mother Sigbrit as the real ruler of Denmark, governing the king himself with the Devil's aid; and if the Devil held him fast in his grip, it was in the shape of the beautiful Dyveke. All of a sudden, at Midsummer 1517, the royal mistress died. What she died of was never known. Certain of the symptoms suggest appendicitis. But in the Middle Ages sudden death was always likely to give rise to suspicions of poison. So it did now. A man of high estate, the powerful nobleman Torben Oxe, was believed to be the culprit. Oxe was alleged to have sent Dyveke a basket of summer's first cherries poisoned; of which she, eating, had promptly died.

Christian was wild with grief and lust for revenge. He had Torben Oxe summoned before the Council of State, but for lack of evidence the Council acquitted him. Convinced as he was of the accused's guilt, this only infuriated the king still further. Rejecting the verdict, he appointed a fresh court, consisting this time not of Torben Oxe's own peers but his peasants. Overawed by such royal pressure, they could only condemn him to death. The sentence was carried into effect.

Guilty or not? The question can never be answered. There was no looking into the matter then, and it has never been reviewed afterwards. A case, perhaps, of judicial murder. Torben Oxe was also accused of having sought – perhaps even of having enjoyed – Dyveke's favours. Christian himself believed that he had 'defiled the royal bed'. But on this point research acquits him. The Danish nobles had certainly had strong motives for wishing to get rid of the king's mistress. So much is unquestionable. But they gained nothing by her death. If there is a murder which could have yielded political dividends, surely it was Mother Sigbrit who should have been the victim? As it was, she was still alive, and her status remained unshaken. Indeed, after Dyveke's demise, Christian became even more attached to her mother and her influence over him became all the greater, likewise her power over the realm. Ever since his accession, Christian had been opposed by the aristocracy. Now he conceived a violent hatred for these noblemen who – he was convinced – had deprived him of the woman he loved.

In the life of Christian II the death of Dyveke was, as far as we can see, a turning point. Her loss precipitated an acute psychological crisis.

A Danish psychiatrist, Dr Paul J. Reiter, head of a Copenhagen mental hospital, has devoted a major work to the king's medical and psychological aspects. In it Reiter sheds some light on certain of his traits, hitherto unstudied. Christian, he declares, was a schizoid personality with the asthenic features commonly regarded as characteristic of a 'weak character'. At certain periods in his life, Reiter says, Christian's state of mind was such that he cannot be regarded as responsible for his actions. The first such period, according to Reiter, occurred after Dyveke's death in 1517. It was his life's great and decisive catastrophe. His feelings for the woman he loved are described by this psychiatrist as an erotic possession, a storm of 'raging passion, which the young foreign girl had stirred up in his soul'. Several times previously Christian had acted both precipitately and ruthlessly; but on the whole the balance of his mind had not been disturbed. Now it was different.

Reiter is not inclined to label this king a psychopath: under more favourable circumstances he might have developed into a more integrated personality. But the loss of the woman he loved and his conviction that she had been murdered by his enemies shook him to the very foundations of his soul. All restraint thrown to the winds, his blind passions were unleashed.

In this psychiatrist's opinion it was the Dyveke catastrophe which led Christian II into the paths of violence that culminated in the Stockholm Bloodbath, and to his ever afterwards being nicknamed

Christian the Tyrant. During those fateful November days of 1520 the king, Reiter says, was in a state of acute anxiety and excitement, utterly without self-control. Such were the ultimate roots of what might be called Sweden's St Bartholomew's Eve.

Historically the Stockholm Bloodbath is an enigma, and must ever remain so. Historians are still disputing exactly what happened during those November days in 1520. The same year as I sit writing this, a Swede, Professor Curt Weibull, has been involved in mutual polemics with a Danish colleague, Niels Skyum-Nielsen, on this very question. In brief, three candidates have been advanced as primarily responsible for this blood-letting: Christian II, his demoniac adviser Jens Andersen Beldenacke, and the Swedish archbishop Gustav Trolle. In the last resort, however, guilt for the massacre must obviously rest on the king himself. He could have prevented it if he had wished. Except by his will not a head could have fallen.

The course of events, as far as we know, was more or less as follows. When Christian had been crowned king, great festivities were held in Stockholm Castle, the chief notables of the kingdom and the mayors and council of Stockholm being invited. The king was at his most amiable. Walking about in the halls he lavished his favours on his Swedish guests, who, according to a contemporary record, 'fell to gaiety, dancing and games, and gave themselves up to all kinds of amusements'.

Next day the scene changed. The coronation guests were once more summoned to the castle, where the gate was closed. When the king had mounted his throne, archbishop Trolle stepped forward. He presented to Christian an indictment, demanding the severest penalty of the law upon those who on the occasion of the seizure and demolition of the Archbishop's castle at Stäket in the autumn of 1517 had committed so grave a crime against Holy Church, against himself and all his retainers. The objects of this indictment were in the first place aristocratic members of the Sture party; but also the mayors and council of Stockholm. The next person to speak was Kristina Gyllenstierna, recently widowed wife of Sten Sture. Authoritatively and without mincing her words she maintained that both the action against Stäket and the deposition of Gustav Trolle had been decided upon at a parliament held in Stockholm and must therefore be regarded as wholly legal; measures, moreover, for which all those who had participated in them, indeed all the leading men of the kingdom, had been in a body responsible. In evidence of this she handed the king the document which confirmed the parliament's decision. At that moment one of the leading prelates of Sweden, Bishop Hans Brask of Linköping, got up, as he put it, to 'make his apology'. He had been one of those who had signed the parliamentary decision; his seal, together with all the others, was hanging from the dangerous document. But from his own seal he now produced a capsule within which he had concealed a slip of paper. On this were written the words: 'To this sealing I am compelled and forced'. In this way, in a scene which was to become legendary, the Bishop of Linköping is said to have saved his own skin.

A cross-examination of all the others now began. The questions came thick and fast. The atmosphere became more and more excited. The hours passed. And when darkness had begun to fall, the doors were flung open and a troop of soldiers marched in. The arrests were swiftly made and, Olaus Petri tells us in his *Chronicle*, 'Bishop Vincentius of Skara and Bishop Mattias of Strängnäs, and many of the Swedish nobility, together with their servants and many Stockholm citizens, were seized by the neck and imprisoned, some in the tower, some in the chapel and some elsewhere in the castle. There they passed the night.'

Their fate was decided next day, November 8, when the prisoners were indicted before an ecclesiastical court, in which Gustav Trolle was one of the judges. They were pronounced guilty of heresy, a verdict which at once disencumbered the king of his earlier promise of a general amnesty. It was now up to him to carry out the punishments, and this he did with unerring precision.

The situation best appears in the following little scene: the Stockholm headsman presents himself to Bishop Vincentius, who with justifiable amazement, enquiries: 'What news?' And receives the answer: 'Not exactly good news, Your Grace: I have orders to chop Your Grace's head off.'

The executioner's hour had come. One of the witnesses, no less a person than Olaus Petri, has left us a record of what ensued. His description of the sanguinary drama, in the last pages of his Swedish *Chronicle*, is laconically realistic:

'The king caused the trumpets to be blown and an announcement to be made that all should remain within, where they were. And about midday he caused the Bishop of Skara and the Bishop of Strängnäs, with the knights and knights' retainers and citizens whom he had caused to be taken prisoner, to be led out into the great market place, there to take their lives. And when they thus were come into the market and stood up in a ring, some of the kings' council stood up in the oriel window. Nils Lycke spake unto the people who stood in the market place, and bade them take no horror of that punishment which was there to be inflicted. For his Royal Majesty, quod he, had been implored to implement these punishments by Archbishop Gustav, who thrice falling upon his knees had begged and pleaded that the wrong he had suffered might be punished. Much else he also declared, wherewith to exonerate the king. Then cried Bishop Vincentius up to him under his very eyes and said that he spake not truth, but that his king acted with lies and treachery toward Swedish men. And demanded that the others might have judgment passed upon each for himself, and know wherefore they must die; and mighty hard words spake he against the king, and said that God would be revenged upon such tyranny and injustice. Wherefore Bishop Mattias of Strännäs was the first to be beheaded outside the town court, and his head was laid betwixt his legs, the which befell not any of the others. And next thereafter was Bishop Vincentius beheaded.'

After which the turn came to many lords of the Council and other great men and to the three mayors and all the councillors of Stockholm: likewise to a number of prominent citizens. One expert on the history of Stockholm, Nils Ahnlund, has said that 'the number of victims was stated by the headsman to have been 82, a number therefore certainly reliable'.

Finally, Olaus Petri's *Chronicle* tells us: 'And the dead bodies remained lying in the market from Thursday until Saturday. And full pitiful and sorry a sight it was to see how the blood together with water and excrement ran down in the gutters from the market. Yea, it was a horrible and merciless murder.'

The Stockholm Bloodbath was an event which caused greater indignation in Scandinavia than anything else ever to happen here. No action has been more roundly condemned. Mediaeval people were hardened to violence. The occasional execution stirred them not a jot. But this massive slaughter was too strong even for their stomachs. The beheadings took three hours. Which means one head falling about every other minute.

Even from the despot's own point of view to take the lives of so many people at one and the same time and place was an error of judgment. That day too much blood ran in the gutters. People were sickened. If the executions had been phased out in time and carried out in a number of different places, people would not have been so profoundly shocked. As it was, the horror was concentrated in one spot, and became even more ghastly because of the great coronation banquet which, as we have seen, immediately preceded it. One day it was wine that flowed. The next blood.

Its epilogue, too, was utterly loathsome. On November 10, a couple of days after the bloodbath, the Stockholm burghers staged a banquet in the tyrant's honour. His queen, Elizabeth, had given birth to a daughter. In a city 'still steaming with the blood of its leading citizens' the banquet took place in the City Hall, beautifully adorned for the occasion. On their way to it the guests, crossing the great market place of Stortorget where the bloodbath had taken place, can hardly have failed to notice its traces. Ladies were invited – not only the leading citizens' but also the aristocracy's 'wives and virgins' – to this sumptuous banquet with its 'manifold merry-makings'. The wine flowed, and after it was over 'was delightsome dancing'. The newly crowned king was as gracious as could be, kind and amiable as he had been during the coronation ceremonies before the massacre.

Danish historians have been much bemused and confounded by this feast given in honour of the Tyrant after the massacre. How can the Stockholmers have brought themselves to do such a thing? Only a couple of days had passed since their guest of honour had had many of the capital's leading citizens beheaded. How could their surviving peers acclaim the king so soon afterwards? Many relatives of the victims must have been among the guests. The only explanation can be the terror this orgy of blood had instilled into the Stockholmers' hearts. Trembling for their own lives, they tried to assuage the Tyrant's wrath by a banquet in his honour.

This Swedish St Bartholomew's Eve fell most heavily on the aristocracy, on the Stockholm burghers and on the Church. It did not affect the Swedish commons, whose grief at the death of the leading aristocrats can hardly have been inconsolable. The commons had no very friendly feelings for great men. If the peasants revolted against Christian, it was for quite different reasons. First and foremost they resented his efforts to disarm them. To pay the wages of the great host of German, Scottish and French legionaries, without whom he could not have conquered Sweden, he had also imposed a heavy burden of taxes. As far as Christian was concerned, though he had enjoyed a hereditary right to the realm for more than twenty years, he had been obliged to recover it by force of arms and he regarded the Swedes as owing him the military expenses he had been put to.

In the course of a century Denmark had had only four kings. But Sweden had had no fewer than fifteen kings or regents. By getting rid of so many leading Swedes, all of them potential rebels, Christian hoped to stabilize his own royal authority in Sweden and secure for himself the same position as he enjoyed in Denmark. But the very act by which he imagined he had restored the Kalmar Union had in fact given it its death-blow. It is one of history's tragic ironies that the Stockholm Bloodbath can only be seen as a final settlement of accounts between the Union party and the Swedish nationalists. Even if murder was not an argument viable in law, in those days it was in reality accepted and utilized as such. The real motives were usually disguised. Such political murders were made to wear an air of legality by judicial proceedings before the courts. And this was exactly what happened when alleged heretics were executed under Canon law. In my view Professor Lauritz Weibull comes closest to the historical truth of the matter when he declares in an essay: 'the Bloodbath was not an isolated occurrence. It was the final catastrophe in the long and bitter struggle between the two parties who were then rending Sweden apart'.

❋

After he left Sweden for ever at the end of 1520 Christian was only to remain ruler of the North for three more years. But this brief period was marked by a notable achievement, for which he also deserves to be remembered. He became a social reformer. The judiciary, in particular, was radically reformed. Christian devoted the last years of his reign to passing new laws for his subjects. He had set up for himself a great, if at this epoch unattainable, goal: to restructure Scandinavian society.

King Christian II's legislation comprises more laws than that of any other ruler of any of the three kingdoms. And it is here we stumble on the extraordinary contradictions in his nature: the harsh tyrant – the friend of the common people – the Renaissance despot – the democrat before his time – the Devil in human guise – Christian 'beloved of the peasants'.

Danish historians tell me that no book exists which comprehends all Christian II's legislation. After his fall, in 1523, his law books were burnt at the Viborg Assembly. A symbolic gesture, it was the funeral of all his reformist ideas. To learn something of their contents, therefore, I have had to turn to a composite work in several volumes, a collection of documents in Danish history, one volume of which, printed in Copenhagen in 1781, treats of his law books. To go through them all here would take up a hundred pages, so I shall have to summarize their essential content.

The chief impression I have gained from studying them is that the last Union monarch's aim was to establish social equality in mediaeval Danish society. This can be seen most clearly in two laws for the Danish nation; the *Landslagen* and *Stadslagen* (Law for the Country, Law for the Town) dated, in the one instance, late in 1521 and, in the other, January 6, 1522. What he was planning was a thorough-going social revolution.

Christian wished to strip the Danish Church of its enormous privileges. As in Sweden, and indeed everywhere else, the clergy were only subject to canon law. Now a national court was to be set up, before which all bishops and other clerics, in the eyes of Danish law, would be on a par with other citizens. Never a friend of the Church, the king was as little a friend of the nobility. In their well-fortified cannon-proof fortresses the bishops lived like princes. On one occasion Christian is supposed to have observed they could just as well live in barns – a remark which, passing from mouth to mouth, made the 'bishops thoughtful'. Nor, if the king had his way, were they in future to travel sumptuously around the realm with their great trains of several hundred armed men.

Christian's law for the countryside is of the greatest interest to the political history of the Scandinavian commons' long struggle for their liberties. In this code of laws his foresight as a legislator can clearly be discerned. All trace of the ancient Scandinavian institution of thraldom still existing in Denmark in the form of '*vornedskabet*' – i.e. the unfree status of the peasantry vis-à-vis the landowners on their estates – is here abolished. This limitation on the Danish people's freedom, which tied them to their birthplace and prevented them from tilling any soil outside its boundaries, survived until 1702, and in 1733 was replaced by the somewhat milder '*stavnsbaandet*'.

'*Vornedskabet*' was a form of serfdom, under which a peasant was a mere chattel, changing owners with the land he worked. It is this commerce in human beings which is expressly forbidden in Christian's new law: the 'unchristian custom, which hath been in Sjaelland and thereabouts, of selling and giving away poor peasants as other soulless creatures, shall this day henceforth no longer prevail'.

The peasantry's relations with the nobility were regulated in several respects. A Danish nobleman still took the same view of his peasant as the German princes: the peasant had been created a thrall, a serf, a slave. 'Though in the eyes of God he was their equal, the great had no more respect to a poor peasant than to a dog'. That Christian's legislation threw the nobility into a panic and led to an insurrection against him is easy to understand.

A new law for schools, too, stipulates that in instructing their pupils they shall use humanistic text books. Furthermore, the pupils shall no longer stray about and beg at doorways. Even the peasant's children are to go to school, where they shall first and foremost learn to read and write their mother tongue. Hitherto fierce whippings, such as can only be called gross cruelty to children, had been permitted in Danish schools. Christian's new law abolished

such barbaric physical punishment. The '*ferle*', a coarse whip or
stick with a lump at one end, often used for beating children on their
hands, was forbidden.

Such humane paragraphs in Christian's school legislation may
seem self-evident to us. In their day and age they were revolutionary.

The new law promulgated for the towns and burghers, too, was
intended to bring about a radical transformation of economic life.
The country markets were to be abolished and trade concentrated
in the cities. Christian also had plans for a great Nordic trading
company for his three realms, a common market based on Copenhagen and Stockholm. Here he paid special attention to the Bergslagen ore exports. He intended to put an end to the immense powers
of the Hanseatic League which for almost two hundred years had
dominated all trade in the North. This far-sighted project envisaged
the economic union known today as Nordek. Even today, four and a
half centuries after Christian, it remains a utopia.

The king's new laws had many regulatory affects on the economy.
Sometimes they almost seem 20th century in character. Designed
to improve agriculture, the mother of all industries, they devote
great care also to fisheries, where his legislation enters into details.
The country exported a great deal of herring. One paragraph
forbids excessively small-meshed nets, thus guaranteeing a certain
minimum in the size of fish caught.

But what above all characterizes Christian's legislation is the
principle of equality. Burghers and peasants were to be the nobility's
equals before the law. To 20th-century posterity it seems obvious
that this could never have been carried through in 16th-century
Scandinavia. Not until the mid-19th could the Danish peasantry
finally and completely free themselves from '*vornedskabet*'.

And when the king was deposed and his law book thrown to the
flames, this – given the epoch – seems to have been its natural and
predestined fate. Erik Arup, a modern Danish historian, who names
some of Christian's most dangerous enemies among the nobility,
describes their triumphant feelings at that historic burning of the
books before the Viborg Assembly. But the future was to vindicate
the legislator:

'They might rejoice at the sight of these damnable law books being consumed by the flames. But their action was to fail of its effect; ever afterwards the sublime and human law of men's equality would stand inscribed in the hearts of the Danish people'.

As we have seen, the status of the Swedish commons was freer than that of the Danish, but even in Sweden the last Union monarch's concern for popular liberties has given him the name Christian 'beloved of the peasants'. The old song *The old Eagle, the Hawk and the Little Birds*, which was also sung in Sweden (at least in the provinces bordering on Denmark) is evidence of how he survived in tradition as a friend of the common man. Originally written in old Danish, it was afterwards translated into Swedish and all its twenty verses are to be found in print in a famous 19th-century work on Swedish folklore by Arvid August Afzelius.

The song is a dirge, in which the commons lament the loss of Christian, their royal protector. He has been driven into exile by his uncle Fredrik and the Danish and Holsteiner nobility. Christian, that is to say, is the old Eagle; the new king is the Hawk, and the common people are the Little Birds. It is these poor little birds who 'of the Hawk make great complaint: He strips them both of down and feathers and would drive them from the wood'.

In the course of these twenty verses the whole political situation in Denmark ensuant upon Christian's fall is mirrored in a fable of bird-life. The poor little birds who are being hunted by the cruel Hawk are represented by the dove and the sandpiper. The exiled king is apostrophized in each verse's refrain. Twenty times over we are told: 'But the Eagle is nesting in the mountains.' Christian 'beloved of the peasants' 'knowth neither lee nor lair, where he can build his nest'.

Afzelius makes this comment on the song: 'There is more truth in this song than in the chronicles. King Christian was a friend of the people and hated the nobility. King Fredrik, on the contrary, sacrificed the peasants' rights to gratify the nobles. King Gustav in Sweden was of the same mind as King Fredrik, and was long hated by the common people. For in Sweden, too, "The Hawk sat in the Oak crown", i.e. the nobles were elevated and enriched, but "the little birds grieved". '

It was neither the first nor the last time in history that the commons had recourse to allegory when there was no other way for them to make their voices heard.

The insurrection of the nobility against Christian II, his deposition and his unsuccessful attempt to recover his throne have no place in this book; they belong to Danish history. Finally, in 1532, he walked unsuspectingly into a trap laid for him by his enemies and – against a promise of safe conduct – became their prisoner for the rest of his life. His prison was Sønderborg Castle, except during his last years, when he was transferred to Kalundborg. In 1559, at the age of seventy-eight, after twenty-seven years as a prisoner of the Danish state, he died, one year before his opponent Gustav Vasa.

Obviously this last Union king, who became a prisoner for life, is differently viewed by Danish and Swedish historians; but in his own country too, he has been critically appraised; notably so by older chroniclers, who have even called him a loathsome tyrant. Opinions on his character differ sharply. Whilst C. F. Allen and Paludan-Müller call him a strong personality, Erik Arup regards him as a weak one, and the Swedish historian Lauritz Weibull agrees with Arup. Modern Danish historians have done him justice as a social reformer and praised his remarkable far-sightedness, and today his reign is more discriminatingly assessed.

The most positive characterization of Christian II is the one made by Palle Lauring in the sixth part of his great Danish history. Based on latest research, it is, as a biography, remarkable. Lauring draws a fascinating psychological portrait of Christian, whom he finds to have been a most complex personality. In this portrait the king appears as a man of great spiritual and physical capacities, with a wide range of activities, an imaginative man, capable of grandiose plans. His projects exceed all common measure. At the same time he is far from being the man he would like to be. He is indecisive, given to tergiversation, unsure of himself. Conscious of his own weaknesses, he does his best to conceal them from others. To put his plans into effect is beyond him – they remain a mere longing and a dream. In this account Christian the Tyrant becomes a political visionary.

While not defending the king's evil deeds, Lauring explains them as due to fear and anxiety. And those November days in Stockholm – the days of the Bloodbath – were the most anxious of all. Sheer terror drove him to his bloody settlement of accounts, terror of these Swedes whom he had finally, after a long war defeated. If he takes their lives it is to be quit both of them and of his fear. But Christian himself cannot stand the sight of human blood. Where was the king during the massacre in the Stockholm market place? A question which has never been answered. One source declares that 'he is in his privy'. He locks himself in – for reasons we can surmise.

This latest biographer of Christian, in my opinion, has found a key to the actions of tyrants and potentates, for whom power is everything. They are possessed by an ever-present fear: fear of losing their power. In their terror they grab at every means of retaining it – notably the most ultimate and definitive: violence and murder.

Palle Lauring thinks we misjudge Christian II by giving him so exigent a title as The Tyrant: 'he was certainly not equal to it.' To rule tyrannically calls for force, for authority, for energy and resolute decision-making. But Christian was forever going back on his decisions. Weak and timorous, in critical situations he rarely knew how to act.

As to the king's ultimate fate, Palle Lauring writes: 'Christian II's long years of imprisonment were wholly illegal. He was never indicted, never examined or tried, nor was any sentence ever passed upon him. It is the greatest judicial murder in Danish history. This does not acquit Christian II of responsibility for his acts, but it lies wholly outside the rule of law on which the laws of Denmark and the commitments of Danish kings were based.'

As a social reformer and as a legislator it was the tragic lot of the last king of the Nordic Union to be right – three centuries too soon.

Tyrant II : Gustav I

The clan and its founder

AN EARLY 19th-CENTURY Swedish biographical reference book declares: 'Vasa is the only family name in our annals which may be said to have a place in world history ... and of which an educated European cannot be ignorant without it being regarded as a gap in his education'.

In Sweden, too, Vasa, more than any other family name, has penetrated our historical awareness. We come across it daily – we take a stroll in the Vasa Park, eat Vasa bread, take part in the Vasa Race*, worship in the Vasa Church and sport the Order of Vasa on our chests. The name appears in streets and cities, in churches and parishes, in associations and clubs, in orders and medals. We find the word used internationally: in Minnesota, USA, Swedish immigrants have called a town Vasa. I have seen Vasa Bread (a genuine Swedish crispbread, known in England and America as 'Rye King') advertised on several countries' TV. German newspapers advertise a Swedish Vasa Coat, said to be an exceptionally hardwearing garment. The name has become a trade mark. There are Vasa Bazaars and Vasa Companies. The name stimulates sales. Sometimes it seems to possess an inherent value, which cannot be called in question.

It is the name borne by the most illustrious and famous of our royal dynasties. Dynasties in Sweden have come and gone, but if any king has been able to show he has a drop of Vasa blood in his veins it has been counted to his honour and advantage: a fluid

---

* The Vasa Ski Race in March, between Sälen and Mora, commemorates the turning point in the national struggle when two Mora men caught up with Gustav as he fled into Norway after the Stockholm Bloodbath (1520), and prevailed on him to turn back. Some 8,000 skiers participate.—*Translator*.

nowadays so rare that it must not be wasted. Participation in the Vasa heritage means, in Sweden, the very highest lineage.

But where does this family name, the only one in Sweden regarded as entitled to a place in world history, come from? I have visited the place which first had the honour of bearing it. Vasa, the oldest farm belonging to the clan, lies in Skepptuna parish, Uppland. Near the Fyris River, at one time a navigable waterway, it comprises about 300 acres of the most fertile agricultural land in Uppland. Its old castle-like main building burnt down in 1926, and only its two detached wings remain to form the owner's residence. The estate also comprises large areas of woodlands. Today the farm has no cattle; despite its 300 arable acres it buys its milk from the Milk Marketing Board. Since much of the arable land was once river bed, the humus is admirably fertile. Thirty hands used to be employed here – today the owner does his own work, aided by only three.

The proprietor of Sweden's most famous noble estate is not a nobleman. His name is Birger Jansson. These two names, Vasa and Jansson, are symbolic of the changes which have occurred during the five centuries in which Sweden has developed from a semifeudal society into a democratic one.

We do not know for certain how the estate, and with it the Vasa clan got their name. The old word *vase* means a bunch of twigs laid out in the lake to attract spawning fish, but in the Vasa arms it means a sheaf of corn. This symbol, however, was not adopted until after the hereditary Vasa monarchy had been established at Västerås in 1544. Earlier, the clan had worn a *sceptrum liliatum*, a lilied sceptre resembling the point of a lance, on its coat of arms. Lance head or sheaf of corn – whether the Vasa arms are to be taken as symbolizing war or the peaceful arts of agriculture remains an open question.

Two other great Uppland estates associated with the name of the Vasas once belonged to them: Lindholmen in Orkesta parish, and Rydboholm in Östra Ryd. Like Vasa, they lie in the province's most fertile region. Rydboholm, for instance, consists of seven hundred acres of superb farming land, with deep rich soil. The Vasas certainly had an eye to the finest land and knew how to come by it. In other provinces, too, they owned estates.

At school I was taught that Gustav Vasa was born on Lindholmen farm in Uppland; but subsequently he has acquired another birthplace, Rydboholm Castle, one of whose towers bears his name and where household equipment from the early Vasa period is still to be seen. Obviously, the founder of Sweden's hereditary monarchy need not content himself with a single birthplace. The people of Orkesta assert that he was born at Lindholmen, and a monument on the railway station declares that it was here, on May 12, 1496, that Gustav Vasa came into the world. A mile or so away, on a hillock in the forest, the remains of the main building of the old Lindholmen farm are to be seen, and under a gigantic oak a huge stone has been raised, bearing the name of the first Vasa king and his almost illegible year of birth. Today Lindholmen is owned by the City of Stockholm, which, I am told, is going to convert the ancient seat of the Vasa into a holiday home for its municipal employees – another shift of power from noble to populace.

Various years between 1494 and 1497 have been given for the birth of Gustav I. Everyone agrees that he was born on Ascension Day, in the month of May, when the cuckoo was to be heard; but we do not know in which year.

The Vasas, then, sprang from the soil of the Uppland countryside. At the height of the Middle Ages a family of enterprising and ambitious Roslagen peasants had raised themselves above their brother commoners and become ennobled. Though the sources are familiar with this family of magnates from the mid-14th century onwards, it was not until the 15th that it produced any men of real note. The first was the Earl Marshal, Christer Nilsson Vasa, a contemporary of Karl Knutsson.

Supporters, at first, of the Union party, the Vasas had later become allied by marriage with the Stures and joined the nationalist side. Subsequently their influence grew, especially after Gustav Vasa's grandfather had married one of Sten Sture the Elder's sisters.

Gustav Vasa was the eldest son of Erik Johansson Vasa, lord of Rydboholm, a knight and councillor of State. As father of the founder of the Swedish monarchy he deserves more attention than the fleeting mention given him by our historians. He has been cursorily described as a man of moderate talents, an 'honest and mirthful gentleman'. The portrait is hardly exhaustive. Contemporary documents offer us a good deal more information than this about Erik Johansson. I will try to amplify his portrait.

The court records of the city of Stockholm state that on June 1 1489, Erik Johansson has assaulted and killed a man, by name Peder Arvidsson. Dragging his victim off to his estate at Rydboholm, he there 'unhonestly did away with him'. The enquiry into this manslaughter reveals that Peder Arvidsson was a citizen of Stockholm who had 'cut into' Erik Johansson's forest and fished his waters, an intrusion for which he had paid with his life. The Lord of Rydboholm administered his own rough justice, and Peder Arvidsson was obviously not the only man to fall foul of him; for the court records also inform us that, at a settlement reached with the citizens of Stockholm in the town court on July 19, 1490, Erik Johansson had to 'apologize for not a few deeds of violence.' According to this contemporary source, he promises to change his behaviour towards 'poor citizens of the town, who trespass on his property' – no longer shall he 'beat, hammer and treat them like other soulless beasts'. It seems that he had been in the habit of manacling such trespassers.

Seven years later Erik Johansson Vasa again appears in a contemporary record as a man of violence. Together with his men he plunders Frösunda rectory. The rector of Frösunda, Otto Ingelsson, 'weeping tears', complains of this deed. 'They raped a servant girl, forced her to show them Otto's possessions, chopped up a table, broke chests and doors in pieces, ate flesh of a Friday, and more, which neither Russians nor paynims would have done.' Archbishop Jakob Ulfsson asked the Pope to excommunicate the assailants, but we do not know whether the bull was ever issued. Nor do we ever hear of Erik Johansson being brought to trial for plundering the Frösunda rectory. If he never was, then, the explanation lies no doubt in the fact that it was the criminal himself who was responsible for the administration of justice in the district where his crime had been committed. As early as 1493, Erik Johansson is named as being a district judge at Danderyd and Rydbo, in that part of Uppland to which Frösunda then belonged.

Eighteen years afterwards the Lord of Rydboholm committed his last act of violence known to us from original documents. As late in 1515, when he had been both a Councillor of State and a knight for twenty years, he broke into and plundered a county church on one of the Mälar islands. According to a letter from Bishop Mattias of Strängnäs to Sten Sture the Younger, Erik Johansson's squires, acting on their master's orders, had committed 'deeds of violence' in this church, plundering it of much of its furnishings. The bishop had not excommunicated this Councillor of State and knight, hoping that he would repent what he had done; but he had shown no remorse. In his letter Bishop Mattias expresses a hope that the regent will exhort Erik Johansson to restore the stolen goods and become reconciled to the Church. 'The sources do not tell us how the affair developed'. Presumably the bishop had to content himself with his pious wish. The Lord of Rydboholm was the regent's close associate.

Obviously, the grandsire of the Vasa dynasty had a covetous eye to ecclesiastical property.

Hans Gillingstam, a modern genealogist, calls Erik Johansson a 'crude and violent person', and this is no exaggerated characterization of a man whom contemporary sources make responsible for assault and battery, manslaughter, rape and theft, even though in between whiles he administered justice in his own part of the country. His activities as a criminal alone, however – activities not altogether foreign to the class of mediaeval magnates – would not suffice to give him a place in Swedish history; and he would have been utterly forgotten by posterity had he not begotten a son who was to be the originator of the Swedish monarchy which still exists.

God's miracle-worker

When I was a child Gustav Eriksson Vasa seemed almost a super-natural being in human guise. God himself had sent him down to earth to be the saviour of my fatherland from 'that bloodhound and unchristian tyrant Christian.' Even as a schoolboy, Snoilsky's* poem about him was familiar to me:

* Carl Snoilsky (1841-1903), Swedish poet celebrated above all for his collection *Svenska Bilder* (1886), portraits and scenes from Swedish history in a strong national-democratic vein. The poem on Gustav Vasa quoted below is part of this work.

> We read of King Gösta
> in chronicle-book
> God's wonder-worker who shattered
> the Tyrant's yoke.
> His locks are like the silver
> which Eskil's chamber filled;
> From ground to roof our Sweden
> his hand alone did build.

Again and again I read the tales in our history books about the young Gustav's adventures in Dalarna – those famous stories about how, having escaped from Danish captivity and after the Stockholm Bloodbath he wandered northward as an outlawed fugitive and by his fiery speeches contrived to win over the Dalecarlian peasants who chose him as their captain and as leader of a national revolt which resulted in the overthrow of King Christian. For sheer excitement these tales were on a par with my Red Indian books and the volumes within whose blood-red covers Nick Carter was the hero. With tense anxiety I followed Gustav's never-ending flight from the Danish soldiers, as Snoilsky had done before me:

> For fear our hearts in childhood
> had scarcely strength to beat,
> as soldiers' lances piercéd
> the straw where he lay hid.

After I had left elementary school the subject of my very first school essay was precisely that occasion during the liberator's flight when he hid himself in a hay cart and Sven Elfsson of Isala cut his own horse's foot to explain away the blood flowing from Gustav's knee, pierced by his pursuer's halberds – the animal pathetically sacrificing its own blood for the saviour of the fatherland. In itself, an admirable tale. The only thing wrong with it is that it did not happen in Dalarna in 1520, or even in Sweden: it is a Roman anecdote about a man called Marius who had such an adventure long before the birth of Christ, interpolated into Gustav Vasa's adventures by a 17th-century Uppsala student who had been travelling in Dalarna.

Even as late as the 18th century Gustav was still having fresh Dalecarlian adventures attributed to him. The province's tourist industry has known how to make good use of them. In the Ornäs

House the visitor is still shown the privy through which Barbro Stigsdotter helped her hunted guest, the future saviour of Sweden, to escape – a monument throwing its own light on Swedish history. Again, in a loft in the Rankhyttan ironworks, the visitor is shown the flail which Gustav is supposed to have used for threshing. In reality Anders Persson's loft from 1520 disappeared – either demolished or rotted away – several hundred years ago. And with it also, presumably, his flails. Naturally the tourist trade overlooks such trifles.

Gustav Eriksson Vasa's appearance is more familiar to us than that of any other Swedish king. He was fond of sitting for his portraits, of which he has left us more than any other monarch. Anyone who has ever held a five-kronor note in his hand knows what he looked like. For a century and more Swedes have been thumbing his portrait.

> His image with its flowing beard
> So worthy and so dear ...

According to our older history books, Gustav Vasa seized power in Sweden as the result of divine intervention. 'God will find his man' – and when the Almighty eventually found him it was at Rydboholm, in the guise of Gustav Vasa. He was God's miracle-worker – even in the latter part of the last century many historians were still quite sure of that. 'Christian's behaviour was admittedly vile, but God turned it to the benefit of Sweden,' a textbook from 1859 declares. 'Only by the extirpation of the incessant quarrels and warfare among the powerful lords was it possible for Gustav I to reform religion and introduce into the realm the order which was so utterly needful.' That is to say, the Stockholm Bloodbath was a necessary condition of the Reformation. Another author of school history books from the same epoch, describing the bloodbath, draws his own conclusions; 'The people of Sweden were not crushed, but their patience was at an end, and now they rose under the man whom God had appointed to save our fatherland from the hated Danish yoke.'

The same view is found in C. T. Odhner's *History for Upper School Classes* of 1886, after his account of the bloodbath: 'In God's hand Christian's cruelty became an instrument for the rehabilitation of Sweden, to its happiness and honour; the noble instrument which Providence had elected for the redemption of Sweden had already entered upon his high calling'. Odhner had already called the Vikings an 'instrument in the hand of God for the introduction of Christianity'. Now God had supposedly made similar use of Christian the Tyrant, as a tool with which to carry through his plans for Sweden. The older school of Swedish historians based their works on an unshakable certainty that 'our people, led by God, developed in the direction of all which in the true senses is great, noble and good'. Why, one wonders, did Odhner and other historians condemn the Stockholm Bloodbath, if they regarded the last king of the Union as having done Sweden so great a service by arranging it? The answer of course is that without this massacre of nobles God's miracle-worker could not have saved the country.

Gustav Vasa had a motto: 'All power is of God'. Through all his speeches and letters runs the theme that it was the All Highest who had given him the needful means and resources to rehabilitate Sweden and establish his monarchy. None of his rivals for power in the country enjoy this divine support. He alone has been called, is chosen; and therefore has the right to require the confidence of the Swedish people and their support for his policies. It was Gustav Eriksson, himself, who placed himself in the ranks of God's miracle-workers, as the Bible calls them. In several speeches – such as his speech from the throne at the 1544 Västerås riksdag – he likens himself to a new Moses. As Moses had led the Jews out of captivity in Egypt, so had he, Gustav, rescued the Swedes from their thraldom to the Danes. Again, in his farewell speech to the Estates in 1560, he likens himself to David, the insignificant youth and shepherd who overcame the insuperable Goliath, and whom God had raised to royal estate. He reminds them of the time when he 'in forests and shacks, clad in homespun, drank water and ate wretchedly'. But the king gives God the whole glory for his achievement: 'Hath aught been well done, then it is the work of God. Thank Him for it.' Again, when he had filled his treasury in Stockholm Castle with silver treasures, taken from all the poor parish churches of the realm, he had declared that it was God himself who had given these riches into his hands.

It was in elementary school I first made the acquaintance of this father of our country, whose care for his subjects was as tender as if they had been his own beloved children. Even as late as the 1930s Gustav was still being held up as such to Swedish schoolchildren. In Falk-Tunberg's history book of 1931, Gustav I is described as follows: 'In his private life he was providential for his people, God-fearing and pure in his habits. Simple and economical, a good husband and father'.

This image of Gustav Vasa as the Father of his People and God's Miracle-Worker I have long left behind me. It is, in my opinion, false through and through. This king we were told so much about in school was a fairy-tale king, who had never existed in the flesh. The invention quite simply, of Peder Svart and other contemporary chroniclers, an idealized portrait commissioned and in reality painted by none other than the sitter himself. All the time the artists were working away at their easels His Grace was standing behind them, giving them requisite instructions. Yet the portrait was accepted by historians down the centuries as true and genuine.

Not until our own time has it been subjected to critical examination. Twenty-five years ago Professor Erik Lönnroth declared that a certain change had occurred in the view taken by research of Gustav Vasa: 'Though one cannot speak of any radical re-evaluation, there has certainly been a somewhat pronounced modification of lights and shades. In brief, it means that the features of a liberator and father of his country are fading away.'

Lönnroth presents many facts which would have sufficed for a profound revision of our image of this king, and a major work on the topic was expected from him. But though Lönnroth wrote these words a quarter of a century ago, as far as I know he has never returned to the topic. And in the most recently published biography of the king by Doctor Ivan Svalenius (1950), it is largely the same old King Gösta we knew before who reappears. In the main the portrait is conventional; not without nuances, certainly, but insufficient to modify its lineaments as a whole.

Since we are still awaiting a radical re-evaluation of Gustav I by Swedish historians, it is hardly surprising that a foreign historian should have done part of the work which has so long waited upon his Swedish colleagues. The Englishman Michael Roberts, professor at Queen's University, Belfast, has devoted many years to research into Swedish history, specializing in the Vasa period and the 17th century (*The Early Vasas*, 1968.) His book on Gustav is based on incontrovertible facts. and in his account of the man who created the national state of Sweden he is blithely untroubled by such national prejudices as still have the power to inhibit some of our Swedish historians.

Roberts overlooks none of the king's merits as a ruler. His astounding energy, his enormous capacity for hard work, his admirable grasp of practical affairs, all receive ample recognition. But this Englishman's ethical verdict on God's miracle-worker is little short of devastating. Gustav was possessed with an almost pathological greed for power, he was utterly unscrupulous and ruthless and 'his word was decidedly not to be relied on.' He was litigious, but had scant respect for the law, and still less for truth. His mendacity was beyond belief, his greed for wealth bottomless. To put it bluntly, Gustav was a miser. What earlier writers have called his sense of thrift, Roberts calls 'anguished miserliness'; he finds that this quality 'could be pushed even to ignominy'.

With one exception I have been unable to find any counterpart to this portrait of Gustav Vasa by any Swedish historian. Here we have quite another king from the one whom my generation's schoolchildren had to read about at school. It was when I was studying the history of my home district during the Dacke rising that I began to form my own image of Gustav Vasa. I read up on local history as it reflected my forefathers' view of the Father of the Country, and it appeared to be well-grounded. In almost all historical works Gustav Vasa had been represented as the king who had been most beloved by his people. But between the years 1525 and 1543 his subjects' affection had taken the form of five revolts against him; three in Dalarna, one in Västergötland and one in Småland.

Here was something that did not fit the picture!

My new opinion of the founder of the Swedish monarchy became definitive when I read Fabian Månsson's great work, already referred to. And later on this great student of the Vasa period confirmed it for me in person, when we discussed the past of that part of Sweden from which both stemmed. Fabian explained to me that Gustav Vasa had been a ruthless oppressor of our ancestors, who had deeply infringed their ancient liberties and who with his German legionaries, by mass executions and by starving them out, forced them into submission. After crushing their rebellion, of which Dacke was the leader, he had ravaged Värend, the centre of the liberation movement, so thoroughly devastating it that it took two centuries before this part of the country could again recover and reach the standard of living it had enjoyed in the Later Middle Ages.

Naturally I am well aware of the one-sidedness of the picture of Gustav Vasa which now follows. Its purpose is to present the view of God's miracle-worker which found active outlet in the revolts against him. These had historical grounds which have been too little explored. The good which Gustav Vasa did during his reign is well-known. The ills he inflicted on his subjects are less familiar.

As someone who has no scientific reputation to lose, I shall run no risk if I devote myself to this aspect of the matter and write of Gustav I the Tyrant.

The Kalmar Bloodbath

Every Swedish schoolboy has read about Stockholm Bloodbath in his history book. From the same period we have a similar event, but one which has been wholly overlooked by history teachers: the execution of the garrison of Kalmar Castle in July 1525. This massacre, however, though more or less skipped in the history of the kingdom as a whole, has been described in detail by local historians. Among national historians only Emil Hildebrand has paid it some attention. He declares summarily: 'It was a monstrous bloodbath'.

Gustav Eriksson Vasa had been elected King of Sweden in 1523; but even as late as 1525 – and for a good while to come – his position was shaky. He had not succeeded in driving the Danes out of the country by the force of Swedish arms. When faced by fortresses, his peasant levies had proved useless: his siege of Stockholm had been more or less a military fiasco. Not even the Dalesmen, known for their courage during the first phase of the war of liberation and feared for their effective archery, could prevail against this fortress in the capital. And they implored the king 'with the very loudest cries and wailing' to be allowed to go home and sow and reap and till their land. He granted them their wish. They were permitted to go home to Dalarna. But the capital of the kingdom still remained to be subdued. In lieu of his Swedish peasants, therefore, Gustav Vasa recruited German men-at-arms, well trained, militarily efficient folk, with warfare as their profession. From the Hanseatic League he obtained on credit ten men-of-war from Lubeck and a couple of companies of men-at-arms.

The Germans brought the assault on Stockholm to an effective close. Thanks to the foreign aid and after a lengthy siege, the new king of Sweden was able to enter his capital. But Kalmar was an even stronger fortress than Stockholm. Nor could it be taken by Swedish troops. So the king was again obliged to have recourse to foreign assistance. He gave the task of taking the 'key to Sweden' to his chief German commander, Berend von Melen, who had already proved his capacity as a field commander. Von Melen had blamed his own unsuccessful attempt to conquer Skåne for Gustav in 1523 on 'a sudden thaw'; in reality it had not been the consequence of any thaw, but of the peace treaty concluded by the peasantry along the frontier. But von Melen carried out his task at Kalmar to perfection. After astute parleys the garrison was prevailed on to surrender the castle, and von Melen occupied it in the king's name. For this he was amply rewarded by Gustav Vasa: the German soldier was given a seat in the Swedish Council of State, received Kalmar county and Uppvidinge hundred in fief, and Gustav's own second cousin, Margareta Eriksdotter Vasa, to wife. The German who had conquered the 'key to Sweden' became related by marriage to the King of Sweden, and was his favourite. No Swede occupied a comparable position, and among the native nobility the immense and swift success of this foreigner aroused intense envy. Sweden had just been liberated from her Danish overlords. Now the Swedish nobles had every reason to ask: was there to be a new régime of foreigners in the land? Was the king going to replace Danes by Germans in his council and in the highest posts of the realm?

Berend von Melen was every inch an adventurer. A soldier of fortune, he is the very embodiment of a legionary, a type altogether characteristic of that age. All over Europe the great age of the legionaries had begun, and von Melen was a formidable representative of his species. He had served many masters, sometimes even two at once. Earlier, he had served as a colonel under Christian II and taken part in his campaign against the Swedes. Christian's commandant at Stegeborg, upon this fortress being captured by the Swedes, had gone over to them and entered King Gustav's service. The mark of a true legionary was his ability to change masters from one day to another. Such behaviour was hardly regarded in those days as treason, but in much the same light as we view an employee who leaves one firm to take up a better job with another, True, a legionary had to swear an oath of fealty to each new master; but this oath to the colours was nothing but a formality, over in a jiffy, and the cause of no qualms. For in any case he had no intention of keeping it.

And Berend von Melen did not take his oath of fidelity to Gustav seriously, either. Indeed, in view of von Melen's eventful past, it is astonishing that Gustav should have placed such implicit trust in this commander of legionaries. How could he rely on a man who had forthwith abandoned the Danish colours for the Swedish? There can only be one explanation: Gustav stood in such dire need of efficient legionaries and capable military commanders that out of sheer necessity he was obliged to use this German colonel.

And von Melen turned out to be as faithful to him as he had been to Christian. He regarded Kalmar Castle, which he had captured, as his private property. Placing his brother Henrik in command of it, he gave him strict orders on no account whatever to hand it over to the King of Sweden. When Gustav demanded that the castle gates be opened to him, all he got from Henrik von Melen was an apologetic but flat refusal.

By this time the king had already other reasons for suspecting Berend von Melen of guile and treachery. He had sent him to Gotland to seize that island from Sören Norrby, but von Melen had come home empty-handed. Further, it had come to Gustav's ears that while on Gotland von Melen had entered into treasonable negotiations with the enemy. Obviously the legionary was contemplating a fresh change of masters. The King of Sweden had suffered reverses; his new monarchy, only two years old, stood on shaky foundations. Probably the commander of the legionaries was counting on its imminent collapse, and had already begun to reinsure himself against that eventuality. He would not have hesitated for a moment to return to King Christian.

Von Melen can be regarded as a traitor twice over, but Gustav discovered his treachery too late, and this was to cost him dear. Even then he could only proceed cautiously against his military commander. As long as he was in charge of a numerous body of his own countrymen this German was a military factor in the Swedish power game, and a man very dangerous to its king.

In the spring of 1525 von Melen was summoned to Stockholm by King Gustav, who again demanded that the gates of Kalmar Castle should be thrown open to its rightful owner. Expressly promising to hand it over, von Melen set off for Kalmar to fulfil his promise. Naturally, he lost no time in breaking it. Nor had he ever had any intention of letting Kalmar, which he regarded as his own fief, pass out of his hands. This great fortress was in truth worth the keeping. On the eve of a journey to his own country, von Melen therefore required an oath of fidelity from the Swedish and German soldiers of the castle garrison that 'They were to obey and abet him and keep the castle in his possession, and not surrender it, neither to King Gustav nor to anyone else, until such time as he had returned from that journey (to Germany)' – W. Sylvander. And the garrison swore to be faithful to him and defend the fortress to the last man against King Gustav and his people. The man whom von Melen left behind in command of the castle was Henrik Jute, a soldier who had earlier done service under Sten Sture.

Together with his brother Henrik and his own family von Melen went back to Germany, where he joined the king's enemies and for many years to come troubled him with his conspiracies.

But Kalmar had been captured on King Gustav's account and belonged to the Swedish crown. The king's bitterness against this relative by marriage, who had played such a disgracefully double game, was understandable. The legionary had pulled the wool over his eyes. Gustav had showered gifts and rewards on von Melen; and all the thanks he had got was the blackest treachery. Few Swedes of the day were as intelligent as Gustav Eriksson of Rydbo-holm; but in cunning and dissimulation he had met his match in this German, Berend von Melen. Gustav Vasa is noted for his ability to learn from experience. This time he certainly did.

Beautifully situated on a promontory in Kalmar Sound, Kalmar Castle looks as idyllic as can be. Yet the ground around its walls is certainly more deeply drenched in blood than any other in Scandinavia. Every time war broke out between Sweden and Denmark the fight for the 'key to Sweden' was equally sanguinary. Always the struggle came to be focused on Sweden's strongest frontier fortress, and the side which was in possession of it always had the upper hand. But the fortress was almost impregnable by mediaeval military art. Above the castle gates is inscribed the proud legend: 'never captured by force of arms'. During the Sture epoch it had withstood a number of lengthy sieges, the memory of which has survived in popular tradition.

Von Melen's treason had made it necessary for Gustav Vasa to take the strongest of all Scandinavian fortresses for the second time. In July, 1525, he went down to Kalmar with some choice troops, four companies of footmen, all told about fifteen hundred élite soldiers. Obviously the king was well aware that he was faced with a difficult and costly undertaking: but for his men it became even more costly than he expected. Many hundreds of them paid for the castle with their lives.

In the month of July, 1525, one of the bloodiest chapters in the history of Kalmar Castle was written. Gustav's troops tried to storm the fortress and a horrible slaughter commenced. Faithful to their oath to their master, von Melen's legionaries put up the stoutest and most obstinate resistance. Though outnumbered many times over, they repulsed the storm troops. Again and again the assailants were driven back from the walls leaving behind them enormous losses in killed and wounded. The bodies of Gustav's men filled the moats, and the survivors, attacking across these heaps of corpses, only augmented their numbers.

Peder Svart, who describes the struggle in his chronicle, is of the view that King Gustav lost half his force within a few days: 'A good half part of them lay on their necks, and a great part limbless, some with an arm off, some with a thigh, some both arms and thighs.'

The historian of Kalmar, W. Sylvander writes: 'The king wept tears of grief at the terrible reverse and the loss of so many heroes and so many competent men-at-arms.' And Peder Svart adds: 'King Gustav wept so that he must well-nigh have swooned.'

As far as we know it was a unique situation in Gustav Vasa's life. He is not known to have been a weak, lachrymose or sensitive man, nor do we anywhere else hear of his shedding tears. There is therefore something remarkable about this outburst of grief at Kalmar. If Gustav gave vent to his feelings it was only human – militarily, too, he had reason to grieve. The men he had lost in the moats were his élite soldiers. And he could not spare a man.

His troops seem to have done everything humanly or militarily possible. But contemporary chroniclers also relate how the king, beside himself with rage after the failure of the assaults, called his troops a lot of chicken-hearted cowards. 'Tearing off his royal mantle and donning his armour, he declared he would take part in the assault himself, either to conquer or die, either to take the castle or else perish before it. But his men-at-arms implored him to spare his precious life for the fatherland, and for God's sake not to shame them by personally taking part in the storming operations.' They promised him to try a new assault and not yield, 'even if each and every one of them fell in it'. Whereupon the king withdrew his threat, took off his armour and promised to spare his own life.

This is one of the few occasions when Gustav Vasa makes an appearance in a wholly military context. As a leader of armies he is not to be compared with Sten Sture the Younger, who was a man of real military talent; nor was Gustav a warrior king like his grandson Gustavus Adolphus, who was to lead his own troops in the field. So whether he really had any serious intention of risking his life in the struggle at Kalmar in 1525 is hard to say. Perhaps the threat alone sufficed.

New assaults led to new reverses and fresh losses. But the garrison too was being decimated. Finally, against a promise of free conduct, it offered to capitulate. The castle was surrendered on St Margaret's Day, July 20, 1525. No note of the terms of the capitulation has survived, but it is generally supposed that the defenders reserved their right to depart without let or hindrance. And this – in view of what followed upon their capitulation – is the crux of the matter.

Kalmar's trustworthy historian Sylvander, who has studied the matter more thoroughly than anyone else, writes: 'It is almost incontrovertible that the garrison ... on the one hand threatened rather to die fighting than surrender at discretion, and that the king, rather than sacrifice any more of his courageous troops, granted the defenders freedom of life and limb. Without question the garrison had not only negotiated their unhindered evacuation of the castle but also their repatriation at the king's expense, *for he had them given victuals and ships in which to return to Germany.* The king obtained the castle by negotiation.'

Other historians have queried this point, and regard the terms of the capitulation as obscure: they doubt whether the king gave the garrison any promise to spare their lives or let them depart. Personally I regard Sylvander's statement as impeccable. Psychologically, too, it is wholly probable. Why else should the soldiers in the castle give up the fight, unless they were afterwards to be granted their lives? The legionary scorns death. That is his character. If it were not, he would not adopt such a profession. These men would certainly have preferred to die honorably, sword in hand, to a dishonorable death on the headsman's block, and would scarcely have capitulated except against the king's express promise of a safe conduct; unless they had thought their lives were safe. Great weight attaches to this psychological argument.

As a result of negotiations, therefore, the survivors inside the castle expected to go free. Their lot was otherwise. Gustav Vasa broke the safe conduct. The men of the garrison were seized and held prisoner, and the king appointed a court-martial, presided over by himself, before which they were brought and tried as traitors. But neither juridically nor morally, as far as we can see, can they have committed treason. After all, they were not in the king's service, were not his troops, and had never sworn fealty to him. Von Melen was their lord; it was to him they had sworn to be faithful, and to him they had demonstrated their fidelity by fighting on to the last. It was Berend von Melen who had been guilty of treason against Gustav Vasa; not his men.

Nevertheless the court-martial condemned them all to death on the wheel, as traitors. The sentence was commuted to decapitation. Whereafter, with the sole exception of two servingmen 'who were graciously granted their lives at the urgent plea of those who afterwards took them into their service', the entire remnant of the garrison were beheaded. All the others had fallen in the siege. We do not know exactly how many soldiers perished on the block in Kalmar. Fabian Månsson gives a figure of between sixty and seventy. Other writers place the figure either higher or lower. A local historian tells how the edge of the executioner's axe finally became so blunted that it could no longer be used, upon which he finished his task by crushing the soldiers' heads with a mace.

The analogy with the Stockholm Bloodbath of five years earlier leaps, of course, to mind. Christian II, too, flouted his own express assurances of an amnesty to his defeated opponents of the Sture party. Gustav I revoked the safe conduct he had promised to the capitulating defenders of Kalmar Castle. The difference in the victims' numbers cannot have been very great.

But in their effects the events in Stockholm and Kalmar were quite disparate. The first bloodbath stirred up an immense storm of indigation. Its political consequences were decisive. The other massacre occurred in obscurity, and historians have noticed it only in a somewhat distrait fashion. The explanation is simple. Among the Stockholm victims were members of the leading and highest families of the realm, noble lords and prelates of the Church, who bore celebrated names, men known and famed throughout the country. Olaus Petri lists 'those whose heads had fallen and whose names were famous'. But at Kalmar it was only ordinary humble soldiers who were beheaded, nameless men. In the one instance the victims' deaths were of great consequence; in the other, of little or none. In all ages different value has been set on different human lives, according to birth, status and property.

Peder Svart, Gustav I's favourite and ever-willing chronicler, though he finds Kalmar Bloodbath horrible, naturally acquits the king of all responsibility for it. He throws all the blame on that vicious traitor von Melen. Had Gustav Vasa cut von Melen's head off, he would have been entirely within his rights. Instead, he executed the rank and file, who had committed no crime. Peder

Svart, that is, discreetly ignores the crux of the matter. As he had to – otherwise Gustav Vasa's sanguinary orgy at Kalmar would have borne too disconcerting a resemblance to Christian the Tyrant's in Stockholm.

And facts only speak out when historians make use of them. What we have here is a concrete instance of how history is falsified by selection. The facts of the Stockholm Bloodbath have spoken down the ages, for four and a half centuries. Those which have all this time been available about the Kalmar Bloodbath have remained dumb. It is high time they were allowed to speak.

The King's Church

Gustav Vasa broke the Roman Catholic Church's economic hegemony in Sweden, stripped it of its enormous wealth, and deprived it of its military limb, the bishops' cavalry – those trains of horsemen who rode through the country demanding board and lodging from the peasantry. Bishop Hans Brask of Linköping was the last in the long line of lords spiritual who united in their person the functions of prelate and a cavalry officer. The Swedes were also relieved of the tax monies which for several centuries they had been paying to the head of the Church in Rome, and of which God's Vicar on Earth had never rendered any account. Had they known how he used these funds they would at times have been deeply shocked, as must any believing Christian who had learnt not to store up riches which moth and rust consume. During the Late Middle Ages and the decadence of the Papal Church the Peter's Pence were often put to such uses. The Church had also sold heaven to her Swedish members in the form of indulgences. Profitable deals in men's salvation after death certainly ought not to have been the business of those who alleged they represented the man who said his kingdom was not of this world. This was the opinion of the Church reformer Olaus Petri; and Gustav shared his view of the matter.

In liberating his kingdom from its dependence on the universal Catholic Church the king did something which in itself was praiseworthy. He also abolished the power of the bishops, succeeding in Sweden where Christian II had failed in Denmark. But according to the Reformation propaganda the Lutheran Church was to meet a great need among Swedes and salve their spiritual anxieties. In point of fact, however, the common man in Sweden had not asked for any novel doctrine. On the contrary, he would have much preferred to keep his old one, to which he and his ancestors had adhered for more than four hundred years. Many generations had died peacefully in the Catholic faith. What really precipitated the Reformation was the king's and the crown's urgent pecuniary needs.

To judge from Olaus Petri's declarations, Gustav's intention seems to have been to provide Swedes with a Church of their own, a national institution, a popular and wholly independent Church, with no supreme head except God Himself. Even to someone who believes as little in the one doctrine as in the other, this seems a change for the better, and one with which one can sympathize. But what was the upshot of the ecclesiastical reformation which Gustav Vasa despotically – setting Olaus Petri aside – took over? After a couple of decades all that had happened was that, instead of a pope, the Swedish church found it had a king as its supreme authority. It became not a popular but a royal institution. As for its property, Gustav Vasa treated it as his own, deciding all its affairs out of hand. It became the king's Church.

It was Gustav I who founded the Swedish State Church, which still exists. But a state Church is an institution offensive to all commonsense. For more than four hundred years the kingdom of Sweden has had a certain definite religion, a certain definite faith: the Evangelical Lutheran. But how can a kingdom believe in something? And even if the kingdom is called a state, its capacity for faith is just as nugatory. The state is not even a figure of folklore, as the Devil is in the view of modern theologians. It is an abstraction and, as such, can neither think nor feel, nor embrace any conviction whatsoever. Only a living human being is blessed with such a faculty.

This new Church was organized subserviently to the king's surveillance and control. The old Church, with its fortified episcopal residences, had acquired almost one-fifth of the land throughout the realm. All this now became crown property. And with the riches of this cavalry-and-estate-owning Church the king should have been content. The poor little parish churches should have been allowed to keep their possessions. Yet they too were stripped of their belongings, plundered of their silver and other ornaments. Not a single parish church was left untouched. Down the centuries, generation after generation, men had made great sacrifices to enhance the temples which were their parish's place of assembly. Now the king's men came and took from them their bridal crowns, their candlesticks, their chalices, their altar cloths, their monstrances, their images of the Virgin and other treasures, sacred to the common people. Through the ages these objects had been inextricably involved in people's holy days and festivals, in their spiritual life. It is calculated that eighty-five per cent of the silver in the parish churches of Småland, 3,700 kilograms, were taken away. The loss of these gleaming treasures, which had helped to brighten their dark churches, left a great gap. Only the bare walls were left.

It was a gross outrage to the piety of the country folk. To anyone who knows at first hand how profoundly serious are the religious feelings of the countryman it seems only natural that this plunder of his churches should have led to insurrections. To me no rising seems more understandable than the church-bell rising in Dalarna in 1531. The people were being deprived of property honestly earned by them. In their eyes the king's proceedings were nothing but barefaced robbery, an act of burglary committed against their temples. Finds made in various parts of Sweden have revealed how people tried to rescue their beloved heirlooms from the royal bailiffs. Silver treasures from churches, buried in the 16th century, have been found in prehistoric cairns.

To rob the people like this was hardly the right way to create the popular Church which should have replaced the cavalry-and-state-owning Church. As far as we can judge, even the reformer Olaus Petri, himself a man of the people, thought it was the wrong way of going about things.

On one occasion, before Gustav Vasa, on June 6, 1523, had been elected king at Strängnäs, he had sworn an oath never to touch the property of the Catholic Church as it existed at that time. This promise formed part of an agreement concluded on July 25, 1521, between himself and Bishop Hans Brask, the Church's chief representative. Gustav had solemnly promised to defend the privileges of Holy Church, her personnel and her possessions 'as long as I live'. Further, the regent, as he then was, bound himself to be the bishop's friend for better or for worse and 'never to desert him'. Before he had lived much longer Gustav had broken his oath in every detail. After a few years the universal Roman Catholic Church in Sweden had been overthrown and Hans Brask had fled into exile.

Gustav Vasa's actions were dictated by the kind of council given by Machiavelli in *The Prince*: 'And therefore a wise prince cannot, nor ought not keep his faith given when the observance thereof turns to disadvantage, and the occasions, that made him promise, are past. – And ordinarily things have been succeeded with him that hath been nearest the Fox in condition'. The king of 1527 saw no reason to keep the promise made by the regent of 1521. The Västerås *riksdag* of that year is more important than almost any other in Swedish history. It was at this assembly that Gustav finally defeated his most dangerous opponent within the realm, Bishop Hans Brask. In doing so he took a decisive step toward setting up his royal dictatorship. If he needed the wealth of the Church, it was in order to exert his own power and implement his plans – and so he simply seized it, using methods again reminiscent of *The Prince*. Lauritz Weibull has summed up the results of the Västerås *riksdag*: 'Gustav Vasa had been granted the tool of power for which he had been striving. He had come by it after a series of machiavellian machinations. With these implements in his hands he could now proceed further!'

King Gustav lost no time in doing so. In his ecclesiatical confiscations he went further than anyone in the kingdom, in 1527, could ever have imagined. In a royal brief dated January 31, 1531, he requires of each church one bell and also the congregation's entire land tithe for that year – all the church's regular income, that is, except the amount needed for the purchase of wax and wine.

Gustav Vasa implemented his policies by setting off one class of the population against another – a method much favoured by rulers. He played off the aristocracy against the commons, the peasants against the burghers, and one province against another. Soon he was consulting none of their representatives before arriving at his decisions: latest research shows that from the early 1530's onwards Gustav Vasa's dictatorship was complete.

After 1529, the king did not again summon a *riksdag* until 1544. He held meetings of the Council; but they were mere formalities. What really mattered and had to be obeyed were the royal decrees, and these he issued arbitrarily. When the *riksdag* finally met again it was simply in order to approve the decisions already made and long ago implemented by the king. The analogy with Hitler's *Kroll-Opera* leaps to mind.

His confiscations of parish plate continued even after he had paid off the kingdom's debt to Lübeck. In 1541–42 he set in motion a systematic plunder of country churches in the Götaland provinces, and this was one of the causes of the Dacke rising. This time Gustav did not even pretend to ask the lords of the Council for their opinion. Probably it was his new German advisers, Konrad von Pyhy and Georg Norman, who had put the idea into his head. On the king's personal orders, his bailiffs abstracted from the poor parish churches all that might be left in them of value. Altar cloths and copes were removed and handed over to Queen Margareta, who used the superb materials to clothe the royal children.

It is estimated that six and a half tons of church silver were gathered into the celebrated St Eskil's chamber, Gustav Vasa's private treasury. This was one imposing result of the Lutheran reformation in Sweden; and to that extent it was a great success. But there was also a religious aspect. The faith hitherto held by Swedes was now found to be utter error. For four centuries they had been baptised into the wrong church, had lived and died in the wrong religion. Now at last the moment had come for the introduction of the true faith. Now it was decided – to use the words of the Västerås *riksdag* – that 'the pure word of God shall be everywhere preached according to God's command, and not according to uncertain miracles, the fables and vain imaginings of men, as hath been heretofore'. It was to be preached in the vernacular, so that the common man should understand the doctrines of the priesthood. In point of religious enlightenment this was a great step forward. The Church of Sweden was purged of the dogmas of the papal Church, together with the worship of saints, the milk of the Virgin

Mary and so forth, by which the people were no longer to be seduced and confused. Holy Writ was to be interpreted and disseminated in such a manner as could be understood by everyone. Thanks to the labours of Olaus Petri, the New Testament was published for the first time in Swedish. It was he who first tried to teach our people to read.

Gradually, however, new dogmas arose, a Lutheran protestant theology, hardly easier for the common man to understand than the doctrines and Latin masses of the Roman Catholic Church had been. Among other things the Reformed Church set in process an intensive and thoroughgoing study of diabolism, one result of which was some statistics over the total number of devils in hell. A 16th-century protestant theologian at a German university made a precise calculation, running into thirteen figures: 2,666,866,764,664, a figure which, even so, only took into account the 'lesser devils'.

In Lutheran doctrine the Lord of Hell, the Devil, became a good deal more terrifying than he had ever been in Catholic doctrine, and after the lake of burning brimstone had been introduced hell became both more realistic and more horrible. It was the new Church which implanted in the psyche of the common man a terror of hell that was to become a monstrous popular torment, which has survived down into our own time. I have myself known several of its victims. On the lips of the common man the prince of the underworld acquired a multitude of new names, over and above the purely conventional 'Satan' and 'Devil', 'The Evil One', 'The Enemy', 'The Dangerous One', under which he had appeared down the centuries. In my own childhood it was The Dangerous One who was used to terrify me. All these new sobriquets taught folk to understand how deeply the Devil was to be feared.

So Sweden officially became an Evangelical Lutheran kingdom, with its own state Church, but a great deal of time was to pass before people were transformed spiritually from Catholics to Protestants. Here was no question of a spontaneous conversion; and it is quite possible that, but for Gustav Vasa's monetary straits, the Swedes would have remained Catholics to this day. I feel we should be sorry for those many people who would have preferred to keep their ancient faith. The nuns of Vadstena, forced to listen to sermons by Lutheran clergy, are famous for their passive resistance. They stuffed their ears with wool and wax.

Popular discontent at the Reformation was fanned by printed Catholic propaganda, and it did not take Gustav Vasa long to realise that freedom of the printed word could be a serious danger to his régime. Through it his subjects had a chance, which they had lacked before the age of the printing press, of spreading nefarious opinions. Closing a Catholic printing works and exiling its printer, he subsidized those printers who published reformist tracts. Even this was not enough; a censorship was necessary. In 1539, Gustav issued an edict, expressly commanding that no 'print' should be placed in the hands of the common people 'without we first have considered and decided therein'. *This was the first law establishing censorship in Sweden*, a law which made possible a total suppression of the free word. Two hundred years later Gustav's successors on the throne were still applying it, right up to the 18th century. All printed matter, as the expression went, had to be 'seen over' before it came to the eyes of the public.

Even in his care for his subjects' reading matter Gustav Vasa was therefore a pioneer and innovator – not that any of his predecessors would not have done the same, had the printer's dangerous art been invented in their day.

The press policies of modern dictators follow ancient precedent.

Sweden's greatest householder

No Swedish king was ever so deeply knowledgeable about agriculture as was Gustav Eriksson Vasa. That he possessed a practical knowledge of farming is certain. During the years when he was growing up at Rydboholm and on the other Vasa farms he had obviously studied the daily life of the peasantry at each season of the year and, even if he had not participated in them himself, had studied their tasks. He knew when the field had to be harrowed, when the grain had to be sowed, when the hay had to be brought in, and when the sheep had to be shorn. When he became king he wrote to the peasantry all over his kingdom, instructing them in the proper cultivation of their homesteads. Such insights are unique in a man in his position; perhaps he is the only Swedish ruler who had an intimate knowledge of farming. I cannot imagine Queen Christina issuing directives for the proper method of pig-breeding, or Gustav III writing letters to the common people on the best season for planting potatoes!

These commands and regulations, always being issued by their king, hardly amused the peasantry. On the contrary, his interference in the cultivation of their farms certainly angered and irritated them. Such matters they thought they understood better than His Grace. And sometimes they really did. The peasants of Öland, in one famous instance, certainly did. In a royal missive Gustav strictly enjoined them to bring in their hay on St Olof's Day (July 29) at the latest. To this letter the addressees could certainly have replied: 'Your Grace! Are we to take in the hay stooks under roof, even if they've been standing in drenching rain for a week? Are we to harvest soaking hay, which will be utterly ruined in the barn?'

The Swedish peasant had of old been in the habit of cultivating his land as he pleased and thought fit. He had no desire to be subjected to the guardianship of an all-puissant king who intervened in his private affairs with directives, regulations and bans, this authoritarian master who even threatened to take his farm away from them if he did not look after it properly. Were free peasant proprietors to put up with such treatment?

From Eli Heckscher's *Economic History of Sweden* it transpires that Swedish agriculture, taken as a whole, increased its yield during the early Vasa period. The number of derelict farms was reduced, output per homestead of grain, meat and butter rose. The king's concern for the mother-industry would therefore appear to have borne fruit, though we must also bear in mind that such an increment was also favoured by the state of peace which, beginning in the mid-1520s, was only interrupted by the civil war of 1541–42.

Another aspect of Gustav I's great interest in agriculture was his enormous personal acquisitions of land, which in due course made him the country's largest private land owner, with estates comprising at his death some 5,000 homesteads.

When Gustav came to power the soil of Sweden is estimated to have been distributed as follows: 3,754 crown homesteads, 14,340

Church homesteads, 13,922 noble homesteads, and 35,239 taxable homesteads – i.e. farms, owned by the peasants themselves. The Church, that is, had owned almost five times as many homesteads as the crown. Forty years later, in 1560, the distribution is utterly different. Now the state owns 18,936 homesteads, the Church none, the nobility 14,175 and the peasants 33,130. All Church estates have passed to the crown; the nobles have retained and somewhat augmented theirs; but the peasantry have lost a couple of thousand homesteads.

That is to say, in 1560 the king and his clan owned so many homesteads that they corresponded to more than a quarter of the crown lands, and to almost one-sixth of all lands belonging to the commons. No Swedish king has ever possessed anything like such great wealth. In mid-16th-century Europe, according to Michael Roberts, stories were circulating of the fabulous wealth of Gustav Vasa.

His miserliness and avarice for land seem to have been pathological. He only had to be seized with desire for some fertile acres, a forest well-stocked with game or some good eel-fisheries, to became immediately possessed of them. In his day the ownership of the soil was not fixed by law, once and for all. Ownership was a matter of interpretation. Gustav never passed up an opportunity to acquire a good homestead. Further, as can be seen from a declaration made by him on April 20, 1542 he claimed that all common lands were crown property. 'Forasmuch as such lands as do lie uncultivated, they belong to God, to us and to the crown of Sweden, and none other'.

But already in the 1550s the notion that the crown was the rightful owner of *all* land, that peasants only had the right to till it, and that this right could in certain cases be taken away from them, had probably been put into Gustav's head by his German advisers. In Sweden it was a revolutionary concept.

Juridically, the crown in Sweden had never owned any peasant lands which were subject to tax. The peasant proprietor had a right to the land he cultivated. And so it had been, up to the reign of Gustav Vasa. But foreign law asserted the view that *all* land had originally belonged to the crown, which had subsequently ceded it, partly to the nobility with *dominium directum* (full ownership rights), and partly to the peasants, who only enjoyed an hereditary right to its use, *dominium utile*.

This idea of the state having plenary rights of land-ownership had originally been the brainchild of an Italian jurist, Johannes Bassarius, who had lived in the 13th century. Applied in feudal Germany, it was therefore probably brought to King Gustav's ears by Konrad von Pyhy, Georg Norman and other Germans. Such an overriding proprietorship of all taxable homesteads fitted in admirably with Gustav Vasa's policies, and the king began applying it in practice. If, in his opinion, any peasant was mismanaging his farm, he was turned off it; and if a homestead had paid no tax for three years, it was seized by the crown.

Gustav Vasa's new view of land ownership is mirrored in two of his letters to his bailiffs and the commons, dated April 15, 1541, and February 4, 1553. Wherever a tax-paying peasant is found to be allowing his land to become derelict or otherwise ruining it, this land belongs to 'us and to the crown of Sweden. May all take note thereof'.

'Us and the crown of Sweden' – the identification is complete. The two are become one flesh.

All of which was to say that any tax-paying peasant who in ancient custom had been held to be the owner of his land should be allowed to cultivate it only as long as the king and the crown permitted. In reality the crown peasant's status was now to be that of a farmer: the landowner could give him notice and turn him out. A century later this view of property rights was to assume weight and importance. In the great battle between the Estates, the nobles and peasants were struggling fiercely for the soil, and there were peasant revolts. The nobility, namely, implementing Gustav Vasa's idea, had seized taxable lands to which they regarded themselves as having been given all rights of ownership by Queen Christina. Whenever a peasant failed to pay his taxes for three successive years, his homestead was declared forfeit; which meant quite simply that the nobleman took it over and the peasant was evicted from his farm, his own and his family's home. (My novel *Ride To-Night*, whose action is placed in the year 1650, treats of this imminent threat to the liberties of the commons).

This order of things which Gustav Vasa attempted to introduce into Sweden was feudal, and as such utterly foreign to all Swedish juridic ideas, as understood by the people. Nor did it strike any lasting root in our country. But historians have overlooked its connection with the struggle a century later, between the Estates.

For insurgents, the block

In the Late Middle Ages, Dalarna was politically Sweden's leading province, almost a realm within the realm. The great age of the Dalesmen had begun with Engelbrekt's assault on the Borganäs bailey on Midsummer Day 1434, and it lasted right up to the day of Gustav Vasa's razzia among the leaders of the church bell rising at Kopparberg in 1533; that is for a century, all but one year.

Bergslagen, the great mining region, the abode of many wealthy mine-masters, included Southern Dalarna. Otherwise, Dalarna was a province where poverty was indigenous. It was rich only in people. It had no nobles, no estates and no large farms. The land was distributed into small parcels, sufficient to support many peasants. Equality between one man and another was therefore greater here than in the provinces dominated by the aristocracy, such as Uppland, Södermanland and Östergötland. If Dalarna's status was unique, it was partly because of her large population. The province could put several thousand armed men into the field, a force utilized more especially by the Stures who always sought, and could always rely on, getting the Dalesmen's support whenever they needed it. Gustav Vasa, too, had come up to Dalarna on the same errand as the Stures before him. Their feat of arms with their home-made weapons had made the Dalesmen a military power-factor to reckon with. Particularly feared by their enemies were their sharp iron-tipped arrows, which they made for their cross-bows and long-bows. Even today the crossed arrows are a prominent feature of the coat of arms of Dalarna.

In the Later Middle Ages, Dalarna, with her poor but un-feudalized population, had also been the chief source of Swedish insurrections. More risings against foreign and native powers had broken out there than in any other part of the country. Even as late as 1743, at the time of the 'great Dalesmen's dance' (the scornful name given to the revolt by those who tragically and bloodily crushed it) this proud tradition lived on and proved to be a source of inspiration to the Dalesmen. And in 1788 Gustav III, who had read the history of Gustav I with close attention, stood up on the wall of Mora churchyard and, dressed in local costume and wearing the ribbon of the Order of the Seraphim on his breast, raised the parishes against the Danes and Russians.

The Dalesmen had done more than any other Swedes to put Gustav Eriksson Vasa on the throne. Subsequently they made even greater efforts to remove him from it. These attempts had begun as early as 1524. Only a year after Gustav had been elected king they were already wanting to get rid of him. In Dalarna it was a time of famine and bark bread. The cost of life's basic necessities had risen sky-high, and people lacked 'honest coin'. They attributed their troubles to all the Lübeckers the king had brought into the country. In exchange for a loan to finance the war against the Danes he had given these foreigners a monopoly of all trade, and they were utilizing it to skin the population of the very province which had most helped him to seize power.

The Dalesmen's first insurrection against Gustav was led by two Catholic prelates, Peder Kansler, known as Sunnanväder, and Master Knut. Both had been evicted by Gustav from their livings. Now they wanted to see the Stures on the throne. The king was reasonable and prepared to negotiate. At a meeting with the discontented and fist-shaking Dalesmen, at Tuna in October, 1525, he promised to set everything amiss to rights, and for the moment the discontent subsided. As for the two leaders of the rebellion, by and by Gustav got them into his clutches and they were sent to the block.

The second rising of the Dalesmen, in 1527–28, was a considerably more serious affair. What was in question this time was the oppressive burden of taxation – that abiding source of insurrection – bearing on the commons. In order to pay off the state's debt to the Lübeckers the king had decreed the imposition of very harsh taxes. This time the Dalesmen had a suitable candidate to replace Gustav Eriksson on the throne, a youth who claimed to be the eldest son of Sten Sture the Younger, a man much loved in Dalarna. To history he is known as the 'Daljunker', but research has not been able to establish his true identity. Since he was no more than sixteen years old, Sten Sture and Kristina Gyllenstierna can hardly have had a son of his age in their marriage. Pcder Svart calls the Daljunker an 'angry and desperate rogue' *'arg förtvifflad bof'*. In the king's propaganda against him as leader of the insurrection he is called Jöns Hansson, and declared to be a 'rascal', a stable hand who after robbing his first master had run away from his second. All contemporary witnesses agree, however, that the Daljunker behaved like a man of education and assumed all the airs and graces of a gentleman. Nevertheless his alleged mother, Kristina Gyllenstierna, utterly disavowed him. A statement of doubtful authenticity declares that she was forced to do so under torture. The young man himself declared that his mother was ashamed of him; if she would not recognize him, he said, it was because he was born 'before she was wedded'. Recent research (Folke Lindberg) takes into account the possibility that he may really have been the person he pretended to be.

Not all the Dalecarlian villages supported this alleged scion of the Stures, who unsuccessfully tried to invade Dalarna from Norway. After that King Gustav was able to crush his rebellion. In February, 1528, he summoned the Dalesmen to a meeting at Tuna Mead for a settlement of accounts. They were promised, of course, a safe conduct – and of course Gustav abused it. When the Dalesmen arrived at Tuna they found themselves confronted with the king's men-at-arms, in full panoply of war, who ringed them in in the meadow. 'They were rounded up like cattle'. And now the most effective of all instruments for forcing men into submission was brought out: the headsman's axe. After which their terror could be counted on to bring them to heel. The supposed ringleaders were plucked out of the crowd, led to the block and instantly beheaded. 'When the others saw how blood had begun to flow, another sound came into their barking. They feared desperately for their lives, began to shriek and weep, fell on their knees, imploring and begging the king for God's sake to show mercy, and promising betterment' – to quote Peder Svart's chronicle.

These rebels who died on the block in Tuna Mead are anonymous. Nor do we know their numbers. Gustav Vasa also insisted that sentence of death should be passed on the Daljunker, who had fled to Germany. The same year, in the autumn of 1528, the young man – whoever he was – was beheaded in Rostock city market place.

Tuna Mead or compound is a large open place in the southern part of Dalarna. For centuries it had been the scene of popular assemblies. Long before 1528 it was already historic, and after the king's razzia in that year it became bloodsoaked ground. When I saw it, in 1971, the meadow was under plough. A ring of great stones marks this immemorial meeting place. But that historic event in 1528, when an unknown number of Dalecarlians met their deaths, has still not been commemorated in any way. The event lives, admittedly, in a magnificent poem by one of the great Swedish writers of our time, Erik Axel Karlfeldt. But I lack a monument to these nameless men, on the spot where they perished for the Dalesmen's right to self-determination.

In the following year the Västergötland revolt broke out. It began among the commons of north-west Småland: 'the Smålanders made no little noise' says Peder Svart. Their 'noise' spread to a number of other provinces, but the king managed to splinter the movement and separate the men behind it, and it was soon suppressed. Nor could the noblemen of Västergötland and the Småland peasantry really have had the same aims.

The church bell revolt of 1531, the third and last to be made against Gustav Vasa in Dalarna, occurred chiefly in the parishes around Lake Siljan, always the most restless part of the province. Its centre was at Leksand, and it was there it gestated. It was a brief affair, 'a flame suddenly lit, which hastily went out', according to a local historian. The rising's main importance however, lay in its consequences – chiefly in its horrible epilogue, two years later, when the king held another razzia at Kopparberget, Falun.

The resistance movement began among the enterprising parishioners of Leksand, led by their vicar Herr Evert. Leksand church possessed the largest bell in all Dalarna. In a 'Survey of Dalecarlian bells which were seized in 1531–1533' its weight is stated to be 16 ship-pounds, or about 2,700 kilos. The Leksand peasants resolved never to hand over their bell willingly, and were prepared to defend it by main force. Anders Persson, of Rankhyttan, had advised them to 'deal the king's emissaries as many blows as they could well stand, without any being slain'. And when, in the event, the bailiff Lasse Eriksson and his assistants came to fetch the church bell, the insurrection broke out in Leksand churchyard, one of the most beautiful in Sweden. The king's men were 'beaten and hammered with axe-hammers' and 'treated so piteously that none can fully tell the tale.'

None of the sources say that any of Gustav Vasa's emissaries were killed – the insurgents appear to have followed Anders Persson's advice. As far as we know, therefore, the violence offered by this resistance movement amounted to no more than assault and battery, with grave threat to life. But Gustav Vasa, in revenge, took at least ten lives.

At the moment when the bell rising broke out, Christian II was preparing to recover his lost kingdom by invading from Norway, and at first this exterior threat obliged the king to settle matters with his subjects in a conciliatory spirit. The rising in Dalarna against the church levies had never been general. In the end the king even took the great bell at Leksand, the source of the disturbances. Other rebellious parishes offered to compound for their bells by a payment of 2,000 marks – the price of 200 cows – providing they could keep them and the king overlooked the violence offered to his officers. Gustav Vasa agreed and accepted the money, pardoned the insurgents completely and received them back 'one and all' into his friendship, as the settlement put it.

The wretched Dalesmen took the king at his word. Their gullibility, writes one historian, is astounding: 'they should have remembered how the king had settled accounts in Tuna Mead, three years before.'

For Gustav Vasa was a man with a long memory. He never forgot. Two years after reaching this settlement with his subjects, he came back to Dalarna with his men-at-arms, noblemen in full armour, and at the Kopparberget carried out his inquisition. This was in February 1533. The king alleged that after the settlement the Dalesmen had conspired with King Christian. The allegation is not proven, and I have not been able to find more than one modern historian who is prepared to believe it. All others are more or less sceptical, and I am among the most sceptical of all. In my firm opinion this supposed treason was nothing but a pretext to crush a people who would not submit to him. 'We cannot escape the impression that there was something of the spirit of the Stockholm Bloodbath in this final settlement of accounts', writes a local historian.

Again the Dalesmen were penned in a ring by the soldiers. Some were dragged straight to the block. Others were taken to Stockholm, and there beheaded. Among the executed were two of the king's old friends in Dalarna. When 'the noxious weeds had been plucked out' the rest of the Dalesmen were pardoned.

At Kopparberget 'Dalarna's brilliant history was drowned in blood' – is E. Hildebrand's grim way of putting the matter. And it is correct. It was the headsman's axe which finally suppressed this stiff-necked people, whose only wish had been to manage their own province's affairs.

Before being executed, seven of the leaders were imprisoned for a year in the capital. Peder Svart claims that only Måns Nilsson from Aspeboda, Anders Persson from Rankhyttan and Ingel Hansson were 'cut off' in Stockholm. The other prisoners, he says, were granted their lives. But the king's faithful chronicler is given the lie by the minutes of a court of justice. From this document it transpires that, on February 17, 1534, seven imprisoned Dalesmen were condemned by the Stockholm Court to lose their lives and their property. This sentence was passed on them exactly one year after they had been taken prisoner at Kopparberget.

Peder Svart states that one of the Dalesmen's leaders, Nils from Söderby, was 'cut off' at Kopparberget, he being the fifth, and adds: 'several more were there executed'. According to the chronicler the decapitated heads were placed on a plank. The head of Nils from Söderby, as their 'captain', was placed in the centre, crowned with a 'tall crown of birch-bark'. The heads of four of his comrades, like a bloody wreath, were placed two on either side. The macabre plank with the five insurgents' heads was then affixed to a 'rather tall stake'.

Peder Svart mentions 'several more', as if others besides those whose heads were set up on the plank were also executed. How many could they have been? And how numerous were the other unknown rebels who had been beheaded at Tuna Mead three years before? I have asked several specialists on the reign of Gustav Vasa whether they can say approximately how many victims altogether were claimed by the king's razzias in Dalarna. None have been able to. All we know for certain is that seventeen men perished on the block in the course of his reign. One more should be mentioned: the vicar of Leksand, Herr Evert, leader of the bell rising, who was condemned to death but died in a Stockholm prison before the sentence could be carried out.

In his work on Kopparberget, Professor Bertil Boëthius des-cribes the Dalesmen who were 'cut off' at Tuna and Falun as criminals, and their deeds as 'crimes'. This is a view of history to which I cannot subscribe. Did not the Dalesmen's 'crime' really consist in holding different views as to how they should manage their own affairs, their own society, from those held by the king? But Gustav Vasa could assert his view with an argument which admitted of no answer. The headsman's sword.

Nationalist historians maintain, of course, that what Gustav Vasa was asserting were the interests of the realm as a whole, and that to these the provinces' special interests had to yield. The sufferings and deaths of individuals, that is, are of no consequence where the national state must prevail. And if, compared with the interest of the state, human lives are of so little import that those in power have the right to sacrifice them to it, then Gustav Vasa, in taking the lives of the Dalecarlian rebels, acted rightly. But it is also possible to regard his action as political murder. Unfortunately this concept is never juridically defined. From the point of view of the Swedish nation as a whole Gustav Vasa's execution of the rebels has generally been accepted as justified.

Gustav Vasa and Machiavelli

In the preface to his translation of Machiavelli's *The Prince*, the great Swedish novelist Hjalmar Bergman, known as an authority on Italian history and culture, writes: 'The author has given the reader nothing less than a portrait of the human being – a portrait so crucial that one can say it is coeval with, and will probably only die in the same year as, mankind itself.'

Machiavelli was working on *Il Principe* in 1513 – I have not been able to discover when it was finished. Written in Italian, it was translated into Latin, but not until 1532 was the original edition published in that tongue. Up to then it had been circulating in manuscript copies. Danish historians are of the opinion that Christian II had a copy in his hands as early as about 1520. He commanded Poul Helgesen, a deeply learned cleric, to translate a book the title of which is not given but which on good grounds is believed to have been *Il Principe*. Helgesen translated the beginning of the work, but it was not long before he came to the conclusion that it was an 'evil book' and refused to go on with it. Instead, he translated for the king Erasmus of Rotterdam's *A Christian Prince's Education and Doctrine*, indubitably a somewhat different kind of book from *The Prince*.

It is known that copies of *Il Principe* were being read in the courts of Europe in the 1520's. Palle Lauring is of the view that Christian II may have obtained a copy from the Hapsburg court in Vienna, with which, as brother-in-law to the Emperor, he was in intimate contact. And we certainly have every reason to believe that Christian the Tyrant derived great profit from his reading.

In his dedication of the book to Lorenzo di Medici, Machiavelli explains that in his work he wishes to 'draw up rules for how princes should govern'. In a word, *Il Principe* is a handbook in the art of seizing, exercising and retaining power. The work was written for Renaissance princes, but in the modern age its principles for political action have been applied by virtually all despots, kings, dictators and presidents. Thanks to its influence on them it has had a hand in deciding the destinies of nations.

According to *The Prince*, force, treachery, guile, lies, hypocrisy and dissimulation are all necessary and defensible instruments of policy. Unless he uses them no prince can hope to rule successfully. This is why, among all humane and sensible people, this author has acquired such an evil reputation. But I wonder whether this has not been to do him an injustice? I ask myself: What he gives us here, is it his innermost, sincere view of life? In view of his own fate – Machiavelli was imprisoned and tortured – I cannot believe that he had a very high opinion of princely tyrants; and, when all is said and done, the book concludes with a call to rebellion against the princes who were terrorizing the Italy of his day. Should not *The Prince*, perhaps, be read as a satire on potentates, as an icily logical parody on tyrannical government? At very least the book is double-bottomed, and open to divers interpretations. Its author tells us what this world of ours is like. But does he not really mean it should be otherwise?

Machiavelli presents the human being under two guises: as a wielder of power, and as its victim. His prince exploits all his insights into human nature, all its shortcomings and weaknesses, its cowardice, its fear, its ingratiation, opportunism, selfishness, meanness, vanity – above all its lackey-like soul. Only by cleverly exploiting such knowledge can he keep his power and govern successfully.

The ideal prince described by Machiavelli in *Il Principe* is strikingly like King Gustav I of Sweden. In the main, Gustav Vasa ruled according to the principles of statesmanship expounded in this book, and without a doubt he was a most successful monarch. But did Gustav himself ever read Machiavelli? Though not out of the question, it is hardly likely.

When *Il Principe* first appeared in print, in 1532, Gustav had already been king for nine years and had long been putting its lessons into practice. It is possible of course that a copy of the work had already reached the Stockholm court at an earlier date, though this does not mean the king had necessarily read it. Gustav was no bookworm. What we know about his person – and we know surprisingly much – does not suggest that he had a thirst for self-education. It was not in learning that he was pre-eminent.

Nevertheless in his youth he may well have become acquainted with the spirit and principles of *Il Principe* – through Doctor Hemming Gadh. This hypothesis deserves closer study.

As I have said, Hemming Gadh had come home to Sweden after living in Rome for twenty years as Sten Sture the Elder's envoy. The last decades of the 15th century were the time when the ideas of statesmanship which Machiavelli was later to expand in his books were burgeoning in Italy. Since Doctor Hemming was then continuously resident in that country he must have been familiar with and impressed by these ideas. After his return to his own country he put them into practice, notably on the occasion of the death of Sten Sture the Elder – as I have related before – and later on when he became a traitor to the nationalist party and went over to King Christian. Many of his temperamental letters, preserved in the Sture archives, bear witness to his unscrupulous attitude – in the spirit of Italian Renaissance – toward political problems.

Gustav Vasa had become acquainted with Hemming Gadh when, as a youthful junker, he had entered Sten Sture the Younger's court, some time around 1515. According to Peder Svart, Doctor Hemming became Gustav's tutor. And Gustav appreciated the old and widely experienced politician. Despite his later defection to Christian, Gustav once called him 'a right-thinking and honest Swedish man' – but admittedly not until the Union king had cut Gadh's head off.

It seems perfectly natural, therefore, that Doctor Hemming should have instructed his pupil in the arts of politics and statesmanship, and that in doing so he should have drawn on his own experiences in Italy, where in the course of his long residence he had become acquainted with a thrusting nationalism that had developed into what later came to be called Machiavellianism. Thus it is at least possible, that while Machiavelli was writing *Il Principe* in Italy, its ideas were already being presented orally in Sweden by a man familiar with its author's environment; and he no lesser a person than the tutor of junker Gustav. The spirit of *The Prince*, that is, may have been implanted without either pupil or teacher even being aware of the book's existence. Without ever having read a single word by him, Gustav Vasa may well have become Machiavelli's pupil.

Unfortunately we have no eye-witness accounts of the lessons which Hemming Gadh gave to junker Gustav, and this hypothesis – that he may have influenced the founder of the national state of Sweden with lessons drawn from Machiavelli's Italy – can only remain a hypothesis.

It is also possible that Gustav Vasa was perfectly able to acquit himself without any influence from his teacher or any instruction in political ideology. He may have been born with the traits of character typical of Machiavelli's *Prince* – perhaps he was a natural despot, who had no need at all of any 'rules for how princes should rule'.

Gustav Vasa the man

Of all figures in the history of 16th-century Sweden, Gustav I is the one who is most alive for us. No one else has left to posterity so many documents and eye-witness accounts of himself. He made sure he should be known to future generations. Above all it is in his own letters that we come closest to Gustav Vasa the man.

The State Archives have published *Konung Gustav Den Förstes registratur* containing several thousands of letters in twenty-nine bulky volumes. So far I have not found time to count them, the task would take a couple of days. For Gustav I wrote more letters than any other Swedish ruler – perhaps more than any Swede, whether man or woman, with the possible exception of Strindberg.

Were all these letters dictated by His Grace to his clerks, in person? Besides an amanuensis he probably had several collaborators who assisted in their composition. Nevertheless these thousands of letters show a quite remarkable uniformity of style and expression. As one reads them one gains an overall impression of their being the work of a single author. For the king to have conceived and written so vast a corpus of documents would have called for a super-human capacity for work. That they could have been written from beginning to end by one and the same person is incredible. Can the explanation be that his collaborators gradually came to be so deeply versed in the king's style and manner and they acquired an illusory ability to mimic his own masterly language?

For Gustav Vasa is both a master of the Swedish language and one of its innovators. His letters overbrim with pithy and trenchant expressions, with drastic imagery, striking similes, authentically popular turns of phrase and stock phrases. Often the author of these letters simply takes the speech of the common man, and transfers it on to paper. We are all the time aware of his origins, all the traits of a Roslagen peasant. This king wrote a language his subjects could understand, a faculty which was a great political asset to him when he had to pacify a rebellious and threatening commons. During the Dacke rising, especially, numerous documents were written by him to allay popular discontent; and probably they had the desired effect. He knew how to use words which, when his letters were read out to them, the people understood. We are told that the commons enjoyed being addressed by His Grace in person.

Gustav Vasa is the author of many household sayings and turns of speech which we Swedes still use without knowing where they originated. To educate his subjects he resorted to precepts, germinal ideas, moral *obiter dicta*. He played the schoolmaster. Among his maxims I find this one the best: 'To speak once, and abide by one's words, is better than to speak a hundred times.' Himself, Gustav abided but rarely by his word, but certainly people's confidence in the utterances of our modern politicians would be augmented if they could translate this rule of life into practice.

Gustav Vasa was a forceful personality, of monumental proportions. What did this man not achieve in his forty-year reign! He never lost sight of a goal until he had attained it – as in most cases he did. No methods were beneath him. In *The Prince* rulers are warned against 'misusing leniency'. In the case of the King of Sweden no such warning was needed.

Gustav Vasa exhibits traits both fascinating and imposing – in some instances even likeable. Fabian Månsson is obviously ambivalent in his attitude to the despot. Sometimes, in spite of himself, he admires him. In his novelistic depiction of the young junker Gustav at the court of Sten Sture, Fabian gives us a portrait of which he is half enamoured, a portrait fraught with insight into Gustav's milieu. Gustav, a young nobleman among his peers, joins in the games and pleasures of youth. He is a great favourite with the opposite sex, whether married or not. He is a tall, handsome, imposing young man – 5 ft 7 in in his socks, someone has calculated – with blue eyes the colour of cornflower and 'blooms in his cheeks'. His sister's son, Per Brahe, who once saw his uncle naked, bears witness that his skin was without birthmark or trace of smallpox.

Nowhere on Gustav's 'well-formed' frame was there a blemish large enough to place a needle's point. Arriving in Stockholm to help him drive out the Danes, the German legionaries were delighted at the sight of their new master. To serve such a king was wholly to their taste!

These physical endowments may have contributed to his successes. In social life he was no dullard. On the contrary, he was a charmer. When, on occasion, he let himself go in the society of other people, he was always happy to 'make merry.' For Junker Gustav also played and sang to the lute, may even have been a pioneer of the lute-song as a characteristic Swedish pastime. One experience which made a deep impression on him was probably his captivity. In 1518 he had been one of the hostages at a negotiation outside Stockholm between King Christian and the regent, Sten Sture the Younger. The king had broken his pledge: he forcibly and treacherously brought the hostages on board his ship and sailed for Denmark. This experience very probably left its mark on the young Gustav Eriksson. To some extent it explains the development of his character. Understandably enough it made him hate the Danes even more heartily than before. But it was also a youthful adventure from which he had profited. Since others do not keep their troth with you, neither need you keep yours with them! So says *The Prince*, but the prisoner at Kalö, – the Danish castle where Gustav was kept in captivity between 1518 and 1519 – having himself experienced the truth of this saying, did not need to read it in print.

Gustav Eriksson Vasa was the first of his clan to sit on the throne of Sweden. He was an upstart king, and his colleagues in the neighbouring kingdoms looked down their noses at him. This was why he sought to increase his own prestige by obtaining a real princess of the blood for his queen. First he approached the royal house of Denmark; and was turned down. His next overtures were to the Polish royal family, with the same negative outcome. Gustav was regarded as a usurper, and therefore no peer of such princely families as had inherited their elevated status from many generations of forbears.

As a suitor Gustav I had to bear many humiliations. When, at long last, he managed to get a prince to accept him as a son-in-law he had already been on the throne for eight years; and even then his father-in-law was only a petty German prince of no importance. After long and troublesome negotiations Gustav obtained the hand of Princess Katarina of Saxony-Lauenburg. Though his father-in-law's princely status was of the type of which there were thirteen to the dozen, even he hesitated a long while before he could bring himself to hand over his daughter to a Swedish king who occupied so uncertain and rickety a throne.

Whether or to what extent Gustav suffered from an inferiority complex is impossible to say; but some of his actions must be regarded as a self-made man's imperious need for self-assertion. And assert himself he did. While many of his contemporaries' thrones have long ago collapsed, the monarchy which he established still stands.

How Gustav Vasa was viewed by other princes in his day can be seen in a letter from the Tsar of Russia. Sweden and Russia were just then at war, and the despotic ruler of all the Russians felt it necessary to denigrate and mock his adversary. In his letter he alleges that Gustav Eriksson was the son of a Småland peasant. We do not know how Gustav reacted to this insult, but he could hardly have been more pointedly taunted. Not only was he declared to be the son of a common peasant, but of a Småland peasant to boot! This was after the Dacke rising, and Gustav Vasa's feelings about Smålanders can be surmised. But in a letter of 1575 his son Johan responds to this gross accusation, refuting the Tsar's allegation that his father had been of low birth: 'One of our forefathers of the fifth generation before us, his name was Christer Nilsson, he was of the most noble family, wherefore none knoweth the beginning of His noble lineage and origin or was so highly Esteemed here in the Realm, even as the Constable (*cusabel*) is in France.'

It has been claimed that Gustav killed his first queen, Katarina, in a fit of rage. The rumour was widespread, but is unsupported by any evidence; so the king must be acquitted of this particular charge. At the same time it is interesting to note that he was so famed for his violent temperament and savage moods that people could have believed him capable of such a deed.

His second marriage, to Margareta Leijonhufvud, turned out

happily. The dynasty was secured by numerous children. The marriage also brought Gustav some political advantages. By it he became related to several of the leading families of the Swedish aristocracy. His third marriage, on the other hand, in which he took the sixteen-year-old virgin Katarina Stenbock from her betrothed, comes unpleasantly close to baby-snatching.

All sources agree that in his three marriages Gustav Vasa was and remained an exemplary and faithful husband. No amount of research has ever unearthed a single concubine, not even in his bachelor days before his first marriage. Not that any of his historians have gone so far as to allege that he had remained continent up to his first marriage in 1531, when he was already a man of thirty-five – that would be to put the case too strongly. But, once married, he did his best to bring up his children in the fear of the Lord, in the fashion of his day. Did he exhort his sons Erik and Magnus to follow his example in point of extra-marital relationships? Perhaps. But if so, they certainly did not obey him. Both had many illegitimate offspring by their mistresses.

Several of Gustav's children caused him grief and darkened his old age. His worries for his eldest son Erik, the heir to the throne, are famous. By his inane courtships in Europe, Erik made a fool both of himself and of the new dynasty. At one time he was simultaneously courting a German princess and Queen Elizabeth of England. Such an escapade on the part of a future king of Sweden must have affected his father deeply. Erik was also responsible for the great scandal at Vadstena Castle, when he spied on his sister Cecilia's illicit love affair and arranged matters in such a way that one night the castle guard found a man in her bed. This was no way for a brother to treat his sister, and his father let him know it.

But the king's paternal anxiety must also have been extended to his other son, Magnus. In him the streak of insanity which runs through the Vasa clan – according to genealogists since the beginning of the 15th century – comes out very strongly. Our modern psychiatric experts regard it as likely that Duke Magnus of Östergötland was a schizophrenic. According to contemporary documents he was sometimes 'kept in custody', how or where we are not told. Yet he must have had lucid intervals. Erik XIV tried to exploit his half-brother for his own political ends by presenting him as a suitor to Mary Stuart. There is a remarkable notice concerning Duke Mägnus in an autobiography entitled *Annales*, published by an Italian, Antonio Possevino, in the early years of the 17th century. Possevino was Pope Gregory XIII's envoy to Johan III of Sweden, and one of his tasks was to find out how things stood at Vadstena, after the Reformation the last surviving nunnery in Sweden. In his *Annales* the envoy laments divers acts of violence and outrage against the nunnery's inmates in the reign of Gustav I. Among other matters he wishes to let it be known to all 'that the man who took the lives of three Vadstena nuns after subjecting them to gross violence was King Gustav's son, Duke Magnus'.

Duke Magnus lived until 1595 and was buried with all pomp in the nuns' church at Vadstena, in the presence of the regent, Duke Karl, and members of the Council. He has a magnificent tomb in St Bridget's own church. Heidenstam has written a poem acclaiming his memory. Had the poet realised that in Antonio Possevino's autobiography the man he celebrates is called a rapist and murderer, it is unlikely he would ever have penned it.

The Swedish public's view of Gustav Vasa has been deeply influenced by Strindberg's play about this king. The finest of all Strindberg's historical plays, it is my belief that even historians have been swayed by it. The strong man who appears on the stage with a hammer in his hand had a certain basis in reality, and his utterances are cast in the authentic style of the king's own letters. It all sounds thoroughly genuine. Gustav, in his lifetime, may well have spoken just like this. But in one respect this kingly figure is utterly unhistorical. He thanks the All Highest for having punished him; and this is something utterly untypical of the real Gustav. In none of the sources are we told that he ever felt the least remorse for any of his actions, or regarded himself as deserving to be punished for them. None of his broken oaths, none of his sacred promises or solemn assurances, seem ever to have caused him the least twinge of conscience. And indeed on one occasion he expressly defended his actions when he wrote: 'Necessity knows (*bryter*' – lit. 'breaks') no law; not the law of man and at times not even the law of God'. That is to say, he did not even acknowledge God as his judge or as having the right to punish him.

Even on his deathbed there was nothing of the remorseful penitent about Gustav. When his private chaplain and confessor Master Hans came to his death bed and required him to confess his sins, Gustav sent him packing.

The conscience-stricken king in Strindberg's play, therefore, is no one but the author himself. It is Strindberg, who had just gone through his 'Inferno Crisis' and was still wrestling with God; he uses the king as his mouthpiece.

In his farewell speech to the Estates of the realm, however, Gustav Vasa does concede that his reign *may* have had its faults and shortcomings. He takes into account 'that all things are not conducted (*'drivne'*) so right or well as they should be'. If so, 'I will gladly be prayed for: do it for God's sake and forgive me for it'. The king calls on God to witness that it has not 'befallen out of iniquity or reluctance, but from human weakness, that I have not been able or had the strength to better it.'

This speech is the only document I have been able to find in which the king conceded that he is no more than a man; and even this admission is hedged with reservations.

As a modern view of Gustav Vasa, based on scientific research, I will quote Michael Roberts' final words, in which this English historian sums up his reign. As the verdict of a foreign historian I find it to be of peculiar interest: 'But with all the flaws in his character he was indubitably a great king. For he died with most of his objectives realized, and with things achieved which would have appeared incredible in 1523. Of no Swedish monarch can it be said with greater certainty that his reign was a solid success. What he minded he compassed.'

If success is the measure of a king's greatness, it only remains to agree. But there are other footrules, too, and it is these I have mainly used in this chapter.

In Olaus Petri's *Chronicle* these standards were used to measure other kings, even in their own lifetime. There is no book I would more wish to read than an uncensored history of the reign of Gustav I, written by Olaus Petri, the greatest of all 16th-century Swedes.

Life in the Villages

In the first part of my History I have explained how the '*byalag*', or village community, was an independent factor in society. I called it a fortress of popular liberties. Within its own confines the village was a closed community, a little world of prehistoric origins, all on its own. Linguistic research into place names has proved beyond all doubt that the village must have come into being as early as the period of the Great Migrations, about A.D. 500. Within this village community the inhabitants joined forces in order to be able to manage themselves and their own affairs. As long as they stuck together, they could assert themselves against the outside world. The '*byalag*' was based on a natural community of interests, which gave rise to a living village – a form of life which has persisted in Sweden right up to the 20th century, for more than a thousand years.

If I am now to describe what life was like in the old village community, on work days and holy days, my account will pre-suppose a time when the realm was at peace, when the villagers were allowed to attend to their own tasks without interference from troops extorting board and lodging as they passed through the countryside. It would appear from the source materials, that they were in fact never free from one or another of their great torments: war, crop failure and plague, or indeed from all three at once. Mostly it is the evil events which have been remembered. Yet there were long periods of peace and good harvests, free from pernicious and infectious diseases. At such times, relieved of their three torments, the villagers were able to derive some satisfaction from life. Compared with that of later generations, their existence was austere. They were unenlightened and had none of our material conveniences.

On the other hand, they did not suffer from the lack of things they could not even envisage.

The most positive aspect of the village community was its un-written laws for mutual aid and assistance. Here their fellowship was without flaw. People behaved above all helpfully toward one another, as if it were the most natural thing in the world. Anyone needing help must at once be given it. 'You help me, and tomorrow I'll help you', was the rule. 'Neighbours are brothers' is an old Swedish saying. Whenever a villager fell ill or suffered an accident, when he could not sow his field or do his haymaking in time, then his neighbours got together and did it for him – without compensation. All they asked in return was themselves to be helped in their turn. Otherwise, cash wages were unknown among the villagers. When some job was finished and had to be paid for, payment was always in kind: food, a loaf of bread maybe, or a piece of pork.

This peasant community knew nothing of the commercialism which has overwhelmed modern society. Neighbour did not exploit neighbour for profit. So their need for joy, one of mankind's eternal longings, was satisfied communally without any individual making a profit on it. The entertainments industry may have had its modest forerunners, but as a major and highly profitable, affair it did not come into being in Sweden until our own century.

One remarkable feature of peasant culture was the long-vanished work feasts. All the villagers' more important tasks were carried out jointly, and within the *'byalag'* troubles and joys, toil and merry-making, profit and pleasure were rolled into one. These work feasts can be traced back to heathen times. They were rooted in the rational arrangement for carrying out tasks on a basis of mutual help; but in another respect, too, they served the villagers well. Work done jointly was greatly preferable to the thraldom of solitary toil. Any man who did heavy and solitary work in field or meadow was liable to be assailed by melancholy reflections or fall to pondering the sense of his lot in life. But many hands make light work. To be able to chat as one worked was an asset. Anyone who has ever done heavy manual labour knows how contact with one's mates can help offset its monotony. Good comradeship and friendly chat enliven men's spirits, make the long working hours seem shorter. 'With both hand

and mouth we can lend each other a helping hand', says an old Swedish proverb.

The villagers' work feasts had many names, varying from province to province. That the Swedish word for ale ('*öl*') often appears in these names as a suffix witnesses to the crucial position of this most important of mediaeval beverages. There were '*slåtteröl*' (haymaking feast), '*taklagsöl*' (the feast when the roof was completed on a new house), the '*byköl*' (when the laundry had been done) and many others. To these must be added such family occasions as the '*barnsöl*' (on the birth and christening of a child) and '*gravöl*' (funeral feast).

Certainly, most of the village's teamwork was therefore carried out to an accompaniment of food and drink. There was no stinginess toward the participants. Amply regaled, they found relief from the plainness of their everyday fare.

The major feasts were held at the conclusion of some seasonal work. The hay-feast, marking the conclusion of haymaking at the end of July, was one of the greatest events of the peasant year.

In the days of the old village communities more time was devoted to livestock than to agriculture. This was above all true of those parts of the country where the farms were small. Here the meadow meant more than the ploughed field; second only was the peasant a ploughman. Little of the land attached to each farm was arable. But the hayfields, the grazing lands, the watermeads, the swamps, mires and bogs which would have to feed the cattle during the long winter, that was the vital crop. During summer the beasts were let out hoof by hoof to graze on the common lands. The big problem was how to find fodder for them during the six winter months. All grass growing on the farm fields would be cut, dried and brought into barns and sheds erected out in the fields, thence to be brought into the farm as soon as the sledges could run over the snowladen ground.

This was why, of all summer work, haymaking was the most gruelling. The size of a meadow was calculated according to the number of haymakers needed to mow it in a day. To scythe a whole field was slow work. The ground was not only littered with stones but also thick with bushes and shrubs. As a boy I went haymaking with my father every weekday in July. Our small farm measured a

sixteenth of a hide ('*mantal*'). Our scythes were for ever striking
against loose stones, and this prevented us from swinging them
freely. Instead we had to poke about with the point, whose edge
became notched and jagged from the stones and frequently had to be
rewhetted. But we had time to spare – a whole long month. Every
blade of grass was utilized for hay. Once a peasant in our village was
bitten by a snake when tearing off grass he could not get at with his
scythe.

The days around St Olof's Day saw the last blades of grass fall to
the scythe. By St Olof's Mass, the 29th of the haymaking month, all
haymaking had to be finished, and in the evening on the last of July
the hay feast was held. It was the time of year when the contents of
the storehouse were beginning to be exhausted. By then the mistress
of the household would be sweeping up the last flour left in the bin
and scraping the pork barrel for this great summer feast. For then
the workpeople would have to be plenteously regaled with food and
drink. Dancing and games in barns or on rock ledges were all part of
the feast, which went on all night long. Finally, towards morning
and long after sunrise, a flock of weary haymakers went off home to
bed. They had been working hard; but also enjoyed themselves.
Toil had blended with merry-making.

This great feast of the hay-harvest, which went on all day at the
height of summer and continued through the mild warm night has
something idyllic about it; an idyll which seems the more golden
the further it recedes from us. The village hayfeast has vanished
from people's lives – but survives in Swedish literature. Strindberg
has devoted a chapter to it in his novel *The People of Hemsö*.

From the grasses of the field the villagers took fodder for their
cattle, and therefore food for themselves. From the ploughed field
they took their clothing. It was there their garments grew. Flax is
one of the oldest cultivated plants in the world. It is known to have
been grown before 2,000 B.C. In Egyptian tombs believed to be
4,000 years old, archaeologists have found flax seed. This useful
plant had probably reached Scandinavia in the Bronze Age, when it
had brought about a revolution in people's clothing. Until the
introduction of flax our forefathers had wrapped themselves in
skins, first in the furs of beasts of prey, mostly wolves, then in the

hides of their slaughtered domestic cattle and sheep. But as soon as they had learnt how to grow and treat flax they began wearing cloth. At about the same time, perhaps, they had learnt how to use sheep's wool and goat-hair for the same purpose.

The flax fields with their blue flowers added a dash of colour to the old village lands and were a splendid sight to the eye. Even in my own childhood such a field was still occasionally to be seen. But to turn this new plant into cloth called for lengthy and troublesome work, not to say a great deal of patience. From the day when the flax seed was sown on the ploughed field to the day when the linen cloth was finally spread out on the ground for bleaching a whole calendar year had passed. The process began one spring and ended the next. Before it could be turned into clothing for the body, or sheets and bolsters for a bed, the flax had to go through a long and complex process. No fewer than eleven different stages were involved – I fancy I can name them all: 1. Sowing, 2. Reaping, 3. Drying, 4. Beating, 5. Breaking, 6. Tawing, 7. Heckling, 8. Spinning, 9. Winding, 10. Weaving, 11. Bleaching.

Both men and women, young and old, took part in the villager's work feasts in connection with the flax's preparation. The flax was treated in a special shed, a '*basta*' where it was broken, scutched, swingled and heckled. Its preparation was mainly woman's work. The men saw to the sowing, reaping and breaking, but the other stages in the process were done by the women. And in the end it was the women who with their needles and thread transformed the linen weave into garments.

These village festivals were not without their magical aspects. The draught animals which participated in the work were decked out with flowers and foliage; leafy twigs were tied to the horses' forelocks and floral wreaths were hung on the horns of the oxen. Such adornment had originally been a sacrifice to ensure happiness by propitiating and invoking the blessing of fertility gods. Such is still the custom today. The 'roofing feast' ('*taklagsöl*'), still a feature of Swedish life, is held when the roof trusses are raised on a new building. The wreath which is then hung up at the apex has magical significance, though today few workers in the building trade are aware of it.

A singular instance of such immemorially ancient magic is connected with the women's great autumn feast, their cheese-making:
This was held at a time when the cows, still on their autumn grazing
grounds, were yielding plenty of milk. In order to make many
cheeses at one and the same time from a collective milk supply, the
women exchanged milk at a feast put on by each in turn in her own
farmhouse. The origins of this cheese-making ('*ystmöte*') are demonstrably mediaeval. In his *History* no lesser a writer than Olaus
Magnus has left us an initiated description of this feast. He praises
the women of Västergötland, more especially, for their gigantic
cheeses. It seems they weighed hundreds of kilos:

'Among all the inhabitants of the North the people of Västergötland are most in demand for their cheese-making, wherein none other
folk can be called their equals – very often they make such great
cheeses, that two strong fellows are hard put to it to carry even one
of them a short way. Nevertheless, cheesemaking is never the men's
work, but the women's. From divers villages in that province they
gather in summer at the home of her, whose intent it is to make
cheese. Now the milk is boiled in great kettles, rennet is added, and
the content pressed in great wooden forms, mostly four-sided. – But
no man is thought worthy to be present at this women's work, and
should any beg admittance, it were in vain.'

Sweden's last Catholic archbishop wrote these words in the mid-
16th century. In the early years of the 20th I several times helped
my mother to carry her milk jugs to the farm where the cheese-
makers were to gather. But I was only allowed to carry them as far
as the threshold; to enter the house with mother was forbidden.
Though I often wondered why, I only came across the explanation
in the pages of Olaus Magnus. Naturally, it was because I was of the
male sex! The mediaeval historian omits to explain why no man was
'worthy' to be allowed inside, merely states it as a fact. The explanation can only be magical. The presence of a male would have
disturbed the influences curdling the milk, and spoiled its coagula-
tion. Men could cause the same damage to the butter-making. If a
man came into a house where a woman was churning butter, no
butter would appear in the churn until he had gone out again.

All important family events, too, were celebrated with a feast, to which the villagers invited each other. Whether a mournful occasion or a joyful, the whole village had to celebrate it. Theirs was the fellowship of participation. And people took their time over such feasts. As a rule a single day did not suffice. It called for several, and perhaps the nights too. A wedding feast went on day and night, only interrupted by the intermittent need for a few hours' sleep. But lengthiest of all was the feast held when the *byalag* was to change its alderman. The outgoing alderman, who had preserved order in the village, had to be thoroughly thanked and feasted. We are told that an alderman feast in the fertile and wealthy Söderslätt plains of Skåne could last as long at ten or twelve days.

Communal life obeyed an order of things which the village folk had themselves designed and established. Although known in Sweden since the 17th century, this autonomous village law is certainly of considerably older date. Some of its regulations could be harsh; and sometimes it intervened in private matters which should have been no concern of the village as a whole. Evidence exists, for instance, that a village could arrogate to itself the right to forbid anyone living in it to marry outside its confines. Baskemölla village council in Österlen, Skåne, required a fine of any man marrying exogamously. This, though probably exceptional, shows that a village could claim an absurd degree of autonomy and self-sufficiency. No one was yet aware, of course, of the dangers of in-breeding.

But though offences against village custom were punished by a fine, the fines – charmingly enough – went into the council's entertainments account. The offenders were allowed to participate in the feast paid for by their fines, and therefore received a certain rebate on what they had paid.

The village community operated a communal assistance scheme that was greatly to the advantage of anyone who found himself in any of those situations in life where one is most in need of help. If a young man and a girl wished to get married, the village council made a collection to help them set up house. In several Swedish provinces we hear of a *'fästmögång'* – or betrothal round. This meant that the girl who was setting up house went around the village collecting flax, wool and hemp, each household making its contribution, a contribution sanctioned by custom. Meanwhile her fiancé went the round of all the farms, carrying a sack, into which each farm poured half a peck of grain for the new householder to sow his field for the first time.

Finally, when the wedding took place, the village council gave the bridal couple gifts. And again when, in due course, the *barnsöl* was celebrated, the new member of the community also had to receive a gift. A woman in childbirth was an object of special care, and all sorts of attentions were showered upon her, the village community having a tender interest in the continuation of the race. During her confinement the women brought her a particularly tasty porridge boiled from barley-grain with a liberal addition of butter. 'Whenever there was a new-born child, they lived it up for weeks on end', writes one observer of folk-ways. This custom of bringing porridge to a woman in childbirth still survived in the Småland countryside in the 20th century.

The village community followed its members with a helping hand, literally from the cradle to the grave. When someone died, the coffin-bearers assumed their function. The road to the parish churchyard, though many miles long, might be impassable to horse and cart. In that event the coffin had to be carried there by the men of the village, two six-men teams taking over from one another at regular intervals.

The '*byalag*', as a social assistance organization, was always at work. Its care for individuals began at birth and ended only with death.

The closed conformist peasant society, however, had one serious drawback for young marriagables: the narrow choice of partner. Contacts with people outside its little closely-confined world were rare. People living in other parishes were 'foreigners', and regarded with suspicion. For this reason extra-parochial marriages were rare. The elective scope of persons hankering after marriage was limited to perhaps a radius of half a dozen miles. Further, marriage was usually determined by the size of homestead. The parties ought to be approximately each other's equal in respect of property.

The village was therefore the great marriage market within which a man or woman had to find their better half. Gradually, as a result, all the villagers became interrelated. The family groups held the individual within their grasp and dictated his destinies. Young people, especially, had to bow completely to the dictates of village custom. Their freedom of movement was notably restricted.

For the village community was severely moralistic. No young couple not yet betrothed might show themselves publicly arm in arm or even holding hands. If a boy and a girl behaved in this way it roused intense indignation. Only at nights could young people consort with some intimacy, and then in a specially authorized *'natt-frieri'*, a term which might be translated – to use the New England expression – 'bundling'. The custom seems once to have been general in all Swedish provinces, but it survived longest in Dalarna and Norrland, where it was still being practised at the close of the 19th century.

This form of nocturnal association made it possible for individuals of the opposite sex to get to know one another with a view to marriage. Indeed, it was the only way for them to make intimate approaches. A boy could visit a girl in her bed and spend the night with her with her parents' knowledge and permission, on con-dition that both young people should remain fully dressed and that their cohabitation should not lead to any act of a sexual nature. Presumably no limits were set to their caresses; but these might not turn into coitus. If they did, then the concept of sin immediately put in its appearance. Whoredom had been committed, and that was a breach of the Sixth Commandment.

Naturally any young fellow and maiden who found themselves physically attracted to each other were exposed to severe temptation. If they did not have the strength to resist it and the girl became pregnant, then the problem would be solved by a shotgun marriage. The community's morals had been besmirched by a premature birth. Otherwise little harm had been done.

These bundlings, however, had a sensible purpose. Marriages could be entered into on a basis of free choice. Husband and wife had already learnt to be fond of, devoted to, one another.

The Lutheran Church condemned 'this sinful relationship

among the young' and its clergy energetically combated bundling. But the custom, popular and not easily abolished, persisted down the centuries. As late as 1889 the rector of Bjursås in Dalarna got his church council to adopt a resolution, under which 'nocturnal runnings hither and thither should be regarded by all right-thinking people in the parish as shameful'. Probably the right-thinkers were not in a majority. These nightly encounters were a tradition, had always been popularly approved, and the clergyman in his pulpit was powerless against them. Not until they were no longer necessary – i.e., when moralistic attitudes became less severe and the young were at liberty to walk arm in arm through the village in broad daylight – did bundling come to an end.

But there was one night in the year when all the sexual laws of peasant society were suspended. The shortest Midsummer Night. This exception had its roots in the fertility rites of the heathen millennia. In the days when our forefathers still worshipped the god of fertility they had celebrated Midsummer as a festival of nature, with an uninhibited sensual joy. Afterwards it was Christianized – as far as possible. The image of the fertility god was shattered, and the cross raised in his stead. But the Church did not entirely succeed in transforming this festival of nature, with all its magic, into St John the Baptist's Day. In the popular mentality it was altogether too deeply rooted in immemorial custom. Some heathen cults showed a remarkable capacity for survival. Even if their origins have been forgotten they have persisted down the ages.

An unwritten law applied to all young people: no one went to bed on Midsummer Night. And while it lasted actions were permitted which during other nights of the year were strictly forbidden. One of these, in all certainty, was the sexual act. During the night of the solar festival the moral code was suspended. 'Midsummer Night is not long, but it sets many a cradle rocking' says an old saw, certainly justified by experience.

During the village's work feasts, too, relations between the sexes became more free and easy, in a way that apparently deviated from the rules of official morality. A note on one Blekinge parish mentions a custom which obtained at its '*brytegille*': the young man and maiden who in the course of the day's labours had worked on the same '*bråta*' (pile of timber) should pass the night in the same bed. A local history from Västergötland relates the following. At a wedding it was the general custom to make up common beds for the young folk, as for brothers and sisters, during the three nights of the '*brytegille*'. No mention is here made of any requirement that the young people – as in their nightly bundlings – should remain clothed. From Delsbo, the 18th-century theologian Samuel Ödmann tells of a wedding at which he had himself been a guest. Afterwards, together with other young men, he went to a sleeping-cottage ('*sovstuga*') where 'brother-and-sister beds had been made up, and all the girls were already abed, with room for one boy between each'.

As far as I know, no one has yet made a methodical study of sexual life and manners in peasant society; nor indeed is there enough material to entice a thesis-writer. On the other hand, though I believe most writers have romanticized its realities, the subject has been a favourite theme for poets and novelists. In his poem on his forefathers, Erik Axel Karlfeldt has beautifully depicted their love-life. It seems to have been virtually ideal:

> In the springtime of life they kissed their girls.
> One became their faithful bride.

But in his diaries Johannes Rudbeckius, a 17th-century Bishop of Vasterås, gives us a more nuanced picture of the moral state of affairs in the see where Karlfeldt's ancestors had lived. The bishop mentions many offences of whoredom which had occurred among the people of Västmanland and Dalarna. Fornication, i.e., extra-marital intercourse between the sexes, is one of this watchful ecclesiastic's greatest headaches. He notes an astounding number of exceptions to the virtuous life-style for which our poet praises his forefathers.

We have, too, many well-documented cases of assault and battery, drunkenness and fornication in peasant society. Old court rolls mention breaches of the Sixth Commandment, 'Thou shalt not covet another man's wife', more frequently than breaches of the Seventh, 'Thou shalt not steal'. The punishments for fornication were harsh; but legislation against nature's gift of a strong sexual instinct have always been of limited effect. The threat of eternal punishment and the torments of hell, held perpetually over his parishioners' heads by the clergyman, probably had greater effect on people's way of life.

I have already discussed the positive aspects of the village community, and they are worth commemorating. But such a society must not be viewed through a romantic haze. There is no basis for such a view. Nowhere in the past do we find a popular golden age. Our ancestors revealed a hardiness and strength of character in a tough existence which can tempt us to overlook the intermittent crudity of their behaviour. They were primitive people, and their daily life does not yield the stuff of moralistic tales suitable for inclusion in an elementary-school reader. Their way of life was saturated with prejudice and superstition. Nevertheless we must always bear in mind that these were unenlightened folk, a race of illiterates, and that their prejudices and superstition were the fruits of their environment. Their breaches of God's Ten Commandments were numerous. The astonishing thing is that they were not even more common.

I wish neither to praise nor condemn the generations who lived in that peasant society. Only to understand them.

*

'The fundamental notion of human collaboration and common interest on which the *byalag* is based seems to me so timeless that it could well be realised even in our latter-day environments.'

This sentence is to be read in the first part of this work. I wrote it a few years ago: Even before then the *byalag*, in a few tentative instances, had been seeking its modern form in Stockholm and these experiments had turned out successfully. In the three years which have passed since then, the idea has been put into serious practice in many of our cities and communities. It has been the young who have taken the lead in setting up these new *byalag*. To those who are young today and still have life with all its possibilities before them, who want to seize them and make themselves the masters of their own destiny, it is a natural, obvious development.

The generation which is now growing up has begun to be aware of the sort of existence which awaits people in industrialized and mechanized society, a society of technocrats and bureaucrats. The older generation has created for them a society in which cars, killing on an average four people every day, have taken up so much space that in the near future there will soon be no room left in our cities for human beings. Meanwhile our Swedish countryside, perhaps the richest and most varied in Europe, is being irrevocably destroyed for all futurity. In our national anthem we Swedes acclaim Sweden's 'meadows green'; but today the dark clouds of sulphur oxide which hang over these fields forbode their death.

There are many signs that today's youth do not accept the great city as an environment to live in and wish they were back in the little country town or village. This is a healthy reaction. Youth has realised that people can survive without the automobile, but not without breathing unpoisoned air. As a result of this insight the *byalag* has been resurrected in a new form. Its goal is a society at whose centre the human being shall take his rightful place.

In this respect the old peasant village community was a model, especially in the strong human fellowship, both at work and in its feasts, which made life's burdens easier to bear. It knew nothing of environmental ravages; its air was not polluted; nor did it have to combat pollution in its waters. No one had to measure the percentage of poison in the air they breathed. No one was afraid to eat the fish from its clear lake and stream waters. The village council had other pre-occupations than those of its 20th-century successors.

What I wrote about the idea of the *byalag* in Part I has brought in a great number of letters from my readers. Many of my correspondents assert that it is above all in the depopulated areas of Sweden that the idea ought to be applied. Such an association would look after the abandoned, the isolated and the helpless who have no say in the society whose citizens they are – a society arranged in such a way that they no longer understood, or even feel, they have a part to play in what is going on in their own country.

Recent experience of the state of affairs in the Swedish countryside at this moment of writing is suggestive of the tasks awaiting a modern *byalag*.

In 1970, in order to visit historic places in various parts of the country, I toured five provinces, namely Dalarna, Närke, Västmanland, Uppland and Småland, partly by bicycle. My experiences were everywhere identical, or anyway varied little from one province to another. My journey took me mainly through districts with small farms. Never on the road did I meet with a pedestrian; now and then a cyclist. But I was passed by several thousand cars. When I did not know my way there was no one to ask. After all I could not stop the motorists who were rushing past at top speed. Who then, should I enquire from? These roads were bare of any encounters between human beings.

So I had to enquire inside the houses. But everywhere the villagers' dwellings seemed empty and deserted. Out of doors not a soul was to be seen. No one was scything the meadow. The fields with their deciduous trees, once kept alive by cow-muzzle and scythe, had all disappeared. Nor was anyone at work in the ploughed fields, where clumps of spruces were spreading out.

I knock at the front door of the main building of a farmstead.* No one comes to open. I go on knocking – until it dawns on me that the house is uninhabited. Dark eyes of curtainless windows turn away the intruder.

I go on to the next house, and it is the same story. No one opens. No one is at home. At last, in the fourth or fifth cottage, the door opens. So someone must be living there. But from the occupant's speech and clothing I can see at once he is not from the village. Quite right, the man who has opened to me is a summer visitor, knows almost nothing, and can tell me nothing of the roads in the vicinity. In the next house lives another summer visitor. And when I ask these temporary villagers about the natives, the race of people who cultivated the village's lands and occupied it for something like a thousand years, I always get one of two answers: 1. They've abandoned their farmlands and moved out, or 2. They're dead.

Finally, in some other houses, I come across people who really do belong here and are still alive. But these are old men and old women,

---

* The typical Swedish farm or manor house consists of three buildings set on three sides of a square, detached as a precaution against fire. The '*manbyggnad*', or main building, is in the centre.—*Trans.*

none under sixty, most over seventy. And they tell me: 'We're the last people left in the village. And we're of an age when we can't have many years left. After us there'll be no one.'

When these old people have gone, the village will be quite dead. A thousand-year-old way of life will have vanished.

The Women Outside History

A great many of the people who made history are still visible to us, their latter-day descendants, frozen into bronze or marble. Their image, preserved in these indestructible materials, has escaped annihilation. They are statues, standing there for us to contemplate in their timeless elevation. But once they, too, were people of flesh and blood like ourselves, lived under the same sun as we do. But can we, as we stand in front of these statues, intuit any of life's own warmth or movement? For me these bronze and marble figures exude only the desolate chill of eternity.

Here stand the great dead, those who have done memorable things in various fields of life. The principle upon which these immortals have been selected is itself illustrative of certain approved patterns of greatness, and of each age's way of evaluating actions. But in itself this very mode of selection is almost a reason to ask ourselves: Did humanity in the past consist, then, only of *one* sex?

A year or so ago one of our magazines compiled an inventory of the Swedish capital's statues. It had found 44 statues of men, and only four of women. Eleven times as many men as women, that is, have been accorded the abiding dignity of bronze or marble.

By and large this ratio, 44:4, accurately mirrors the real state of affairs, though I should have thought that 44:2 would have been still nearer the truth. Few women's faces appear in Swedish history. They have not been able to distinguish themselves on the field of battle; nor, unless they have been reigning queens, have they had a seat in the Council of State. Women have been excluded from the council chamber, *riksdag* and government. In a few instances where, regrettably, male heirs to the throne were lacking, we have had to

206

make do with women as our monarchs. Only once was a woman ever elected to the throne – Queen Margareta – and she was a singularly happy choice.

True, two female personalities whose portraits I have already drawn, Saint Bridget and Queen Margareta of the Union, figure in our mediaeval history. To these should be added a third: Kristina Gyllenstierna, wife of Sten Sture the Younger. Not only does she have a niche in our history; she has even had a statue raised to her. After her husband's death she became famous for her brave defence of Stockholm against the Danes. Annalists concede to Fru Kristina a male intelligence, the highest honour, of course, any woman can aspire to.

In our history books her namesake, Queen Christina, has occupied a good deal of space, as she reigned over Sweden for ten years. But a lady like Ebba Brahe only features in Swedish history in a purely feminine capacity and then thanks to a man, King Gustavus Adolphus, who loved her in her youth. Agneta Horn was an unmarried 17th-century aristocrat who kept a remarkable diary that lives on in our literature. In memoirs from the period when Sweden was a great power we also encounter the wives of the fighting men. While their men were occupying important positions abroad they had authoritative tasks to carry out at home. In General Archibald Douglas' biography (1957) of his ancestor, the 17th-century Field Marshal Robert Douglas, we are confronted with a typical and most impressive representative of this class of women – the Field Marshal's wife, Hedvig Mörner. In her husband's absence – he was campaigning in many lands – she had many matters to attend to. After she had become a widow on May 28, 1662, the task of preparing a worthy funeral for her husband, in November of that year, occupied her for six whole months; just one instance of the sort of tasks that devolved on the wives of the military nobles in Sweden's age of political and military greatness.

But generally speaking representatives of the female sex chiefly appear in our history as the wives of kings. As far as we can see from the available sources, the lot of most queens who sat on the throne of Sweden was not a happy one. Gustav Vasa's first marriage was brief and unhappy: his queen died very young in circumstances which gave rise, as we have seen, to horrible rumours; and his third marriage was imposed on a sixteen-year-old girl whom he took away from her betrothed. Queen Maria Eleonora, Gustavus Adolphus' German spouse, was of an hysterical disposition. As the wife of a warrior king who neglected her, she had to pay heavily while allowing her husband 'the hero king' to fulfil his mission on the stage of world history.

Karl X Gustav (1654–1660) devoted himself even less to a calm domestic existence than Gustavus Adolphus did. Hardly had he been betrothed to the eighteen-year-old Princess Hedvig Eleonora of Holstein-Gottorp, than he set out for the war in Poland, in 1656. Nevertheless the couple met now and again; a son was born and the succession secured. The marriage had fulfilled its purpose. After the king's death Hedvig Eleonora survived until 1715, fifty-five years of widowhood. One of her main interests, we are told, was card-playing. As dowager queen she must certainly have found time hang heavy on her hands.

What a soldier-king's marital life could be like can be seen from Karl XI's marriage to the Danish princess Ulrika Eleonora, in 1680. The young king was exceedingly shy and in order to celebrate his wedding in peace and quiet he arranged for it to take place at Skottorp Manor in Halland, in the neighbourhood lay a military encampment, which he had to inspect! But Kärl was France's ally, and the French ambassador, Feuquières, was keeping an eye on his every step. In his despatch to Paris, Feuquières describes the King of Sweden's manner of passing his wedding night. By three in the morning he was out of the bridal bed, donning his uniform to ride out and inspect his troops.

It should be added, however, that Karl XI only fought one war, and that was enough to last him a lifetime. For the last eighteen years of his reign he was a friend of peace.

But his son Karl XII – or to give him his ever-renowned anglicized name Charles the Twelfth – prided himself on being wedded to his army. Such a marriage no doubt brought great happiness to whatever woman might otherwise have become his queen.

A queen who has excited the sympathy of historians is Charles' sister, Ulrika Eleonora. She occupied the throne for two years without leaving any mark on history. In his youth her husband, Fredrik I, had been a soldier, but his military interests subsequently gave place to an intense womanizing, which made people feel sorry for his wife. In his old age he wanted to act as commander-in-chief in a war against Russia, 1741–1743. But the king demanded so many and such costly conveniences for himself in the field – among other impedimenta he wished to take with him his mistress Hedvig Taube – that for economic reasons the government prevailed on him to stay at home. As it turned out, the defeat which followed in this war could hardly have been greater if the king had been permitted to charge at the head of his army.

The Danish-born wife of Gustav III (1771–1792), Sofia Magdalena, too, arouses intense sympathy in the reader. No marriage in which the man, as was the case here, takes no interest in the opposite sex can fail to be unhappily affected. But Gustav III's brother, Karl XIII, so far from being indifferent to women, loved all too many of them. His spouse, Hedvig Elisabeth Charlotta, one of the most neglected of our aristocratic women, consoled herself for her husband's notorious infidelities by keeping a diary, which has become a classic.

Karl XIV Johan – ex-marshal Bernadotte – was Sweden's last soldier king (1818–1844). His married life must have suffered from the circumstances that he had spent the greater part of his time in the field before becoming King of Sweden. Later on, when he had settled down on the Swedish throne, his queen, Désirée, also came to Sweden. After a short while she fled back to her native France, appalled, so we are told, by the Scandinavian climate and by the chill which pervaded the rooms of the palace in Stockholm – a chill, no doubt, not only of the kind measurable by a thermometer. At all events, Désirée stayed away for twelve years, bravely resisting any desire to visit her husband.

With one or two exceptions our Swedish queens have not been Swedes by birth; as a consequence, the Swedes, since the days of Gustav Vasa and his two younger sons, have not had a single king of pure Swedish blood. All our later queens have been imported from foreign dynasties. For the most part it has been German princesses who have been honoured with the task of procreating ours, the last time when this happened being in the 1930's. The women who have sat on the throne of Sweden, therefore, have been strangers in a strange land, with friends and relatives in another. For various reasons, mostly linguistic, they have led an isolated existence in their adopted country. As wives they seem mostly to have been neglected and, as human beings, unhappy.

But these women who, as queens and solely thanks to their husband's position have found a place in our history, are exceedingly few. Let me pass on to the women of the people, the soldiers' wives who stayed at home on the smallholding after their men had been conscripted for the wars. For these women are to be counted in their hundreds upon hundreds of thousands, a nameless mass, a vast unknown segment of the Swedish nation. Historians have ignored them. Swedish schoolchildren and students have never read a word about them in their history books. Nameless women, history has passed them by.

I try to imagine what the women's lot was like in a warlike nation. As I have already suggested in my chapter on the Vikings, their destiny was largely to *wait* – wives who went about their business at home, waiting for the return of their husbands and sons serving in the Swedish armies abroad. For years, for decades they waited. How could they do anything else? They could not vote against the war, or demonstrate – there was absolutely nothing they could do to bring their men home again. All they could do in their loneliness was – wait.

The longest waiting the women of Sweden ever had to endure was during the Great Nordic War, 1700–1721; therefore I will make a leap forward a couple of centuries in time, from the 16th century to the first decades of the 18th. In my journey through our history I take the liberty of moving to and fro across the centuries. That these soldiers' wives who had to stay at home had no contact whatever with their husbands during their long absence is a fact which should be stressed. The common soldier could not usually write letters, nor send any message home to his closest relatives. Year after year the war went on, and on their smallholding his wife had no means even of knowing whether her husband was still alive or not. Probably, once in a while, through the clergyman or the officers' families, she would receive news of the war and its more important events. No doubt in the age of Charles XII she would hear about the Swedes' great victories at Narva, Düna and Klissow, strange foreign-sounding places. But what chiefly interested her can hardly have been the success or otherwise of a campaign. What she wanted to know was – is my husband still alive?

Our military archives have preserved only a single letter from a private soldier. In this document from 1710 trooper Lars Rask of the Life Guards writes from Dorpat in the Baltic States to his wife Brita Johansdotter at Flista, in Götlunda, describing his predicament. He writes about comrades who have fallen. He has himself been seriously ill, but has recovered. Deeply moving is his complaint at having received no reply to his two letters. All his comrades have had news from home:

Since his letter is unique, I shall quote it in full:

> Most honoured D[earest] Wife and
> Most honoured D[earest] Parents.
> God with us.
> As time permits I can
> not let it pass, but I must
> write [to] my D.Wife and my
> M[ost] D[ear] Parents and my Master and Mistress
> And let you know that I am
> in good health God be praised, and
> horse and equipment are still
> intact God be praised, and I
> have been most sick but now
> God be praised am I well and hale;
> and many are sick and many
> are dead, but none in our troop
> other than Jöns Travare was killed at
> the first engagement and Arvas Ryttare of
> Valby died of sickness. 11 troopers are
> shot dead in our company.
> But I have written 2 times
> and never had a word, but
> I believe that God the all highest
> he will help us home to you
> this summer with Jesu's help, and I

intend before midsummer together with
my comrades to be in Sweden.
Greetings to my brother and his M[ost] D[ear] wife
and children and
Jon and his dear Wife.
All the troopers have had letters
except me and Erik.
God give us peace.
Dorpat the 29 March 1701   *Lars Rask.*

This letter-writer's hopes of his comrades and himself being home again 'before midsummer' that year were not to be realised. Trooper Rask could not know that the campaign was still only in its initial stages. His regiment would have far to ride before the enlisted men could return to their smallholdings. Twenty more years, twenty midsummer feasts, would pass by before peace came and they could again see their homeland.

God give us peace – the last words of the only letter home we know of, written by a Swedish private soldier. Comment is supererogatory. As a Carolinian portrait it comes closer to the truth, I believe, than any other.

As I try to find my way back to the past, to my forefathers' destinies and the circumstances under which they lived, I pause before those people who once trod the same soil as myself and who therefore arouse my keenest curiosity. This fellow-feeling for our ancestors first came to me before a 17th-century soldier's cottage which I have discovered. Old enlistment rolls preserved in the War Office archives gave me the name of the soldier who was serving for ward (*rote*)* no. 132 Moshultamåla at the outbreak of the long period of hostilities in 1700. His name was Anders Swensson. And he was the occupant of the soldier's cottage where, two hundred years later, I was born; the same little plot of land on which I took my first steps. Here I shall not write of my own antecedents; but the information we have on this private soldier is documented and

---

* A *rote* was a unit of one hundred homesteads, together responsible for providing and maintaining one soldier or seaman with his equipment. He lived in a *soldattorp* or soldier's cottage, specially provided for him and his family. *Transl.*

incontrovertible. It is illustrative of the history of the Swedish people.

The earliest of the sources known as the *General Mönster Rulla* (General Muster Roll) are from 1683, the year when Karl XI first inspected the Calmare Regemente – the Kalmar Regiment. It formed a section of the *indelningsverk* – the regional system of recruitment – which the king declared would remain 'unshakable for all futurity'. At the outbreak of war in 1700, No. 132 Swensson, who belonged to the Konga Company of the regiment, was mobilized and put to sea. The navy transported him overseas to Cureland on the East Baltic coast. Afterwards he and his unit took part in Charles XII's triumphal march through Europe, through Poland, Saxony and Russia – until he reached Poltava, where it came to an end. At the battle, which in 1709 put paid to Sweden's imperial epoch, almost every man of the Kalmar Regiment fell. Therefore it had to be recruited afresh. Three days later the few soldiers of the regiment who had survived its annihilation were taken prisoner at Perevolotjna, where the entire army capitulated.

Soldier No. 132, Anders Swensson from Moshultamåla ward, was one of those who escaped with their lives at Poltava. But not with their liberty – his march went on, this time as a prisoner-of-war into Siberia. There he spent thirteen years in captivity. Not until the spring of 1722 did this enlisted man return to his soldier's smallholding. Whereupon he was found to be no longer 'serviceable' and naturally enough, after all he had been through in the last twenty-two years, was classed as 'useless'. He was given his papers and cashiered. The general muster roll which makes note of Anders Swensson, who 'had come home from captivity', adds: 'received the Royal War College's dismissal, 17 Aug. same year' (1722).

Being cashiered, he lost his smallholding, and another enlisted man moved in instead.

And that is all I know about private Anders Swensson, who held the same number in his regiment as my father was to do, almost two hundred years later.

But Anders Swensson had a wife; and about her neither I nor anyone else knows anything at all, not even so much as her name. No military documents record it. The General Muster Roll had no interest in soldiers' wives. Their business in wartime was simply to stay at home, run the smallholding, and look after the children.

But Wife Swensson once lived in a cottage on the hillock in the forest where I first saw the light of day; I know the surroundings and can imagine what life was like for her during the twenty-two years her husband was abroad, defending the fatherland.

One day in 1700, the first year of the new century, she stood on the stone doorstep of the soldier's cottage, bidding Anders farewell. Around them they had their children. She remained standing on the slope where the cottage stands until she had seen her husband disappear along the path up by the meadow. Then she went into the house, shut the door, blew her children's noses as they asked her where father had gone, and told them to pull themselves together. After which she resumed not only her usual chores, but also her husband's. Who else would have?

And she waited. She waited as she worked on the ploughed fields around her cottage where her bread was growing, she waited as she did the haymaking on the great meadow by the Bjurbäcken stream, from which she brought in her cow's winter fodder. In the springtime, when the pike spawned, she fished in the stream. And when the autumns came she picked lingonberries in the fenced woodland meadow and boiled them into a mash. All year round she had the children with her as she worked out of doors. They were too small to be left in the cottage.

In the winters, when the only outdoor work she could do was to chop wood and stack it in the shed and feed and milk the cow, she had time to work indoors. Then she spun flax and tow yarn for the peasants of the ward, which helped her to keep her family alive. Payment was made *in natura*, in bread and something to put on it: perhaps a pound of pork for five times its weight of spun yarn. Women who did such work were called spinstresses, and some of the common people's jingles have survived concerning their terms of payment:

> Monday and Tuesday the spinstress span,
> Wednesday and Thursday with chips she ran;
> Friday and Saturday she ate up her pay;
> On Sunday she goes to the church to pray.

During the dark winters there was little daylight for the women to sit at their spinning wheel, and illumination was always a problem. Either they had to sit close to the fireplace and spin by the light from the flames, or else be put to the expense of candles. Another jingle runs:

> When the candle's burnt down
> And the woman has spun,
> Much more she has lost than she's won.

The years passed away, as they had always done since the beginning of time; and as each new year began Wife Swensson thought to herself: 'This year Anders'll be back.'

But no letter ever reached her from her husband, never a word. Knowing he could not write, she expected no letters. It was for him she was waiting.

Sometimes people got news of the war through the parish priest. But it was mostly rumour, and often totally untrue. When the first news of Poltava arrived, the battle – which had put paid to the Swedish Empire – was made out by the royal propaganda to have been a victory. Not until after a long lapse of time was the nation told what had really happened. And not until peace had at last been concluded did the women whose husbands had been in the Kalmar Regiment learn that the regiment had been annihilated, long ago, in 1709, twelve years earlier, and with it their husbands.

In this way Wife Swensson waited for her Anders for twenty-two long years. And many times she looked down the road to see if he was coming along it. Then, one spring day in 1722, here he comes, walking among the trees in the meadow. Since 1700 there has been a great change in his appearance. His thirteen years in Siberia, more especially, have left their mark on him. It is a strange reunion. At first she doesn't even recognize him; she has to look at him again and again. It had been a young man who had left his wife behind. It is an old man who has come back to her.

And the soldier has come home to an old woman.

In defence of his fatherland, his own part of the country, he has been thousands of miles away; even, in the end, deep into the Ukraine. Meanwhile his wife has been living out her solitary lonely life. And now, when at long last he has come home, it is only to be cashiered. Anders is unfit for further military service. So he and his wife are evicted from their home.

Such, amid a warlike people, could be a woman's destiny. How many other families shared the same fate as the Swenssons of Ward 132, Moshultamåla, Konga Company, the Royal Kalmar Regiment?

The history of Sweden's wars, viewed from inside the soldiers' cottages, still remains to be written.

I have paused a moment before a vanished race of people. But in the forest regions which make up the greater part of Sweden we find traces of them in a countryside whose very soil is a state archive of incontrovertible evidence. Its memories of them have never been distorted or falsified. The little hillside cottage, that monument to a long-forgotten habitation, is only susceptible to one interpretation: *Here lived human beings.*

Often, the traces of this extinct race are to be found deep in the forest. In some little glade or on a small hillock a few grey stones, laid out in a rectangle, are still visible above the ground. Long ago these uncut and untrimmed stones were laid out here to provide foundations for a cottage; a primitive shack whose floor, often, was only the bare earth. The rectangle's dimensions enable us to assess the size of the dwelling.

Nearby, usually on the fringe of the forest, can be seen another trace of the cottagers who once lived here: a little cairn, overgrown with moss and nettles. Here the cottagers had their baking oven. But the monument which speaks most vividly to my imagination is a little hollow, not far from the cottage's foundations. Whether dried out or still full of water, it, too, is documentary evidence. Here was the cottagers' well, where they once drew their water. A well-spring in every sense, it gives rise to vivid images of those women's lives and labours.

Water is indispensable to human life. Nothing replaces it. And it was the women, who carried the water home on their shoulders in buckets slung from a yoke. In winter's biting cold they had to trudge through deep snowdrifts, a circlet of icicles forming round the folds of their skirts. Slipping and stumbling on the ice, bowed against the gale, soaked by autumn rains and sweating in the summer heats, or fumbling their way through the winter darkness, they brought up their heavy buckets from the well to the cottage. In youth they walked erect. Shouldering their yoke they went with swift healthy strides down the path and came back again. But under the heavy weight of their wooden pails, the women's backs, as the years went by, became bent and crooked. On ever slower footsteps they went their laborious way, leaving the cottage's warmth for the rain and cold. This brought on rheumatism, pains in limbs and muscles. The torment fell on them. Arms and legs grew stiff. The pail hung ever more heavily from the yoke.

Slowly the young women turned into worn-out old crones who bore their watery burden on trembling swollen legs and painful feet. Silent and taciturn, to and fro they went with their buckets between the well and the cottage, to the end. Calm and reticent they ended their days, and their old bodies, bent and grimed with charcoal, were placed in a coffin and laid to rest in forgotten graves. No monuments have ever been raised to their life-work.

One such half-overgrown hollow, marking the site of a well deep in the forest, moves me more deeply than all the others. Here a cottage once stood. Its occupant was Private Nils Thor, who served for Rörshult ward in my home parish. He was my great grandfather. He was married to Lisa Jakobsdotter, with whom he had ten children. Known in the village as 'Thora-Lisa', his wife is said to have been a '*hurk*' woman, i.e., strong, self-willed and mannish. Hers was the woman's lot I have just depicted. On this spot, during the greater part of her life, she carried her pail from the well to the cottage.

I have also discovered some written evidence about Thora-Lisa Jakobsdotter, my great-grandmother. To the entry giving her date of death the parish register adds a few words: *Found dead on the ground.*

When I think of her it is always on her way from the well, with her pail of water. It is there I imagine she collapsed.

Such a death has nothing glorious about it. Identical with hundreds of thousands of others it was not in the least remarkable, merely the fulfilment of a woman's fate. Indeed it was quite ordinary – all too ordinary, too universal, to attract the interest of historians; too commonplace to be worth recording. Such, in times past, was the lot of altogether too many Swedish women – which is why Wife Swensson, Lisa Jakobsdotter and all their sisters in misfortune have found no place in our history books.

The men went abroad to wreck other men's lives. The women stayed at home to preserve life. But it was the men's exploits which, on wings of fame, flew out across the world. No one noted the women's, no one recorded the names of those who had stayed at home to care for the race.

The Dacke Rising –
Our Greatest Popular Revolt

From forest thief to the idol of modern youth

To my chapter heading should be added three words: 'against
native oppressors'. The Engelbrekt rising had been a revolt
against a foreign power, against the rule of Danish bailiffs.
The Dacke rising was a freedom movement aimed at the rule of their
Swedish successors; a civil war between two estates, Swede fighting
Swede, nobleman against commoner. This difference between the
two revolts has been crucial to our historians' way of seeing them.
The first rebellion they have regarded as justified. The second, not.
In the nationalist view, Engelbrekt's triumphal progress was a
blessing; so, seen from the same angle, was Dacke's defeat – for it
was against a native overlord, the founder of our Swedish national
state, that the Småland peasants revolted. And this has settled their
posthumous reputation. 'Incontrovertibly it was fortunate for
Sweden that he (Dacke) failed', writes Gottfrid Carlsson.

Our latest professional historian to carry out research into Dacke,
Dr. Lars-Olof Larsson, declares that 'surprisingly enough, we have
no modern all-round scientific account of the Dacke rising'. But
this is perfectly natural, exactly what one would expect from the
evaluations which, right up to our own day, have been our historians'
lodestone. Not until the last few decades has research demonstrated
that this insurrection, led by the crown-cottager Nils Dacke from
Flaka, was a real popular revolt, the biggest in Swedish history.
Dacke had a majority of the Småland population behind him, as
well as a large part of the population of Östergötland, and the
struggle lasted for more than a year. Not until Gustav Vasa had

mobilized all the nobility's men-at-arms throughout the entire kingdom, called in Danish auxiliaries and recruited 6,000 men in Germany, was he finally victorious. So I should like to ask: Which side were the true nationalists?

Compared with Dacke's freedom movement, the three Dalecarlian revolts against the king seem to have been no more than riots. Only Dacke's insurrection constituted a real threat to Gustav's new monarchy.

Anyone who sets out to write the history of the Dacke rising in terms of an overall new and radical view of history, therefore finds himself on virgin soil. He keeps coming up against a host of un-answered questions and obscure unexplored connections between one fact and another. All this obliges him to do his own research. I have tried to form an independent idea of my own concerning this great popular revolt. As long as I can remember – for natural reasons – the subject has fascinated me; for it was precisely in my own part of the country, in the hundreds of Möre, Konga and Uppvidinge, that the flames of revolt were first lit. As a schoolboy my imagination ran riot around Odhner's account of this rebel who was hunted down through the forests of my own countryside by the king's soldiers, until 'in Rödeby Forest they caught up with him and shot him through with arrows'.

I have tried to understand why my forefathers joined Dacke in his revolt, and I shall try to describe their struggle, their sufferings, and the catastrophe which befell our Småland countryside. Although I have been gathering materials for the task for the last forty years, I am far from happy with the results. Dacke's peasants were mostly illiterate. They have left no records. They composed no chronicles of their struggle. From Dacke's side the documents are few and meagre. It was left to the king's party to write the history of the revolt, and this confronts research with an almost insoluble problem: historians can only hear one party in the case. Nevertheless, in local history, I have found much valuable material not yet exploited by our national historians; likewise in still living folk-tradition; naturally my account is based on the latest professional research.

What really happened? And why, and how? These are the eternal questions always confronting the critic of source materials, questions to which he can never arrive at a certain or unambiguous answer that excludes all others. All he can do is choose between the various *possible truths* offered him by the sources. I have made my own – a layman's – choice. Another writer might well choose otherwise.

The portrait of Nils Dacke to be found in our history books is in the main the portrait drawn by Gustav Vasa and by the three chroniclers who have written about his reign: his nephew Per Brahe, the royal secretary Rasmus Ludvigsson, and Erik Göransson Tegel, son of Göran Persson, King Erik XIV's secretary and adviser, of evil repute. It is the portrait of a forest thief. As the king depicts him, Dacke was not even a human being. He was a beast, a monster: 'a gross beast and forest spirit, little better than a soulless animal.' The word here translated 'forest spirit' ('*skogsäle*') means a heathen spirit created by the Devil and sent out into the world to seduce and destroy Christian men. This monster resided in holes and hiding places in the forest, to the ineffable terror of the population. Its name was therefore the most horrifying label the king could apply to Nils Dacke, the rebel leader.

In the king's first letter, dated July 3, 1542, in which he writes at length about the revolt that had just broken out in Småland, he calls the participants 'a mob of forest thieves'. This way of seeing his rebellious subjects he reinforces, in his later missives, with such expressions as 'scoundrels', 'criminals', 'traitors' and 'murderers'. Hardly an opprobrious epithet exists which Gustav Vasa does not fling at their leader. Not only is Nils Dacke a thief: he is a great scoundrel, a heretic, an assassin, an incestuous whoremonger. Hardly a single major crime exists but the king includes it among his offences. Gustav's repertoire of invective was rich indeed; and he brought it all to bear on Nils Dacke.

By his letters to the peasantry in the restive hundreds the Most Puissant, High-Born Prince and Most Christian Lord, King Gustav I, did his best to inspire loathing for the rebels' leader. But this time, as subsequent events were to show, his eloquent penmanship was to avail him nothing. The peasants of Möre, Konga, Uppvidinge and elsewhere elected to follow the 'forest thief'.

In what follows we shall see Gustav's and the royal chroniclers' lists of Dacke's crimes for what they were: namely, special pleadings. But for almost four centuries more or less all our historians' assessments of the Dacke rising have succumbed to their influence. A victor writes not only his own history but also that of the vanquished. Dacke himself is not permitted to speak. He can neither defend nor explain either his motives or his actions. His tongue has been silenced for ever. The maxim 'truth wins out in the end', as applied to history, is the greatest lie ever printed.

Even if one or another among our older historians feels a certain sympathy for his revolt against Gustav Vasa's régime, most of them see Dacke as a criminal and a rebel. A popular historian like Anders Fryxell, one might have thought, would have judged him less categorically. But even he calls Dacke 'a horribly wicked man'. The fact is, the rebel was also a protagonist of the Catholic cause, and this may have had a certain influence on the Lutheran dean's view of him. In imaginative literature, too, the 'forest thief' has survived up to our own day. At best he becomes a sort of Robin Hood. In literature it was in a novel by Ivar Ljungquist, *Nils Dacke* (1927), that he began to be re-evaluated. Here the Dacke rising is seen in its proper historical context: as a conflict between the province and the kingdom, a struggle of the peasant republic of Småland against the national monarchy, a struggle whose outcome was doomed from the beginning. The Värend folk are crushed by the central authorities in Stockholm. Ljungquist's account is based on a profound knowledge of time and place. Next to Fabian Månsson's works, which appeared later, this is the best book on the subject in our literature, outside the works of the professional historians.

His essay on the life of the peasant leader prior to the insurrection makes Gerhard Hafström, a historian of law, the pioneer of Dacke research. In the new materials presented by Hafström, the footpad and forest thief who lived by murder and plunder disappears and in his stead appears a man of superior peasant stock who, for political reasons, had 'gone to the forest' and whose deeds of violence are a reaction to the insufferable tyranny of bailiffs. This student declares that among the 'woodsmen' were 'men from the district's leading families'. Dacke was no footpad. Materials found by Hafström show him in fact to have sprung from a family of wealthy and powerful border peasants.

A modern historian who has continued this new line in Dacke research in a popular-scientific work is Dr Alf Åberg. He gives the peasant leader the most positive obituary so far. Åberg compares Dacke to the greatest of our freedom-fighters: 'From these materials a free-born peasant, cunning, combative and indomitable, a leader among his peers. A Småland Engelbrekt, steps forth.' As far as I know, Åberg is our only professional historian to see the 'forest thief' in this light.

The latest sizeable scientific study of the Dacke rising is a major academic thesis by Lars-Olof Larsson (*Det medeltida Värend*, 1964), a Lund historian who comes from Dacke's own part of the country. Here appear, for the first time, some hitherto unknown source materials which must considerably change our notions of the insurrection's spread. Many aspects, however, remain to be researched.

Just how controversial a figure in Swedish history Nils Dacke still is can be seen from a dispute which broke out at Växjö in 1955, when it was proposed to raise a monument to him. The city council had allocated funds for a monumental sculpture by Carl Milles.

The statue was to have been erected in the main square, facing the governor's residence. The artist produced a sketch of his monument which showed Dacke reposing under a spruce tree. He called it *Dacke dreaming*. Milles explained that his inspiration was derived from a tale about Dacke's flight, in which he had been 'stripped, had his clothes stolen, and was left lying in the forest. It can be a beautiful sight, to see him lying there, dreaming'. In this vision of the wanted man, resting there under a spruce tree, the sculptor wished to embody mankind's ageless dream of freedom, both in the Middle Ages and today. And this was the interpretation Milles wished people to place on his work.

The upshot was a furious quarrel, partly of a political nature. Conservative voices were heard, protesting loudly that to place a monument to a 'rebel' in front of the governor's residence in the county capital would be an act of provocation, an insult to the King of Sweden. Other opponents to the scheme objected to the work on aesthetic grounds. Scorn was poured on Milles' Dacke, lying there snoring. Milles defended his sketch for his work and told everyone how fine it would look when finished.

In the end the city council allowed the matter to drop, and the work was never carried out. Not long afterwards Carl Milles died.

The following year, however, in 1956, Nils Dacke got his statue. Elsewhere in his own province, in the community of Virserum, he stands erect, battle-axe in hand, his crossbow on his shoulder. It was near this place, in March 1543, his revolt suffered its decisive defeat. Four hundred and thirteen years later he has returned in triumph.

To the authorities, to civil servants, politicians and all who wield power in the kingdom of Sweden, Nils Dacke is still a controversial personage. No jubilees celebrate his insurrection. Nor is his name – unlike Engelbrekt's – considered a suitable citation for official occasions. When the King of Sweden visits Växjö, Kalmar or some other part of Småland no one reminds him that he is in Dacke country, a part of the realm which once revolted.

But for the inhabitants of that countryside Nils Dacke's name is far from controversial, nor has it ever been. True, for a whole century after his revolt (as we see from the court rolls) it was a name uttered only at the speaker's peril. But Dacke's memory was preserved and silently revered by the common man. Dacke found a place in legend and anecdote. In time he became a kind of myth. Today, Nils Dacke's popularity is great among the inhabitants of his own part of the country. Just how highly the district esteems him can be seen in the commercial uses to which his name is being put – we bake Dacke Bread, brew Dacke Beer, make Dacke Sausage, run in the Dacke Race, and play football on the Dacke Field. At Virserum there is a Hotel Dacke, and not far away a Dacke Ski-Jump. Clubs, societies and associations all bear his name. But the Småland Tourist Association has still not exploited the insurgent to the same extent that Dalarna has exploited Gustav Vasa, Dacke's enemy.

Småland students rate him high, something they never used to do. The newspaper published by the Småland Nation* for its

* Students at Swedish universities do not belong to colleges but to mediaeval-style 'nations'. *Transl.*

members at Lund University is called the *Dacke-Kuriren*. The Småland Nation has also built a large and roomy student hostel and named it Dackegården, where it annually holds a Dacke Ball at which evening dress is *de rigeur*. Members of the Småland Nation at Uppsala, too, have opened their own Dacke Night Club, and hope his name will attract clients.

Though not based, perhaps, on any profound knowledge of his great insurrection among the Småland peasantry, there is also an academic cult of Nils Dacke. I have read the script of a play about him, written by a young academic. Here the crown smallholder from Flaka is represented in the guise of a modern communist leader, the prototype being Che Guevara, the Cuban freedom-fighter. Of course there are superficial parallels between the careers of the Cuban and the Swede. Both led freedom movements. Both were defeated. And both sacrificed their own lives in the struggle. But their political goals were utterly different. Che Guevara fought to establish a new society and bring freedom to a people who have never known it. Dacke fought to preserve an old one and to recover the immemorial liberties of his people, of which Gustav Vasa had deprived them. In his extreme peasant individualism Nils Dacke must even seem reactionary. Revolutionary goals change with the passage of time and changing society. Yet the two men do have one quality in common: their indomitable love of freedom.

Parallels between 20th-century political ideologies and this 16th-century Swedish peasant rising can therefore easily seduce us into misunderstanding the latter's nature. It all depends, of course, what one means by 'freedom'. But as a spontaneous liberation movement, as a struggle for elementary human rights, the Dacke rising still possesses actuality, is a timeless revolution.

And this is why Nils Dacke has become popular with today's radical and rebellious youth. His very name suggests the rebel: its hard consonants, suggestive of defiance, indomitable will, every stiff-necked quality one can think of, rings out defiantly.

No figure in Swedish history has been so variously assessed as Nils Dacke. After four hundred years this 'forest thief' has become the idol of the young.

Guerilla fighter and crown-cottager

Who, then, in real life, was Nils Dacke? Of the *person* behind this name our knowledge is extremely scanty. I have already shown how little we know about Engelbrekt. About Dacke we know even less. At least we know that Engelbrekt was short of stature. Concerning the Smålander's appearance, though he has been depicted by a peasant painter on the plank wall of a cottage at Hovby, in Östergötland, we have no certain knowledge at all.

But one fact, at least, has been established by modern research. Dacke was a very different sort of man from the one presented to posterity by Gustav Vasa and the 16th-century chroniclers. Gerhard Hafström calls the king's image of him 'exceedingly doubtful'. Accounts preserved in the Public Record Office reveal that Dacke came from a large peasant family which owned farms on both sides of the Småland-Blekinge frontier, but which was mainly concentrated in the Småland hundred of Södra Möre. One of Nils' uncles, Olof Dacke, owned the homestead of Lindö, in Möre. The leader of the insurrection himself came from the allodiary peasants of Värend – peasants, that is, who owned their lands absolutely, and who in no sense were subject to any landlords. In the Late Middle Ages they had become relatively wealthy from the large-scale export of cattle across the border.

Gustav Vasa alleged against the peasant leader that he was a foreigner, born in Blekinge, where he had his 'traitorous family'; an attempt to exploit anti-Danish feeling. The sources prove that the family had its roots on both sides of the border, and therefore demolish this allegation. Even Per Brahe states that Dacke was a Småland peasant, 'dwelling in Konga hundred'. But the question of which side of the frontier he was born on was utterly irrelevant to the thousands of peasants who joined his revolt. In the border country, as we have seen before, no distinction was drawn between Swede and Dane. It was the same folk who lived on either side of the frontier.

Both our great Swedish rebels, Engelbrekt and Dacke, make very brief appearances in history, the former for little more than two years, the latter for a little more than one. And both died violent deaths, the natural destiny of rebel leaders. We know no more about Dacke's youth and childhood than we do of Engelbrekt's, so we cannot follow his destiny until after he had reached years of manhood.

Two portraits in oils, both supposed to represent Nils Dacke, are extant, but since he did not sit for either they tell us nothing about what the living Dacke looked like. They are pure works of fantasy. Experts who have examined them are of the view that one was painted in the 16th century and the other in the 18th. Mainly they interest us as reflections of two wholly disparate historic views of Nils Dacke. The 16th-century portrait is a picture of a high-ranking chieftain, a knight wearing contemporary dress. He wears both the sword and the chain of chivalry, all knightly emblems. By contrast, in the 18th-century painting, the work of the celebrated court painter Pilo, we see Gustav Vasa's 'forest thief'. Here Dacke's physiognomy is wily and cunning. It is the face of a criminal. A writer in the newspaper *Stockholmsposten* in 1822, who had just seen this painting, declares that Dacke 'looks like a crafty criminal'.

In art, therefore, Dacke has survived both as knight and as bandit.

It is after 1535 or 1536 – the year is uncertain – when Nils Dacke made his first guerilla attack on a bailiff, that we can begin to follow his life in outline. By this time he was married, and his wife – whose name was Gertronsdotter – came from another of the district's respected clans, the Gertrons. During the resurrection the sources speak of him having a son, 'a boy of ten years', who was captured by Gustav Vasa. Dacke may be supposed to have married at about the age of twenty-five, the usual age of first marriage for the sons of peasants. This would mean that when he makes his first appearance on the stage of history he is a man in the prime of life, aged at most thirty-five.

Since Dacke's youth and childhood are obscure, we do not know whether he had any book-learning. The question whether he could read and write – so experts whom I have consulted declare – cannot be decided with certainty. In those days the sons of prosperous peasants were sometimes educated by the parish priest or by the monks in some monastery; and it is possible that the boy Nils, who came from the highly respected Dacke family, attended such a school. But there is no evidence to show he could read and write. Gustav Vasa has left us several thousand letters; Nils Dacke, putatively, only one. But no document survives that bears his signature.

The State Archives do contain a contemporary letter bearing his 'mark'. This typically peasant-like signature with the mark looks like this:

But after the revolt had broken out, its leader had literate persons around him to write his letters. Catholic priests who had joined him for religious reasons were particularly helpful. Lars-Olof Larsson gives the names of three rectors who were his faithful adherents: Thord of Älghult, Karl of Åseda, and Rolf of Nöbbele. But there were many others. So we have no words from Dacke's own hand to help us form an idea of his character, and the utterances attributed to him in the sources, too, are meagre in the extreme. Therefore we can only judge him by his actions. And they yield us a convincing picture of an indomitable rebel.

In a 19th-century reference work we can read of the man 'who shook the throne of Gustav I': 'He was suited to be a popular agitator in an age of savagery and ruin; the worst among the rebels found in him their peer'. Dacke's own men would have taken this assessment as high praise. At the negotiations with the king's commander-in-chief, Gustav Olofsson Stenbock, at Bergkvara in July 1542, the latter demanded that the peasants should hand Dacke over to him. They replied that they had every confidence in their leader and would follow him: 'Dacke was a good man, who always desired the commons' best'. This certificate of the commons for their chieftain is quoted by Rasmus Ludvigsson, whose sympathies cannot have been with the rebel leader.

In his chronicle Per Brahe calls Nils Dacke 'a weak traitor', and the royal party accused him of cowardice 'in open battle'. Yet we know of no occasion when he played the coward. Throughout the rebellion, if the sources are to be believed, Dacke marched at the head of his peasants. Even when he stood alone, abandoned by all, he did not give up the fight.

Without question Nils Dacke had many of the qualities needed in a great popular leader. He could measure the extent of his power in his enemies' fear of him. Just how afraid Gustav Vasa was of Nils Dacke is obvious from all the king's attempts to get him into his clutches, as we shall see shortly. On one occasion the king proposed to his Council that the leader of the insurgents should be got out of the way by assassination. Gustav Vasa was fully aware of Dacke's importance as the very soul of the freedom movement. It was Dacke who kept the forces together, playing the same rôle in the Småland insurrection as Engelbrekt had in his.

So we can understand how great was Gustav Vasa's relief when, one day in August 1543, the news reached him that Nils Dacke was dead.

The Dacke rising seems to have had its origins in the disturbances which occurred in the border country during the so-called Counts' War, in the first years of the 1530's. Even at that date we hear of murders of royal bailiffs, and it has been established that from the middle of the decade onwards Dacke was acting as a guerilla leader. At least this is the best modern expression to describe his activities. He seems to have been the ablest partisan leader, and the most successful, in all Swedish history. But during the great uprising he became more than that. Leading whole armies into pitched battles, he waged a full-scale war. In an essay Professor Arthur Stille, a conservative military historian who has given an account of the military operations during the rising, recognizes Dacke's abilities as a field commander. More especially he praises Dacke for his tactics. As a commander of troops Dacke was a man who had to educate himself from scratch; yet against royalist commanders who were professionals and old hands at the game he acquitted himself admirably. He had received his training as a guerilla fighter. This

Värend peasant had had practical experience of forest warfare. King Gustav's aristocratic colonels had not.

Lurking in the forests, mediaeval guerillas ambushed royal bailiffs and shot them down with their arrows. As a form of warfare it was cruel and ruthless; yet not so cruel as modern warfare in Vietnam where pilots, themselves well protected, are indiscriminately murdering from great heights a defenceless peasant population, millions of men, women and children. The progress of technology has brought war to the utmost limits of barbarism, compared with which mediaeval cruelties seem almost child's play, ham-fisted in their primitivity. But it was the best men could do with the lethal instruments they then possessed.

Six or seven years before the insurrection broke out Nils Dacke had taken part in the murder of a bailiff. This murder has been regarded as a prelude to the revolt. Dacke was then living on Södra Lindö farm in Torsås parish, Möre hundred. In company with Jon Andersson, an allodiary peasant from the border country, he shot down and killed Inge Arvidsson, a royal bailiff, in a forest near the state boundary. Their victim had long been hated by the Möre peasants for his outrages against the commons. Inge Arvidsson, that is to say, did not fall victim to a footpad or lawless poachers: he was killed by two of the district's peasants, two men of standing who came from the landowning peasantry. Their violent deed had been provoked by the bailiff's oppressive behaviour. This fact is important. It gives the Dacke rising its historical character.

After their deed Nils Dacke and Jon Andersson fled to the woods – that immemorial recourse of all men in their predicament. While living in the forest they could cross the frontier at will, into 'the other cottage', as the saying went. In the border forests, groups of discontented Smålanders – partisans – had come into existence. Fleeing from the countryside, they persistently harried the king's men.

Gustav Vasa decided to punish his disobedient and rebellious subjects. In 1537, he instituted a stringent razzia among them. This inquisition was led by no lesser a personage than the Earl Marshal, Lars Siggesson, who proceeded to deal rigorously with the commons of Värend and Möre. All peasants condemned for refusal to pay taxes or other crimes and unable to compound with a fine were seized by the bailiffs and flung into the dungeons of Kalmar Castle. Rasmus Ludvigsson writes: 'By the king's command, the stiff-necked and closely inter-married families along the borders of Blekinge were to be more harshly punished than the others'.

But this punitive expedition did not suffice. Instead of snuffing the flames of revolt it only fanned them, and a year after the king's razzia they burst out again. This time Dacke remained in the background. The leader was Jon Andersson. As yet Gustav Vasa had never so much as heard Dacke's name. In March 1538, the partisans sent the fiery cross into Värend, summoning the peasants to a council on the border. Against this incitement of the populace Ture Trolle, lord of Bergkvara and the chief nobleman of Småland, intervened with vigour and succeeded in suppressing the perilous fiery crosses. Instead, Trolle himself summoned the wrathful peasants to an assembly, and for the time being was successful in pacifying them. This time there was no revolt.

Obviously their attempts to raise a rebellion had failed; and equally obviously this was why Jon Andersson, Nils Dacke and eight others who had been involved in the action sought a reconciliation with the king. In August, 1538, an agreement was reached. Under its terms the rebels were to make good their offence by paying fines. Murder and manslaughter, though among the gravest crimes, did not necessarily entail forfeiture of the offender's life – unlike the theft of a horse or an ox, which usually led straight to the gallows.

According to extant documents specifying the fines paid, Nils Dacke and Jon Andersson now had to pay 40 oxen apiece for the murder, several years earlier, of Inge Andersson. Valued in cash, these expiatory oxen amounted to a heavy fine. The price of an ox at Kalmar was sixteen marks – at Ronneby, in Danish Blekinge, a good deal more. And this means that Dacke had to pay the king 640 marks. This would be about the value of a farm at that time, and was a very large sum indeed for a peasant to have to pay. 'Dacke lost all his property', one source declares.

Already, after his attack on the bailiff, Nils Dacke had 'gone to the woods' for two years, and probably been reduced to poverty. From one document it transpires that it was not Dacke himself who paid the fines on returning to the community, but his relatives. Such was the rule. The clan was responsible for most such expenses, which were known as 'clan fines'. A statement that for a while he had been imprisoned in Kalmar is of doubtful authenticity. Clearly, Dacke moved back to his old farm at Södra Lindö.

But only for a little while. After a year had passed he had left the homestead – probably because he had to – and moved to a crown small-holding on the frontier, where we find him during the last three years before the rising, 1539–42.

Nils Dacke's new abode, in those days called Flaka, today's Flaken, was one of the smallest farms in Torsås parish, an out-cropper's smallholding 'newly taken up and built upon'. The spot is incorrectly described as a crown homestead. Actually it was nothing but a crown outcropper's smallholding, so small that it was not even obliged to offer any 'hospitality'. A member of a highly respected family of self-owning peasants, that is to say, had sunk to the economic level of a backwoodsman, tilling rough newly cultivated crown land in the midst of a wilderness.

Flaka lies on the east bank of the Lyckeby river, just south of the point where it widens out into Lake Flakesjön. In Dacke's day the river constituted the frontier between Sweden and Denmark. Flaka being the last habitation on the Swedish side, its occupant could easily cross over to Denmark. The little farmstead is still in use. Flaka being so important and historic a place, and wishing to see for myself what sort of conditions Nils Dacke lived in during the last three years before the outbreak of our greatest popular revolt, I have paid it a visit.

The present owner of Flaken is an elderly farmer. He is keenly aware of the historic character of his homestead, and proud of it. An earlier owner, Gustaf Olsson, who was a juryman, was not. According to one student of local history in these parts, he was even ashamed of it, going so far as to deny that Dacke, that traitor and miscreant, had ever lived in his farmhouse. It was altogether too shameful a blot on his homestead's scutcheon.

The present owner, however, knows all about the Dacke traditions which still live on in the countryside all around. He spoke of Nils Dacke and Jon Andersson as if these men had been his contemporaries and daily associates; as if he had spoken to them only yesterday.

Today Flaken belongs to Rödeby parish, in Blekinge. But this farmer could show me exactly where the old frontier used to run. It had been only a stone's throw from Dacke's cottage. And he was familiar with all the legendary spots along the border mentioned in narratives and tales of the rising. Here had lived Jon Andersson, the rebel leader's neighbour and close friend, though in the end they became enemies. Here in a cave in the forest Dacke had lain hid when on the run from the king's soldiers. A mile or so from Flaken my guide pointed out the very spot where they finally caught up with him and shot him to death. Likewise the ancient cattle track along which, on a wooden sledge, his corpse was dragged to Kalmar.

My informant declared – certainly not quite truthfully – that he had never read a single word in any book about Nils Dacke's rebellion. All his information, he said, had been gleaned orally from old people in the district, who in turn had heard them from people who had been old when they were young, and who had heard them in *their* youth. In this way the story of the insurrection's leader had been passed on down the centuries, from generation to generation. In his own village the 16th-century crown cottager of Flaka is still a living legend.

Even from a cursory inspection of this farm it is obvious that today's Flaken is not a profitable smallholding. Four hundred years ago, when it had only newly been cultivated and had to be tilled by primitive methods, it was certainly even less so. The soil is thin and consists of shallow humus mingled with sand. The small ploughed fields are plentifully sprinkled with stones. This little holding lies in the 'kingdom of stones', as the district is called.

But the occupants of Flaka have been able to supplement their income with fish from the Lyckeby River, which flows close by. The upper reaches of this river flow through my home parish, and when I was a child had plenty of fish in them. In the Middle Ages they certainly had even more. Formerly, eel seems to have been the most important catch. And Professor Hafström has discovered documents from a legal dispute over eel-fishing rights in the Lyckeby River between Nils Dacke and a neighbour on the Danish side, which give us a tangible picture of the life led at Flaka by the future peasant leader.

Eel is a nutritious and much sought-after fish, and could be sold for a good price at the market town of Ronneby. Dacke's neighbour on the Danish side, the peasant Sven of Ledja, claimed a monopoly. But the man who farmed the inhospitable soil of Flaka also needed the eel-fishing, and acted as his own interests dictated. 'When Nils Dacke had dwelt there some while, he had taken unto himself the fishing waters'. A protracted dispute over the eels in the Lyckeby River broke out between him and Sven of Ledja. Finally the court gave its decision and Dacke lost out.

For the crown cottager at Flaka it was a serious setback. Its soil had yielded him only a minimal income, and this legal decision still further reduced his already slim chances of earning a living. Documents from the province show that, somewhere about the beginning of 1542, he surrendered his holding. Rent rolls for the same year show it to have been unoccupied.

Why did Nils Dacke leave his home? The loss of the eel fishing cannot have been the decisive reason which may have lain in his neighbour's claims as a whole – not only to the fishing waters but to the whole of Flaka. According to this theory, Dacke had been deceived by the bailiff who had given him Flaka in the first place. That he was deeply indignant we see from a statement made on oath before Rödeby parish court: 'If the bailiff hath lied to me, I shall tell him the truth.' Whereupon he used the same arguments to settle accounts with the bailiff as he had used before: his cross-bow. His land had been taken from him. Now he committed a new murder*, and again became an outlaw. He went back to the forest.

In Nils Dacke's personal predicament we may have a psychological explanation why he became the leader of the great insurrection. A tiller of the soil, he had found himself obliged to abandon his house and land. He was destitute. What else had he to lose? Nothing. In our day a man in his predicament would be regarded as a member of the agricultural proletariat. Had he lived three hundred years later he could have left the kingdom of stone and emigrated to the United States, *at that time* the home of liberty

* *'dråp'*—strictly speaking manslaughter, second-degree murder. *Transl.*

and a refuge for other countries' rebels. In 1542 no such opportunity existed. America had only just been discovered. Obviously Dacke felt he had no option but to return to his former mode of life. Weapon in hand, he would seize whatever he felt he had a right to. And in the border forests, he knew, were many others who, being in a like predicament, were of the same frame of mind: men who had decided to defend themselves against the bailiffs' oppression by the only means available. Without any doubt they regarded their violent deeds as committed in self-defence.

In May, 1542, Nils Dacke is again referred to in the sources. This time he has gathered around him a partisan force which, emerging from the forest, has commenced a guerilla war. Some time around June 20 – 'just before St John's Day' – it makes an assault on Voxtorp, a bailiff's farm. At the head of his men Dacke attacks the farm, an action which can be regarded as a counterpart to Engelbrekt's attack on that other 'nest of bailiffs', Borganäs, at the same time of the year, one hundred and eight years earlier. The second great rebellion in Swedish history had begun.

In this way one of the poorest crown outcroppers in the realm, a man who had just been obliged to leave his land, 'shook the throne of Gustav I'.

Causes of the rebellion

Concerning the outbreak of the Dacke rising, Strindberg writes in his *Svenska Folket*: 'It did not have its sources in the agitation of a malcontent, for no popular movement can arise unless its causes have sufficiently deep roots. For lack of any proper parliament the peasantry had no other outlet for their dissatisfaction with this new form of personal government, which was infringing their ancient rights and liberties. That the forms taken by their discontent were savage should not surprise us, in view of the savagery prevailing everywhere else'.

A single discontented and embittered man cannot, on his own, make a revolution. Nor can ten, twenty or thirty such men. And it was with only a little force of thirty men that Nils Dacke had attacked the bailiff's castle at Voxtorp. A week or so later, at the head of a thousand, he had invaded Värend and held a '*ting*' at Inglinge Mound, the commons' immemorial place of assembly. Two weeks more, and he is marching on Växjö, the main town in Värend, with a body of three thousand followers. In less than a month his original guerilla group has multiplied itself a hundred times over, and become a host of peasants, men not otherwise given to leaving their homes.

The heartland of the rebellion was Möre, Konga and Uppvidinge, where the fiery cross had called the peasants out of their farmhouses. A contemporary source declares that Dacke 'in a single night' raised the commons of three hundreds. What is more, all these peasants had joined him at what, in this land of cattle-breeders, was the busiest time of year: during the haymaking season when, as we have seen, the most crucial work of the entire year had to be done. Like a great natural force the movement, spontaneous and irresistible, swept over the countryside, borne up on a general deep-rooted discontent. All earlier attempts at revolt had finally been smothered. Now, at last, popular resentment had grown so strong that it had found outlet in action. All the crown cottager of Flaka had done was to precipitate it. No agitation had been necessary. No letters. No inflammatory speeches – his fiery crosses had sufficed.

This is how every revolution worth its name begins – as a perfectly natural unleashing of forces so long dammed up that their final release results in an explosion. But with the Dacke rising the suddenness was only apparent. The popular movement had long existed covertly.

Its causes – its leader's personal motives apart – can be divided into four main groups: political, social, economic and religious. Historians disagree as to which should have most weight attached to it. P. G. Vejde, a leading student of the history of Småland, is of the view that it was the king's ban on all trade across the frontier. Värend supported itself chiefly by cattle breeding. Its people were dependent for their very existence on their cattle exports to the Danish provinces. But in a royal decree of 1532 it had been promulgated: 'None shall hereafter drive oxen or horses out of the realm, whether small or large, at risk of their neck.' That is, the penalty for selling an ox to one's neighbours in Blekinge was death – and this presented a grave obstacle to the Smålanders' economy, which they can only have regarded as a flagrant outrage.

Erik Lönnroth considers the chief cause of the general discontent to have lain in the grievous burden of taxation oppressing the commons in the late 1530's. Alf Åberg, for his part, thinks the rising was primarily a popular reaction to the king's ecclesiastical policies, which were 'a knockout blow to the peasants' own churches, to the congregations' property and the parishes' self-government'. I have already discussed this policy. Around 1541, the king was again plundering parish churches. The small and indigent temples of the Smålanders had been stripped of 3,700 kilos of 'silver, gilt and ungilt,' or about four-fifths of all the precious gleaming metal they had acquired in order to help illumine their murky churches.

Taken together, these causes more than sufficed to precipitate a major popular revolt. But historians draw from them their own conflicting conclusions. To come closest to the truth, perhaps, we should turn to the participants themselves. They, if anyone, should know why, one day in 1542 at the height of their hay-making, they shouldered their crossbows, took up their poleaxes or swords and, knapsack on back, left their cottages to go to war.

We have only one such source, but it is one which in this instance is to be regarded as reliable. Erik Göransson Tegel's chronicle contains a list of the Smålanders' complaints presented to King Gustav's colonels in the autumn of 1542 at the armistice negotiations at Slätbacka, in Skeda parish, Östergötland. The list is a long one. It comprises seventeen articles. Yet Tegel says that it is only a summary.

As it happens, the list agrees remarkably well with the complaints which the peasants of Swabia had made in 1525 during their revolt, seventeen years earlier. At many points indeed the parallels are striking. Was this mere coincidence? Or did Dacke and his clerks know of the German peasants' remonstrance? The question cannot be answered. Between the two revolts there was a difference. Whilst the Swedes were fighting to recover a freedom they had lost, the German commons were fighting for liberties they had hardly known at any time during the Middle Ages. But both lists of complaints were drawn up in the same century, the century of the great peasant revolts, and the points of resemblance between them are sufficient to place the Dacke rising in its European context.

Here is a summary, in modern language, of the original list of shortcomings and complaints, 'in which the men of the Småland commons humbly requested improvement'.

In the first article, the lords and bailiffs are accused of not keeping their promises to the commons. The next attack all the new illegal taxes being exacted by the crown and the nobles. No one asked whether the peasant had anything left when all his dues had been paid and the tax-gatherer had pocketed his share. For a 'very small oak wood', felled for building purposes, a poor man was being taxed 'high above the law'. Acorn-fed pork, too, was subject to a heavy tax: the bailiffs were taking every fifth pig from the peasant. Further, they were exacting 'shirt-linen' (*'skjortelärft'*) from poor widows and from sons' and daughters' dowries. The bailiffs certainly had a right to so-called 'lawful hospitality' – viz. board and lodging in the farmhouses. Not content with this, however, they were improperly taking half a peck of corn as well as a man's load of hay. Further, a custom prevailed by which the peasant, over and above the actual tax, had to bribe the tax-gatherer; and anyone who found this beyond his means fared ill. If a poor man fell into debt for 'a paltry bailiff-bribe' he was driven from his farm.

One article is a remonstrance against the plunder of churches. Everything their fathers and forefathers have bequeathed and given to God's honour, it declares, has been taken away from churches and monasteries, so that it will soon be as delightful to walk in a ravaged forest as into a church. Another article demands that the Swedish Mass and other ancient religious rites be reintroduced. As it was, a child would soon know how to whistle a Mass beside a dung cart.

The prevailing state of lawlessness recurs several times. When a poor man suffers damage in some matter and cannot pay his 'bailiff-bribe', he is left no peace either at home, in church or in the monastery; he is neither allowed to compound for it nor reach a compromise. Justice is being weighed out according to the parties' purses – a popular saying from that time which accords well with this remonstrance.

The direst object of complaint is the threat to their very lives which the peasants feel constantly exposed to. The bailiffs are for ever holding the threat of a 'Dalecarlian visitation' over their heads – i.e. that they might suffer the same treatment as had been meted out to the Dalesmen at Tuna and Kopperberget.

The rebel, writes Tegel the chronicler, 'pretended' countless other complaints against the bailiffs and nobles, wherefore he restricts his list to a mere seventeen. On all points betterment was promised.

In this remonstrance the king's ecclesiastical policy occupies only a subsidiary place, two articles only. Yet they are mentioned in all our histories. Nevertheless it is the new taxes, arbitrarily and illegally imposed, which dominate. They are ruining the common man. The peasant is being taxed 'above the law' – so that, after paying his taxes, he hardly has anything left to live on. This accusation is repeated over and over again. Then there are the bailiffs' outrages against persons unable to pay their bailiff-bribe. The remonstrance leaves us with a definite impression that the Smålanders were virtually being stripped of all their rights.

The bailiffs' régime and impoverishment of the commons through taxation were the insurrection's main causes.

Yet these bailiffs were no more than the henchmen of those in power. The ultimate cause of the popular rising was political. It had its roots in the remote past, in this rebellious province's peculiar status in the kingdom. The five hundreds of Värend, 'the heart of Småland', had always been governed by their own assembly. In their declaration of neutrality during the war of 1520, for instance, they had reiterated their rights as an independent peasant republic. Even earlier than that, indeed, the Värend peasants had defied the central authorities in Stockholm. At a provincial assembly of April 7, 1507, they had rejected Svante Sture's demands that they should join in the war against the Danes: 'On no wise were they willing to lie before [i.e. besiege] cities and castles, but rather [preferred to] stay at home and protect and close off their own land. Full oft had their country been exposed to ravages, and none had aided them but themselves.'

Gustav Vasa had the same experience of the disobedient peasants of Värend as Svante Sture. At the very outset of his reign he had tried to bring them to their obedience by force. In 1526, at the head of a strongly armed band of retainers, he had entered Småland and carried out one of his razzias. But the populace had continued to defy the government in Stockholm. Although forbidden, the border traffic had gone on, and the new dues and taxes had not been paid. In 1537, the king had to repeat his visitation, and this led to an attempted rising in the following year. And now Gustav I's attempts to incorporate the popular democracy of Värend into his realm by threats of armed force resulted in the Dacke rising.

A beautiful name for the pre-Gustav Vasa period has survived in this part of Sweden: for the Smålanders it was 'the golden age of the peasantry'.

It was this era which Dacke and his peasants now wished to bring back.

The king and the 'pack of thieves'

Most of the fourteenth and fifteenth volumes of King Gustav I's records, containing his letters for the years 1542–43, are devoted to the Dacke rising. Every second letter either refers to it directly and in detail, or else obliquely in some other context. The king admonishes the commons in those provinces which are still quiet: Let no man be deceived or seduced by the rebellious Smålanders, whom Gustav vilifies as a gang of traitors. Further, he writes to the nobles and the commandants of his fortresses, castles and other strong places, warning them. The nobles he terrifies by describing Dacke's band as a mob of thieves, firebugs and assassins. The nobles are to put their farms into a state of defence, and so support the king until such time as he can 'put down this pack of thieves'.

Gustav Eriksson Vasa had once been an insurgent himself. It was a role in which he had enjoyed great success. After all, it was his insurrection which had put him in power, led to his being elected king. But here all resemblance ended. Gustav's rising had been made at God's express command – such was Gustav's conviction, often expressed. And our older annalists, as we have seen, have agreed with him. One 18th-century historian, Johan Göransson, writes: 'Gustaf Eriksson was raised by a Gracious Heaven to the throne of Sweden'. As God's miracle-worker he had been fully entitled to revolt.

It was a right he conceded to no one else. Gustav Vasa had brought his own war of liberation to a happy conclusion. But Nils Dacke's revolt – from the king's point of view – was utterly reprehensible; it lacked all semblance of divine sanction. The insurrection of the Smålanders and Östergötlanders led by this crown outcropper from Flaka, therefore, constituted a threat to the entire kingdom. It was nothing but an ungodly conspiracy of a mob of thieves and murderers.

In a royal letter to the commons of Kalmar County, dated July 3, 1542, Dacke's folk are persistently described as 'forest thieves and traitors'. In six places this document refers to the rebellious peasants as 'forest thieves', an epithet repeated in the king's ensuing correspondence more times than one can count. Even after their numbers have swollen to tens of thousands, Dacke's peasant army is still nothing but 'the thieving mob'.

On July 3, too, the king gives his version of the assault on the Voxtrop bailiff's farm at midsummer. The bailiff, Nils Larsson, and a courtier, Arvid Västgöte, had been handcuffed, stripped naked, tied to a tree, and shot with arrows – 'as unchristianly and mercilessly to death as other dogs'. Gudmund Slatte, an aged nobleman who was just then breathing his last and who had already 'held candles in his hands', had also been killed by Dacke's men. In all essentials this account of the matter, obviously based on reports from Germund Svensson, the king's commandant at Kalmar, is probably correct. Other sources attribute the deed at Voxtorp to motives of personal vengeance: a few days previously Nils Larsson, the bailiff, had shot to death Nils Dacke's brother-in-law, a peasant of the Gertron family.

The events at Voxtorp are symptomatic.

The revolt which they sparked off was chiefly aimed at the bailiffs and their oppression of the commons. In a letter from the same time – July 6, 1542 – even the king has begun to realise that the revolt does not lack its causes, and he seeks them in his bailiffs' behaviour. He sends the bailiffs Hans Skrifvare and Jören Nilsson a severe reprimand for plundering and ruining the commons. They

and others, he says, are skimming the wretched peasantry of everything they possess until, impoverished, they are being obliged to
leave their homesteads, wives and children and become forest
thieves.

Unbeknown to himself, Gustav Vasa here depicts the personal
predicament of the leader of the revolt when he had left Flaka.

This letter must be regarded as an indirect admission that the
Småland rising was not without its justifications. Yet for his part
the king admits no guilt; he throws the whole responsibility on to his
subordinates. Closer investigation, I believe, would reveal that these
bailiffs whom he is reprimanding and making an example of had
merely been implementing the king's orders and demands. Who,
after all, had decreed these taxes which had been the revolt's chief
cause?

Even in the 16th century the responsible wielders of power were
not above laying the blame for indefeasible actions on their subordinates or civil servants who had done nothing but carry out their
orders and implement their will. Among those who hold office
today Gustav Vasa has many emulators.

Between King Gustav I of Sweden and King Christian III of
Denmark there was a defensive alliance, under which each monarch
promised to come to the other's aid against any rebellious subjects.
Now Gustav asked for help against the Smålanders; and a Danish
force invaded Småland.

In King Gustav's letters we can follow the spread of the rebellion.
It is not long before the counter-measures applied by the king prove
inadequate. With at most two hundred men Gustav Olofsson Stenbock invades Värend from Västergötland and in the Växjö district
joins forces with the Danish auxiliaries under Peder Skram. But
Dacke faces them with 2,500 men, and the two monarchs' enterprise
ends in a fiasco. On July 22, Stenbock parleys with Dacke at Bergkvara. All the while the king, though apparently ill-informed, seems
to be well aware of the situation's gravity. On July 16, he had
already written to his bailiffs in Finland, ordering them to recruit
'able fellows' as soldiers; and on July 19 he repeats the same order
to his bailiffs in Gästrikland and Hälsingland. On August 2, he thanks

the inhabitants of Uppsala for their contributions in men and money against Dacke's peasants. As early as July 6 he had written to Germund Svensson explaining that the basic purpose of these measures is to ravage the rebellious Smålanders and bring them to their obedience and senses again.

At the same time King Gustav mobilizes the entire nobility of the realm and – most important of all – sets in motion new major recruitments of legionaries in Germany. Thus the greater part of the royal army sent against the Swedish peasants consisted of troops of the Swedish aristocracy, a Danish auxiliary army, and German legionaries.

During the summer and autumn of 1542, Nils Dacke enjoyed almost uninterrupted success, and from Gustav Vasa's letters we can see that the royalist side is being hard pressed. On August 6 the letter-writer has received information that the citizens of Ronneby and its mayor Henrik Hoffman have been providing 'the rebellious company at Konga' with weapons and ammunition, billhooks, lead, shot, gunpowder and other things; and that this is causing him deep concern. In September the rebels' successes culminate in their victory at Kisa, where an advancing royal army is caught amid the 'felled trees of the peasants' and perish almost to a man.

Immediately afterward Dacke himself invades Östergötland with his main force and pitches his camp only three miles from Linköping, where the king himself is temporarily stationed. Now the way seems to be open for the rebels to advance into Kolmården, in whose enormous forests they hope to find a base. This possibility troubles the king no end. He knows that the forest is the Smålanders' best ally, and writes of Kolmården as being a district 'where are great forests, wherein is all their consolation'.

By and by Gustav Vasa is obliged to enter into an armistice with the 'pack of thieves'. The situation has become so extremely serious for him that he has no choice. Perhaps it is at this juncture that he tells his nephew Per Brahe, according to the latter's chronicle, that he wants to leave Sweden and buy himself a county in Germany.

The armistice concluded at Linköping on November 8 is confirmed in a royal brief issued by Gustav Vasa on November 25.

According to this document, the truce has been concluded with Nils Dacke and his people – with 'the commons of Småland'. So now the 'pack of thieves' have been transformed into respectable peasants, with whom the king concludes an agreement on an equal footing. Dacke's peasants promise to return to their former allegiance to the king, and he for his part promises to send magistrates and other sensible men into Småland to listen to the commons' complaints, to 'better' all short-comings and see to it that one and all shall be treated 'as is right and reasonable'.

King Gustav, however, is in no hurry to fulfil this promise, the foundation of the whole armistice. In a letter written that very day, November 25, he writes that he does not rely overmuch on this 'hen's treaty' which he has made with the Smålanders. Obviously he has only accepted the truce in order to gain time and rearm against the insurgents. Again he commands the nobility to equip themselves, and in Germany his German chancellor, von Pyhy, is carrying out large-scale recruitments of troops and shipping them in all haste over to Sweden.

In the letters which follow, the commons of Småland reappear as a 'pack of thieves'. Soon Dacke's peasants are being accused of breaking the truce by robbing, burning and plundering the nobles' estates. How far this accusation was true cannot now be determined; but if breaches of the armistice occurred they were demonstrably not sanctioned by the peasant leader. In an order issued from Kronoberg, Nils Dacke had told his people to respect the armistice rigorously.

The king also concerns himself with Dacke's private life. In a letter of March 12, 1543, Dacke is accused of lying with 'two sisters of his own flesh'. Wherever he goes, the king says, he has his lawful wife in bed with him on one side and 'the said lawful wife's niece on the other'. The royal letter-writer's moral indignation knows no bounds: Such is the Christianity and such the divine service practised by this traitor!

On March 31, Gustav again returns to the chief rebel's sex-life, a topic which he still finds of absorbing interest. Wherever Dacke stays he has two women with him in bed, his wife and his wife's niece. Here the letter-writer gives us an interesting picture of the time. Adultery was a very gross crime. The king was trying to arouse the people's loathing for whoremaster Dacke.

Three times during the first phase of the rebellion King Gustav invited its leader to meet him face to face, promising a safe-conduct. The first occasion was on July 25, after the negotiations at Berg-kvara, when Dacke was invited under safe conduct to Stockholm. The same invitation was repeated after the military convention reached between the peasant leader and the king's field com-manders at Slätbacka on October 7: 'Likewise he (Dacke) was informed that he could freely betake himself to King Gustav at Stegeborg and there negotiate'. Two noblemen were to accompany him, 'for his greater safety sake'. The third invitation to Dacke to avail himself of such a safe-conduct was made in December.

Each time the crown cottager from Flaka declined to meet the king personally, 'well understanding how little such a safe-conduct was to be relied on'. And indeed, in a letter written at Gripsholm on February 21, 1543 Gustav Vasa reveals the real intent behind these invitations. In it the king expounds a plan to have Nils Dacke, with whom he has just signed a treaty of peace, privily assassinated. The letter is addressed to one of his councillors, Herr Måns Johansson. The king proposes to his councillor that either 'a bullet could be put through Dacke or he could be got hold of in some other way. If this could be done without any harm or danger to the assassins, it were not unwelcome'.

To get Dacke into his clutches – such was the simple purpose behind the king's three offers of safe-conduct to the rebel leader.

Gustav Vasa's project for assassinating Dacke if he could not get him into his power in some other way adds nothing to our knowl-edge of the king's character. It is already quite clear and complete enough. But it does characterize the intended victim. It shows how much Nils Dacke meant personally to the great popular rising. A bullet through the leader – and the revolt would soon be quashed.

Though it took Gustav I a whole year and all the troops he could muster in Sweden and abroad to suppress the liberation movement, according to his own letters it was never a question of opposing a popular rising against his government. In his version of its history the great army of rebellious Smålanders and Östergötlanders was, and remained, nothing but a 'pack of thieves' who were giving him a certain amount of bother. One would have thought a much less sizeable force would have sufficed to deal with such a little band of vagrants.

This disparity between the king's official version of the Dacke rising and its historical realities seems utterly comic. In a royal letter of March 16, 1543, a statement is repeated that 'Dacke is said to be at Jönköping, fourteen thousand men strong.' This figure for Dacke's forces troubles the letter-writer – if it is correct, then 'there will be perils enough'. Even so, this army of 14,000 men is still only referred to as a 'pack of thieves'!

If we are to believe Gustav I's records, that immense collection of royal missives, this would mean that in 1543 the greater part of the male adult population of the province of Småland consisted of criminals.

No one really believes that Gustav Vasa was unaware of the Dacke rising's true character. But in his letters he carried through his lies about the great popular insurrection with admirable persistence and logic. The superb mendacity of rulers is familiar in all ages and all societies. In our own age it has in many quarters reached gigantic dimensions. There are, always have been, régimes which are unable to retain their power without help of the lie official. But in the days of Gustav Vasa political mendacity reached one of its apexes in Swedish history.

Triumphal progress of the rebellion

Nowhere in my history shall I devote space to campaigns and battlepieces. Those already to be found in the pages of our professional historians are quite enough. Therefore I shall restrict myself only to the decisive events of the civil war.

Of course there was no question of a war in the modern sense of the term, a war in which each action was carried out on orders from a headquarters. During the first phase of the insurrection, more especially, bands of Dacke's men operated independently, out of their leader's control. Bailiffs' and noblemens' farms were burned down and plundered. The Swedish commons' long-standing hatred for bailiffs had found violent outlet. There was a hue and cry after the king's tax collectors. They were many. Fabian Månsson states that there were 727 in Kalmar County alone.

Many tales of the popular reaction against the king's servants, 'the red-garbed' men, have survived the centuries. Widespread is the tale of the peasant's wife who received a visit in her farmstead from a royal bailiff, on his usual errand, just when she was making pea soup for dinner. When he claimed some peas as 'tax cover' she replied: 'You shall have them boiled!' Upon which the good wife took her pot, which contained the measure of six tankards, and emptied the pea soup over her guest. Fabian Månsson has a somewhat different version. Here it is the peasant himself who empties the pot over his 'guest'. It is possible that this tale has its root in a legend which had found its way to Sweden from Graubünden in Switzerland. A castle bailiff from Fardün had spat in some pea soup which was getting ready for a peasant, Johannes Calzar, who promptly ducked the bailiff's head in the boiling pot and drowned him, shouting: 'Eat up the soup you've peppered!' This dinner is said to have set in motion a great peasant rising in Graubünden.

For the rebels, the first four months of the rising were an almost unbroken series of triumphs, a campaign which took them from Voxtorp bailey in Småland to Östergötland's capital and cathedral town of Linköping. A latter-day student is amazed at such swift progress. How could a levy of unpractised peasants defeat professional soldiers, their superiors in weaponry, training and general materiel?

That the rising was a sort of forest warfare, where the German legionaries were lost, confused and 'terrified of every bush', I have already explained; and here lies the explanation of the peasants' numerous victories. Further, in his '*sackakarlar*' – as the woodsmen who had been in it from the outset during its guerilla phase, were called – Dacke had a well-trained body of picked men. As the war expanded they made admirable officers for smaller bodies of his peasant troops. In his conduct of his army's movements Dacke revealed an admitted ability, outmanoeuvring the king's field commanders. But the main explanation of his successes seems to me to lie in the good fighting morale of his peasants. The Germans were fighting for their pay; it could even happen that, when the king did not pay them their wages, they mutinied and refused to fight. And what bones could these foreigners have to pick with the commons of Sweden? The Swedish peasants, on the other hand, were fighting for their human rights, for the right to till their own soil, to exploit their forests and their waters, for their economy and for their very existence; for the freedom, which they had always possessed before, to manage their own affairs.

How many men fought under Dacke? No one who has looked into the matter regards himself as able to estimate the total forces under his command. Contemporary chroniclers believe the reports from the king's commanders, and state that Dacke when his strength was at its greatest had as many as 30,000 to 40,000 men under arms. In relation to the total population of the two insurgent provinces these figures do not appear unreasonable. But the king's field commanders, of course, made their statements to explain their defeats at the rebels' hands. Their own numbers were too inferior.

I should be inclined to estimate the number of Smålanders and Östergötlanders who went into the field during the Dacke rising as having been at most 20,000, probably 15,000 men.

During the Late Middle Ages men had invented a new and more efficient means of shortening each other's already brief lives: firearms. Dacke's peasants were the first people's army in Sweden to use them. From helpful friends and supporters in Blekinge, on the other side of the border, the Smålanders received a truly modern armoury, consisting of 'tubes', halberds, arquebuses, powder and shot. But the new firearms could only suffice for a small part of the troops. The greater part had to be content with the peasant's classical weapons originally used during the Swiss commons' wars of liberation, namely the halberd, the spiked mace, the battle scythe, the pitchfork and the pole-axe. Probably their weaponry varied from man to man. But the Värend commons had never been disarmed; all attempts by the authorities to take their weapons from them had proved in vain. The weak point in the peasant army's weaponry was its lack of the defensive armour of those days, the helmets, shields and breastplates supplied to men-at-arms.

But the most effective among their weapons, one which hung on the wall in almost every farmhouse – the crossbow – was made by Dacke's peasants themselves. Olaus Magnus and other mediaeval historians describe it as a powerful weapon, peculiarly well-suited for forest warfare. The Smålanders used a crossbow whose bow was of steel and which shot iron-tipped arrows two feet long and weighing two and a half ounces. Modern experiment with these weapons confirms their efficiency. Experts regard the arrows as being lethal at a distance of 160 yards and that at 110 yards they could pierce any ordinary armour. The crossbow played a great part in the Dacke rising. It was feared both by iron-clad knights on horseback and by other professional soldiers, in spite of their armour.

We have no figures for the numbers who fell in our greatest popular revolt, nor is there any possibility of estimating them. Neither side has left any reliable basis for such a calculation. Per Brahe states that the insurgent army lost about 500 men in the great battle of March 1543, when it suffered decisive defeat. But if we add to those who died in battle – as naturally we must – the numbers of those who died *after* it, then the final figure will certainly be a good deal higher. These people may have survived the battle, but what happened to them afterwards? How were the survivors of a battle looked after?

Here we touch on a field that is altogether unresearched. I have been unable to find a single work on mediaeval military medicine. Perhaps, if no one has dealt with the subject, it is for the simple reason that it did not even exist. A special chaplaincy to the Swedish army began to be established in the 16th century, but no mention is made in the literature of any physical care for the men who were being slaughtered. No field ambulance yet existed. The wounded were handed over to the surgeon-barber, the forerunner of the army surgeon, who in fact had been originally a barber pure and simple. The Swedish name is derived from the German word for a beard. In the Vasa period the 'beard-cutter' served with the royal troops, as we can see from the Kalmar city accounts for 1542, which show that 52 marks had been paid out in wages to surgeon-barbers attending on the burghers and their servants who had fallen fighting Dacke outside their city.

But what befell the wounded from a people's army? An expert on medical history whom I have consulted thinks that most of them, sooner or later, must have died of their wounds. And this, presumably, was the fate of those who survived the battles of the Dacke rising. Most of these encounters took place in desolate woods, where those of the maimed and mutilated who could not move off the field had to be left to lie there in their torments, waiting for the only possible end. Insofar as they received any assistance it was from a folk-medicine which could hardly have made much progress since the Battle of Stiklastad, in 1030, where we are told that the wounded were treated only with boiling water. The only other healing fluids were human spittle and urine. I have myself seen people apply their own urine to fresh wounds, supposing it to have a purificatory effect. The juices of certain herbs were also efficacious. Otherwise people's only recourse was to magic signs, incantations and prayers. When it came to sickness and death, mediaeval people were fatalists. It was not an accident or wound which killed a man, but death itself. And if he recovered it was not thanks to any treatment. 'It was so ordained'.

The 'beard-cutters' used their knives not only for cutting beards, but also for operating on the wounded, from whom they extracted bullets and amputated legs and arms. Not that they could do much to relieve their victims' pain: no real anaesthetics are known to have existed before the mid-19th century. In mediaeval operations, strong men held the patient by his arms and legs and bound him down like a beast on the butcher's block. There were attempts at anaesthesia: like a cow at the butcher's, the victim was knocked out by a violent blow on the head, after which the surgeon had to chop off the limb as swiftly as possible before he came round again. A capable surgeon-barber could amputate an arm or a leg in less than a minute. In wintertime, when the cold was severe, amputations were done out of doors. Fierce cold reduces the body's sensitivity. Alcohol, too, was used as an anaesthetic. During the wars of Charles XII brandy had come into use. When any of the king's soldiers had to lose a limb, the field-surgeon would pour a quart of brandy down his throat before he began sawing off the limb.

The sources tell us absolutely nothing about how the wounded were cared for during the Dacke rising. The royal chronicles represent the peasant leader as being utterly callous to their sufferings. In battle, they say, he had the drums rolled to drown the screams of pain from his wounded. It is possible that monks who knew the art of medicine took charge of Dacke's men when they lay 'limbless' and with mangled bodies after a battle. The monks had been expelled from their monasteries and therefore naturally supported this peasant chieftain who wanted to bring back their Church. Probably the clergy also relieved the souls of the dying by bringing them extreme unction, sprinkling them with holy water, holding up a crucifix before their dying eyes and putting a burning candle into their hands to light their way up to heaven. Long before the Red Cross, the cross of Christ made its appearance on the battlefields.

Those who have painted history's battles have overlooked the fate of those who were left lying on the field after the fight was over. Little on this aspect of the matter is to be found in the annalists' pages. Here we come face to face with a suffering of unimaginable extent. When I try to conceive of all the pain which men have suffered in their wars down the millennia, then the sunlight grows dark for me, the grass is no longer green, the flowers lose their scent and birdsong becomes the whimpering of men in agony.

In early September 1542 the rebels gained their greatest victory. It took place near the present-day community of Kisa, on the border between Östergötland and Småland. A royalist force consisting mainly of German soldiers was about to invade Småland. Hardly had they begun their march before they met their fate. The peasants of Kinda rose to a man. Encircling the invaders in the forest, they trapped them in their barricades of felled trees. The battle ended with the royalist army's virtual annihilation. Only a few fragments escaped and turned up at Linköping on September 15. At least a thousand German legionaries lay dead behind the barricades. Today they sleep their last sleep in the Swedish forest.

Local tradition assigns the place of battle to Slätmon, just north of Kisa, where a ten-foot-high stone has been raised as a monument. It stands in the depths of the forest. There is no text on its mossy face, and none of the locals even know when it was erected. Nearby, an old overgrown road passed between two gigantic boulders. The passage between them is called 'The Gates of Hell'. The boulders form a narrow pass through which the royalists had to march, and where they fell into an ambush.

When I was at Kisa, studying the scene of the insurgents' victory, I fell in with a couple of German tourists. They were much amazed when I told them how close they were to a four-centuries-old mass grave containing the corpses of a thousand or so of their compatriots.

In early October Dacke and his whole main army of Smålanders were encamped three English miles outside Linköping, the king himself being in the neighbourhood. Småland was lost to him; and now he himself writes that 'Östergötland is hanging by a thread'. The possibility that Dacke might go on and reach the immense forests of Kolmården, in the north of Östergötland, only thirty English miles from Linköping, and which form the border with Södermanland, terrified him. The region provided an admirable base. From Kolmården the insurgents could threaten Stockholm.

It was in this strategic situation that the Linköping armistice was concluded. So far Dacke had been victorious. His opponents were hard-pressed and in need of a breathing space to recover their strength. By agreeing to the armistice Dacke gave Gustav just such a respite. And therefore the question arises: Did the peasant leader, in doing so, make his great and decisive mistake, and spoil all his chances of final victory for the rebellion? In the position he was in there seems to be no reason why he should have concluded an armistice. But the royalist side certainly had every reason to: it gave them a chance to mobilize all their resources. Dacke had extended his to the limit. He had reached the peak of his successes. But his opponents could draw on many others still unexploited. When the fighting recommenced, Dacke had lost his chances of advancing into Kolmården, which would have afforded his army such an admirable forest encampment.

Obviously Dacke thought that Gustav might be willing to conclude a definitive peace treaty with him, leaving him to govern Småland and hold it in fief. Today the idea must seem naïve. Seen against the background of the provincial separatism of those days it was not so unrealistic. As we have seen, Småland, in the Later

Middle Ages, had only been loosely attached to the kingdom of Sweden; and Nils Dacke was probably assuming that under his own governorship his part of the country could retain its former liberties.

But nothing could have been more unlike Gustav Vasa than to hand over one of his largest provinces, the one, furthermore, forming his frontier with Denmark, to his rebellious subjects, to a 'pack of thieves'.

The king may have scorned his 'hen's peace' with the Smålanders. Yet the historical fact remains: it was his salvation in an exceedingly troublesome and perilous situation.

The Småland chieftain in Kronoberg Castle

On a little islet off the shore of Lake Helgasjön, four miles from Växjö, stand the ruins of Kronoberg Castle. On this little island a fort had been erected in the mid-14th century which, in the Later Middle Ages, was to become the castle of the bishops of Växjö. After the Västerås *riksdag* Gustav Vasa expelled the last Catholic bishop, Ingemar Petersson, and took over Kronoberg as a royal estate and one of his own castles.

Nils Dacke 'occupied the castle with one thousand men from Konga', and it was from Kronoberg that, in the late autumn and winter of 1542–43, he governed Småland. In less than a year he had exchanged his crown outcropper's holding for a castle.

On November 25, he held a provincial assembly at Växjö, where he declared his peaceful intentions and 'exhorted the commons to stand together in defence of their own interests'. He ruled that the armistice, if the king confirmed and abided by it, must be held inviolate. All further plunder of noble estates was strictly forbidden. The leader summoned local assemblies in the hundreds. In nine of these hundreds he appointed new bailiffs to maintain law and order and ensure that any new legislation which might be promulgated should be obeyed, all this in an attempt to re-establish orderly conditions in the province. No man should now be allowed to take the law into his own hands.

But to put an immediate stop to the immediate deeds of violence being committed by errant bands of insurgents was beyond his power. Ignoring the armistice, they were still wrecking the nobles' farms and estates. And this rapine by local rebel leaders, which was going on in defiance of Dacke's orders, provided Gustav Vasa with his pretext to break the armistice.

'Nils Dacke drank Yule at Kronoberg' we read in old histories; he had also begun to implement his political programme. Dacke restored the Catholic Church which the Smålanders had adhered to for four centuries and which was still so popular with them. During the insurrection Dacke had received strong support from Catholic parish priests who, expelled from their churches, for the past fifteen years had been wandering about as refugees – '*The Shepherd has Fled*' is one of Fabian Månsson's chapter headings. According to Hafström, at least sixteen Småland priests, as well as all the clergy of Öland, supported Dacke. Now they were rewarded by permission once again to hold Masses for their faithful parishioners. The tawdry services of the Lutherans, which the Smålanders had likened to Masses that 'could be whistled at the tail of a dung-cart', were abolished. Once again God was worshipped and invoked as He had always been. Once again the Latin words were being sung and spoken under the vaultings, to the laity's edification and consolation. Småland had reverted to its former faith.

But folk missed the sacred 'furniture' of their churches: their gleaming silver, the images of the Virgin, the candlesticks, the chalices and patens, the chandeliers, the monstrances – all these were now in the king's safe keeping, in St Eskil's Chamber.

The rebellion's main objective, however, had been to gain relief from the insufferable burden of taxation. Nils Dacke announced a considerable reduction in the commons' taxes and re-opened the border. This last measure was of great economic importance, the king's ban on all such commerce, as we have seen, having been a death-blow to the cattle trade, the main source of people's livelihood. Once again a peasant was free to sell his ox at Ronneby, where he could get a much better price for it without having to pay with his neck.

For a few brief months the sky brightened over Småland. 'All should be in accordance with ancient law and custom, whereat the commons rejoiced'. For the population of the oppressed province there was now a prospect of a return to 'the golden age of the peasantry'.

In his letters to the king's commissioners Nils Dacke unfolds his plans for the future. He is counting on receiving Småland in fief from the king; on these terms, as his liege, he will serve him faithfully. In a contemporary satirical epitaph over the fallen rebel leader it is said that he 'wished to become a king'. No contemporary source supports such an allegation. That his ambitions were altogether more modest can be seen from the fact that, even during the most successful phase of his rebellion, he offered the throne to Svante Sture – an act of recklessness in the hour of victory. Everything goes to show that, in installing himself at Kronoberg, Dacke had attained his political goal. So far from aiming at the throne of Sweden, he was perfectly content to be governor of Småland.

In Germany the Swedish peasant rising had caused a sensation. The king still had powerful enemies there, notably Berend von Melen. The German princes' incessant intrigues against Gustav Vasa, especially during the 1550's, have been explored in detail by Ingvar Andersson. On its way to Germany rumour had greatly magnified Dacke's successes. Clearly, the German lords believed his victory to be certain and definitive. And now, from the fruits of Dacke's victory, Berend von Melen, Duke Albrecht of Mecklenburg and Count Fredrik of the Palatinate, together with other feudal princes, wished to take their pickings. What part the Emperor himself played in all this is still somewhat uncertain. In Strindberg's play, Olaus Petri convinces the king that he must reply to a letter from 'that tramp' Nils Dacke, his most effectual argument being that 'even the Emperor has written letters to Dacke' And so Gustav Vasa does, too! The king's reaction has a certain psychological truth about it. Now he was even prepared to stoop so low as to conclude an armistice, on equal terms, with the 'forest thief'.

Until recently this letter from the Emperor has been regarded as dramatic licence by Strindberg; but latest research reveals it to have had a solid basis in fact. Dacke's German connections have long been one of the rebellion's least researched aspects. Gottfrid

Carlsson, however, has devoted an essay to them, and quite recently Gerhard Hafström has lit upon some hitherto unknown and still unpublished source material in the shape of a number of letters from Charles V and Fredrik, the Count Palatine, in which they declare their intention to support Dacke. The world's greatest monarch acted the part of a potential ally of the Småland chieftain! And the crown cottager of Flaka had become a factor in European power politics.

A proclamation to the population of Sweden from the Emperor's Secretary of State, Nicolas Granvella, is already known to historians. It exhorts the Swedes to overthrow Gustav Vasa, who has usurped their throne and replace him with Fredrik, the Count Palatine. Husband of Christian II's daughter (Charles V's niece), Fredrik regarded himself as the legitimate heir to the Swedish crown.

Another fact, too, has long been known. One November day, while Dacke was still in residence at Kronoberg, he received a letter from Duke Albrecht of Mecklenburg. Brought by a burgher of Rostock, it offered him military aid. But the letter also contained a request for money, either ready coin or silver, to pay the legionaries' wages. Obviously the Germans entertained exaggerated notions of the wealth of the Småland peasantry, whom they perhaps imagined kept silver spoons in their homes.

So we find German feudal lords, who were keeping their own peasantry in a state of serfdom, offering auxiliaries to these Swedish peasants who had revolted against *their* overlords. Politically the situation was grotesque. And very properly in view of the armistice he had just concluded with the King of Sweden, Nils Dacke declined their offer. If Gustav Vasa kept his promises toward him, he said, 'he would desire none better lord and king'.

Unlike the King of Sweden, Dacke's peasants never received any military help from Germany. Not that Nils Dacke did not realise that Charles V's and the German princes' offer could be an effective means of bringing pressure to bear on Gustav. In letters written to the king's commander at Christmas time he makes use of it, writing that the Emperor has offered him Småland in fief, and implying, of course, that the King of Sweden should do no less.

But soon Gustav has enough forces at his disposal to retake his lost province. Even in the beginning of 1543 Nils Dacke perceives that he will be obliged to resume the struggle.

But now his triumphs had reached their zenith. Two months of the new year have not gone by before he is on the downward path. When he leaves his residence at Kronoberg he has only six months left to live.

From Kronoberg to Flaka

In early 1543, military operations were resumed on both sides. The royal chroniclers Rasmus Ludvigsson and Tegel accuse the 'false and faithless Dacke' of not abiding by the terms of the armistice. By not keeping the peace, he had obliged the king to resort to arms. Latest research has shown the baseless character of this allegation. 'Contemporary sources provide no evidence that Dacke at this time took any steps inconsistent with the truce', writes a modern scholar. What they do provide is evidence that, in his letters to King Gustav, the governor of Småland repeatedly put forward proposals for a peaceful settlement; but got no answer.

Gustav Vasa had used the respite to rearm; and as the new year began he felt strong enough to settle accounts in quite another fashion. It was the royalist side which broke the truce – on the pretext that the other side had already done so.

Against the rebellious Smålanders the king had now had time to mobilize the troops of the entire Swedish nobility. Resorting to methods which have rightly been called 'a monumental piece of sharp practice', he also prevailed on the Dalesmen to go to war against the Smålanders, playing off one province which had revolted and been crushed against another, which had not. A letter, written in the name of the people of Dalarna but in fact dictated by the king, declares the Smålanders to be traitors, and promises 'their most dear lord and king Gustav' to help him against the 'pack of thieves'. The document's alleged signatories also exhort the commons of other provinces to place men at the king's disposal.

This letter Gustav Vasa despatched to Nils Larsson, his bailiff in Dalarna. Still further to confirm its authenticity, Larsson attached the seal of Dalarna to the forgery and sent some of his own servants through the province, dressed as peasants, to prevail upon their supposed brethren. This time the king's literary gifts had the desired effect. A troop of Dalecarlian peasants joined him against the peasants of Småland – a propaganda coup hardly matched even by the Nazis.

In the critical situation which had arisen for him in the autumn of 1542, King Gustav, under the terms of the agreement reached between the two monarchs at a meeting at Brömsebro in 1541, had applied to King Christian III of Denmark for still more assistance against his rebellious subjects. In a letter of October 15 he urgently appeals to his ally to send him ten companies of men-at-arms, i.e., about 5,000 men. In February 1543, Gustav renews his appeal, and in the late winter a fresh army of Danish auxiliaries prepares to invade Sweden. According to Per Brahe's chronicle, this army consisted of no more than three companies of horse and foot, or about 1,500 soldiers and legionaries. On February 24, commanded by Peder Pedersen, it crossed the frontier and entered Småland. Militarily, its exploits were not remarkable; mostly it is famed for its atrocities against the unarmed country folk.

Meanwhile the king had continued to recruit men in Germany, both during the rebellion and during the armistice, and on a considerably bigger scale than has hitherto been realised. Recent research has shown that during the Dacke rising the number of German soldiers in Sweden was more than doubled. When the insurrection had first broken out, in the summer of 1542, there had been six companies of German legionaries, or about 3,000 men, in the country. After only half a year had gone by, they amounted to thirteen companies of infantry and a company of cavalry. By the late winter of 1543, it is clear that the king was in a position to put a German army of at least 6,000 men into the field.

But as far as we know not a single German soldier fought for Dacke. It was the king who brought in the Germans.

At the resumption of hostilities, therefore, the situation had radically changed, a change wholly to the insurgents' disadvantage. Their time of victories was over. The king had rearmed, and now the peasant host was to face a great army of well-trained professional soldiers, for whom they were no match. Militarily, the royalist side now had the upper hand.

The course of events, in brief, was as follows, In late January Dacke launched an assault on Kalmar Castle, held during the rising for the king by its capable commandant, Germund Svensson. The assault is repulsed; the peasants are no storm-troopers. To scotch the king's invasion of Småland, Dacke invades Östergötland with all the forces he can assemble. Earlier he has gained victories even on the Östergötland plains; but in this new campaign his peasants are no match for the regiments of enemy horse. Dacke, forced to beat a retreat, withdraws into the deeply wooded hundreds of north-east Småland, whose commons had all joined his cause.

The final battle was fought in the neighbourhood of present-day Virserum, the little market town where his statue now stands. It was to be decisive for the insurrection. At the site of the battlefield between Lakes Hjorten and Virserumssjön is one of the most beautiful spots in the district, the landscape forms a narrow pass through which the royal army, advancing from the north, would have to advance; and so it was here, in the forest, that the peasants blocked its path. Even a layman in strategic and tactical matters can appreciate Dacke's choice of a strongly defensive position.

The battle was fought one day around March 20, 1543; according to one source, on Good Friday. The lakes were still frozen, and this must have been to the defenders' disadvantage. Several sources state that the royal army managed to outflank the peasants' position by marching over the ice and taking them in the rear, the struggle taking place partly on the frozen surface of Lake Hjorten.

The result was a total defeat for the insurgents. Per Brahe writes that between four and five hundred Smålanders were left lying on the battlefield. At the very beginning of the fight Dacke was shot 'by a hackbut, two balls through the thigh', and was carried from the field. This loss of their leader probably contributed to the peasants' defeat.

Among Gustav Vasa's infantry in this battle was a troop of Dalesmen, whose numbers are given as five hundred strong. Men from the commons of two provinces fought each other, Dalesmen against Smålander, peasant against peasant. A tragedy was played out, often repeated in history – the tragedy which occurs whenever men of the same class, sharing the same vital interests, go to war and kill one another.

In a letter of April 26, 1543, Gustav Vasa thanks the Dalesmen who had taken part in the campaign against the Smålanders for the 'fidelity and manliness they had shown', and for 'willingly allowing themselves to be used' against the Dacke party. Now they are to have their reward, their cash 'consolation'. The king informs his bailiff in Eastern Dalarna that he has sent two clerks down into the country with 'a large sum of money', to reward and pay off his soldiers.

The inexplicable aspect of this tragedy is that the Dalesmen should already have forgiven the king for Tuna Mead and Kopparberget.

After this battle, in March 1543, Dacke's army broke up into partisan groups, each acting independently and fighting hopeless skirmishes against overwhelming odds. In the Kalmar hundreds two brothers of the Gertron family, the leader's brothers-in-law, attempted new risings; but they were quickly crushed. Soon the countryfolk realised that the rising was a lost cause. Parish after parish, hundred after hundred, negotiated and submitted. In the spring and summer of 1543 Småland became an occupied country. And was treated as such.

The Dacke rising had ended as it had begun: as a guerilla war. In Värend, which had been its heartland, men went on resisting to the bitter end. Two months after the great defeat, fresh fighting broke out in Uppvidinge hundred. It was Dacke himself who lit the flame.

The peasant leader, shot through both thighs, had been tended by faithful followers. Obviously his wounds must have been well nursed during the period from the end of March to May, when he had been in hiding. By May he had recovered and was again ready for the fight. The court rolls of Östra hundred inform us where he had been convalescing: Lars, Rector of Näshult, 'sheltered Dacke around Easter time, 1543'. Further, the rolls inform us, Dacke 'lay in the home of' Gröms of Skärvete during 'the time when he was shot'. A whole flora of legends relate how the faithful villagers kept their wounded chieftain well concealed from the king's men-at-arms.

In May, Nils Dacke, having made his way down to Värend, appeared in Ålghult parish, in the hundred of Uppvidinge. Thord, Rector of Ålghult, was one of his most reliable friends; afterwards he had to pay for his fidelity with his life. Dacke managed to gather together a small body of Uppvidinge peasants for a last stand. He had become a guerilla leader again. At Lenhovda, the place where the men of Uppvidinge held their assemblies, he and his companions attacked a party of royal troops commanded by Colonel Jakob Bagge and put them to flight. The royalist side lost eleven dead.

It was Nils Dacke's last fight; and it was a victory.

But thenceforward all the sources refer to him as a solitary man on the run, abandoned by all. Some of the men who had been closest to him in his days of triumph had abandoned the cause and were prepared to betray their leader to save their own lives. In this way Dacke became the last man to go on fighting in the insurrection to which he had given his name – abandoned by all, it was for his own life he was fighting now.

During these last months of his life Dacke was a fugitive, leading a precarious existence in the forests, hunted down like a wild beast by large troops of the king's men-at-arms. Gustav Vasa went to great lengths to lay his hands on this dangerous man. The coast was watched in order to prevent him escaping by sea. Everyone who had joined in the rising but was now willing to help track him down was promised a free pardon.

Many are the tales, passed down from generation to generation, about Nils Dacke's last days. More than anything else, it is the hunted fugitive who has captured the popular imagination. The legends about his flight are innumerable. In all the border country toward Blekinge there is hardly a wood in which he is not supposed to have hidden, hardly a cave or a hollow beneath some boulder or a cleft in the rocks that was not his hiding place.

It is this Dacke – the man lying beneath the spruce tree – who gave Carl Milles his inspiration for the monument which was never raised to his memory.

From May to August Dacke led this hunted existence, probably in the great border forest which had sheltered him before. What we do know for certain is that in the first days of August he was on the Danish side of the border, in Rödeby Forest, which stretches away there, mile upon mile. For it was here he ended his life.

Nils Dacke had come back to the country round Flaka, whose soil he had tilled and where he was so familiar with the lie of the land. From Kronoberg Castle he had come back to his smallholding. The circle was complete. His destiny was nearly accomplished.

No other Swede has ever had a destiny which for its ups and downs of fortune have been comparable to his – first, the self-owning peasant – then the crown outcropper – the guerilla leader – the leader of the insurrection – the governor of Småland – the man who negotiated on an equal footing with the King of Sweden – the man in whom the Emperor Charles V, the most powerful man on earth, thought he had found an ally – the leader of the defeated revolt – then the guerilla again – and at the last the solitary fugitive. And all this inside little more than a year!

Nils Dacke fell in the forest not far from Flaka, the little outcropper's farm which had once been his own. We have no reason to doubt the older historians who say so. On the whole they may be relied on. Two of the leader's captains and closest friends, Peder Skrivare and Peder Skegge, are supposed to have betrayed him, purchasing their own lives by leading his enemies to his forest hiding place. According to another source he was 'spied out' by two neighbours, the Hampe brothers, whom Gustav I rewarded by exempting them from taxes. In Rödeby Forest, somewhere near the frontier, King Gustav's soldiers caught up with him, and Dacke met the fate that usually awaits a rebel. All other versions of his end – that he was taken prisoner, or escaped to Germany – can be dismissed as fiction. That he should have surrendered alive contradicts everything his actions tell us of his character. He was the indomitable woodsman, untameable, untamed; the rebel who never bowed his head to the yoke. In all probability he died as he had lived, defiant to the end.

This picture of him agrees furthermore with a statement in Tegel's chronicle: when Dacke 'would not surrender, he was shot to death'.

So this source, too, tells us he died fighting. Or possibly was ambushed.

According to local tradition his corpse, laid on a wooden sled, was dragged along a cattle track to Kalmar: 'the men-at-arms, who were mounted, did not wish to have the dead man hanging across their horse's back'. The animals, that is, would have been infected by the rebel's body.

Original documents from Kalmar Castle show that Nils Dacke's corpse was chopped into four pieces and impaled. In the castle it was 'quartered and in four places was placed on stake and wheel and on his head [was placed] a copper crown'. The castle accounts contain an item requisitioning 130 nails 'for the needs of Nils Dacke and his party'. These long nails were required in order to impale the rebels and nail up the various parts of their bodies. No fewer than 130 nails were needed; corpses of other captured Dacke men were to be impaled with their leader's. That this was indeed done transpires from the still extant receipt issued by the king's counting house: 'To Nils Dacke and his party, nails 130, which were smithed in Kalmar Castle'.

In *Epitaphium Nicolai Dacke*, the victors' sadistic epitaph over the rebel leader, written on the back of a hand-written folio of Laurentius Petri's *Chronicle* and dated 1559, special emphasis is laid on his copper crown. Dacke's head, with this crown on it, is said to have been impaled on Kalmar town wall. It is Dacke himself who is speaking. He calls himself 'the Captain'. In the year of Our Lord fifteen hundred and forty-two he had begun his insurrection:

> 'Strange was the game I then did play,
> To become a King was my way,
> And thus at last in truth I fare
> sith now at Kalmar this crown I wear.'

Outside the city gates the Smålanders could behold their king.

In the concluding vignette of his *Nils Dacke*, the novelist Ivar Ljungquist draws on this source. In the novel's last sentences the rebel leader's aged mother, herself grievously sick, comes riding to Kalmar on a borrowed horse, to ask after her son. The passage, a poetic interpretation of what had happened, is worth quoting in full: 'One day . . . a little old woman came to the town wall where the rebels' heads had been set up. Twelve were hanging there, and all looked the same, she thought, for eyes and cheeks and all flesh had been pecked off them by the birds and the rest was covered in great swarms of flies. But in the middle was a head with a copper crown on its brow. It could only be his. And as the flies dispersed in a gust of wind and she descried two locks of hair at the dead man's temple, she was sure of it. Such hair had Nils had, brown, soft and shining.

She knelt down close to the wall and prayed for a long while.

Then she went back to her nag and without entering the town rode back the same way she had come. In a cottage by the roadside she was given water, and when its occupants asked her why she, who was so old, was riding abroad alone, she replied:

"I was looking for my son and at last have found him. So now I've only to give back the horse and die before winter comes."

After these words she thanked them for their hospitality and though dusk had begun to fall, rode on her way.'

' —so that Småland should not be utterly ruined— '

The news of Nils Dacke's death had reached King Gustav at Stegeborg on August 7, 1543. He had heard it in a letter from Germund Svensson at Kalmar. The same day he replies to his commandant at the castle. He had learned that 'that traitor Dacke has got his wages, albeit he did deserve a worse departure. But had he been taken alive it would have been most serviceable, for the sake of many things'.

We can form a lively idea of the sort of death the rebel leader would have died, had the king's soldiers taken him alive. But the writer of the letter consoles himself with the reflection that what has occurred 'hath befallen of God's will'. Which may be interpreted as meaning: Any further wages which may be outstanding to him are now being drawn by Dacke in hell.

In his letter the king orders his commandant to seek out Dacke's wife and mother – 'that witch his Mother' – and these orders Germund Svensson was strictly to obey. His emissaries were not to return until they had found and captured both the women. The king's men-at-arms are known to have caught Dacke's ten-year-old son, who was taken to Stegeborg. In a letter to Esbjörn Skrivare at that castle, a few months later, the king orders this officer to keep a strict watch on 'the young Dacke' so that he shall not escape or get up to some roguery. Even the ten-year-old was dangerous to Gustav Vasa. According to the chronicle, Dacke's son afterwards 'died from pestilenzia at Stockholm'. Here we may believe what we like. No outbreak of plague is known to have occurred in Stockholm at this time. But one thing may safely be assumed: the king did not let any person bearing the name of Dacke escape with his life.

Dacke's mother is thought to be identical with a peasant wife, Elin Dacke of Hult, who is mentioned in contemporary documents. She too had to tread the path from an independent homestead to a crown smallholding. In the years 1551–59 she was living on the little outcropper's farm of Lönbomåla. According to popular tradition two bailiffs set fire to her cottage. She was burnt to death. It was the wages of witchcraft. Part of the Dacke family was extirpated after the insurrection. The rebel's paternal uncle, Olof Dacke of Lindö, was taken to Stockholm, where he was broken on the wheel, quartered and impaled. Two Gertron brothers, Dacke's brothers-in-law, underwent the same treatment in their own village. But not all the Dackes were exterminated. Just before Christmas, 1546, Gustav Vasa employed one of them, a man by name Gisse Dacke of Djuramåla, in the parish of Vissefjärda, as ward registrar. And again, in 1624, in the days of Gustavus Adolphus, one of Nils Dacke's relatives was to carry on his work during some disturbances among the peasantry. The name of this peasant leader was Jon Stind; he was stated to be 'Niels Tacke's relation.'

In his letters Gustav I had promised to show no mercy to the rebellious commons of Småland. He would punish them in such a fashion 'that they and their children would never forget it.' The king is not noted for keeping his promises; but this one, let it be said to his credit, he fulfilled to the letter, as Fabian Månsson, the man who is our best witness to this fact, has told me. The rebellious hundreds of Värend and Möre were so devastated, ravaged, laid in ruins and in every way tormented that two centuries had to pass by before they again reached the level of subsistence they had enjoyed before the insurrection.

The great popular rebellion and its defeat were the greatest catastrophe ever to befall Småland. The subject is a large one, and many of its crucial aspects remain unresearched. It would require a long chapter to itself. Here a few last details will suffice. They give us an idea of the horrors and sufferings the Smålanders were subjected to in the mid-fifteen-forties, in one year.

Drawing on the court rolls of Uppvidinge hundred from this time, P. G. Vejde describes an assembly at Lenhovda in the summer of 1543, at which the peasantry of my own native hundred were to be punished for their part in the Dacke rising. The flock of 'criminals' are penned in by a strong troop of the king's soldiers, cavalry and German legionaries, under the command of Colonel Jakob Bagge. New gallows had been erected, and on top of a pile of great logs the executioners, holding their axes as they wait for their victims, bide their time. Seated on his horse, Jakob Bagge fulminates against the commons, commanding the people to denounce their leaders and hand them over – whoever obeys will save his own life. Upon which the terrified and bewildered peasants begin betraying each other, and without further ceremony guilty and innocent alike are led to the gallows or the block, where one after another 'justice is done upon them'. In the face of this massacre panic breaks out. People fling themselves on their knees, shrieking promises with upraised hands never again from this day onward to be disobedient to King Gustav or to ignore his edicts.

The pattern is familiar – from the king's razzias in Dalarna. Their rebellion crushed, great numbers of Smålanders had to 'follow in the footsteps of the Dalesmen', as the bailiffs, according to the peasants' demonstrance, had so often threatened.

In letters to his commanders Gustav Vasa gives the military permission to plunder at will those hundreds which have been infected by the rebellion: 'What part they can get from the enemy, that do we give them to plunder'. To the German legionaries, particularly, the king's permission was welcome. All the sources unanimously agree that they exploited it to the uttermost.

The mentality of these men who made war for a wage transpires from a letter quoted by Machiavelli. Written by his friend Francesco Vettori and dated Florence 1526, it describes the German soldiery's progress through Northern Italy: 'compared with them there is no one who does not prefer the Devil himself'. Presumably they did not behave any more humanely toward the population of Småland.

These men from the Germany of the peasant risings were experts at torture; they were 'practicians'. In their own country the so-called 'Emperor's law', promulgated against rebellious peasants, doomed all traitors to the most monstrous death. Before being executed they were broken on the wheel where every limb of their body was crushed. All the Dacke men who were caught by these German experts perished in this monstrous fashion.

Smoke from burning villages marked the royal troops' path through the rebellious province. Burning, plundering, raping and torturing, the king's soldiery passed through Värend and Möre.

When an author is faced with an event so horrible that he can find no words to depict it, he is sometimes obliged to turn aside and say it 'defies description'. It is just such an occurrence I here find myself faced with. Imagination boggles at it. And in the end Gustav Vasa took a step which seems to confirm the monstrous lengths to which it had gone. After a while, according to Tegel's chronicle, he recalled his German legionaries from the rebellious province, *'so that Småland should not be utterly ruined'.*

Further, as I have said before, a hunger blockade was enforced against Småland. No grain or other necessities of life were to be introduced from other provinces. And when, in the very year of the Dacke rising, there was a severe crop failure, the Smålanders' cup of misery brimmed over. Not only this – the peasants lost most of their draught animals. All who were fined for their part in the rising had to pay their fines in cattle. Several thousands of 'propitiatory oxen' were driven in herds to Stockholm.

The defeated Smålanders were starving, ruined, bleeding to death, impotent. Incapable of further resistance, they were utterly in the power of the victor. Anyone who saw any means of saving his own life seized it. They were defeated, and therefore they submitted. What else could they do? They had sacrificed their all to their revolt – and they had lost. No choice was left them. Professional soldiers might fight to the death, to preserve at least their honour. For Dacke's peasants war held no honours. What use could they have had for such figments? Nothing remained for them but to stick it out, bow their necks under the yoke of a silent suffering, and try to save their own ruined lives. To go on living.

And they survived, and gave life to new generations. Only after two centuries had gone by had my ancestors rebuilt their province.

In this way Småland, the last Swedish province ever to raise the standard of revolt, was forcibly incorporated into the kingdom of Sweden.

And in 1544, the year following his victory over the men of Småland, Gustav Vasa, by the Succession Pact at Västerås, founded his hereditary monarchy. The kingdom of Sweden had been saved, largely thanks to the assistance given to its king by his six thousand German legionaries.

'Those who are victorious, no matter how they gain the victory, are never shamed by it before history' – in these words, in Machiavelli's history of Florence, a spokesman for a defeated people utters an eternally valid truth. It will serve to close this chapter on the Dacke rising, our greatest popular revolt.